CROSS-CULTURAL QUALITY OF LIFE:
Enhancing the Lives of People With Intellectual Disability

Second Edition

Robert L. Schalock and Kenneth D. Keith, Editors

aaidd
American Association
on Intellectual and
Developmental Disabilities

Published by
American Association on Intellectual and Developmental Disabilities
503 Third St., NW, Suite 200
Washington, DC 20001
www.aaidd.org

© 2016 by American Association on Intellectual and Developmental Disabilities

All rights reserved. No part of this book may be reproduced or transmitted in any form or by any means, electronic or mechanical, including photocopying, recording, or by any information storage and retrieval system, without permission in writing from the publisher.

To order:

AAIDD Order Fulfillment
501 Third St., NW, Suite 200
Washington, DC 20001
Phone: 202-387-1968 x216
Email: books@aaidd.org
Online: http://aaidd.org/publications/bookstore-home

ISBN 978-0-9965068-4-7
Product No. 4163

Printed in the United States of America

TABLE OF CONTENTS

Tables and Figures. vii

Contributors. ix

Foreword xiii
    Roy I. Brown and Ivan Brown

Preface xix

Section I: The Culture of Quality of Life 1

Chapter 1: The Evolution of the Quality-of-Life Concept 3
    Robert L. Schalock and Kenneth D. Keith

Chapter 2: The Emergence of a New Moral Community. 13
    Heather E. Keith and Kenneth D. Keith

Chapter 3: The Journey is the Reward 19
    Kenneth D. Keith, Robert L. Schalock, and Karen Hoffman

Section II: Quality of Life at the Microsystem Level 33

Chapter 4: People Speaking for Themselves 35
    Kenneth D. Keith and Robert L. Schalock

Chapter 5: Personal Involvement and Empowerment. 49
    Remco Mostert

Chapter 6: Family Quality of Life in Argentina 59
    Andrea Silvana Aznar and Diego González Castañón

Section III: Quality of Life at the Mesosystem Level 69

Chapter 7: Outcomes Evaluation 71
    Laura E. Gómez and Miguel Ángel Verdugo

Chapter 8: Aligning Supports Planning Within a Quality-of-Life
Outcomes Framework 81
    Marco Lombardi and Luigi Croce

Chapter 9: Continuous Quality Improvement 93
    Tim Lee

Chapter 10: Organizational Transformation 109
    Jos van Loon and Peter van Wijk

Section IV: Quality of Life at the Macrosystem Level 119

Chapter 11: A Focus on System-Level Outcome Indicators 121
    Valerie J. Bradley, Dorothy Hiersteiner, and Alexandra Bonardi

Chapter 12: The Supports Paradigm 133
    Roger J. Stancliffe, Samuel R. C. Arnold, and Vivienne C. Riches

Chapter 13: Positive Psychology and a Quality-of-Life Agenda 143
    Michael L. Wehmeyer and Karrie A. Shogren

Chapter 14: Changing Service Delivery Systems:
An Example from Community Living—British Columbia 149
    Andrea Baker, Brian Salisbury, and Dan Collins

Chapter 15: Human Rights and Quality-of-Life Domains:
Identifying Cross-Cultural Indicators 167
    Claudia Claes, Hanne Vandenbussche, and Marco Lombardi

Chapter 16: The Evolution of Quality-of-Life Perspectives
in the Developing Countries of Sub-Saharan Africa 175
    Elias Mpofu

Section V: The Cross-Cultural Quality-of-Life Agenda 181

Chapter 17: The Global Perspective on the Concept of Quality of Life 183
    Kenneth D. Keith and Robert L. Schalock

Chapter 18: The Role of a Quality-of-Life Theory in a
Quality-of-Life Agenda. 191
    Robert L. Schalock and Kenneth D. Keith

Chapter 19: Setting the Cross-Cultural Quality-of-Life Agenda
to Enhance the Lives of People with Intellectual Disability. 203
    Robert L. Schalock and Kenneth D. Keith

References 219

Glossary 251

Subject Index 261

TABLES AND FIGURES

Tables

1.1.	QOL Domains and Exemplary Indicators	6
1.2.	QOL Measurement and Test Development Guidelines	8
1.3.	Context-Based Application Strategies	11
6.1.	Description of the Latin American Scale of QOL	62
9.1.	Slower PDCA Cycle for Continuous QOL Improvement	101
9.2.	Faster PDCA Cycle for Continuous QOL Improvement	102
9.3.	Slower PDCA Cycle for Continuous Team Performance Improvement	103
9.4.	Faster PDCA Cycle for Continuous Team Performance Improvement	104
9.5.	Slower PDCA Cycle for Continuous Organization Effectiveness and Efficiency Improvement	105
9.6.	Faster PDCA Cycle for Continuous Organization Effectiveness and Efficiency Improvement	106
11.1.	Domain, Subdomain, Concern, Indicator, and Data Source Crosswalk	124
11.2.	Crosswalk of Selected CRPD Articles and NCI Indicators	130
15.1.	UN Convention Articles, QOL Domains, and Indicators	172
18.1.	QOL-Related Moderator and Mediator Variables Studied to Date	195
18.2.	A Proposed Framework to Guide Policy Development	197
18.3.	Quality Enhancement Strategies	199
18.4.	Quality of Life as a Language of Thought and Action	199
19.1.	Disability Policy Goals, Personal Outcome Domains, and Domain Indicators	208
19.2.	Critical Components of Professional Responsibility	212
19.3.	Quality Indicators of QOL-Related Outcomes	213
19.4.	A System of Supports Components, Exemplary Strategies, and Potential Outcomes	216

Figures

1.1	The Context of QOL Application	10
6.1.	QOL Data from PWID Who Live With Their Families or in a Care Home	63
6.2.	QOL of Whole Families	66
6.3.	QOL of Relatives of PWID	67
8.1.	Ecological Matrix	87
8.2.	Supports Matrix	89
9.1.	The PDCA Cycle and Its Components	95
9.2.	PDCA Cycle for Continuous Quality Improvement on Different Levels	96
9.3.	The PDCA Cycle as a CQI Process on Macro and Micro Levels	98
10.1.	Design of a Person-Centered Support System	115
11.1.	ICF Model and Elements Measured by NCI	132
12.1.	Conceptual Framework for Human Functioning (from Schalock et al., 2010)	134
14.1.	Include Me! Logic Model	154
14.2.	Representative QOL Domain Scores	160
18.1.	QOL Conceptual Model	192
18.2.	The Context of QOL Application	194
18.3.	Application Framework	198
19.1.	Cross-Cultural QOL Agenda Components	207

CONTRIBUTORS

Samuel R. C. Arnold—Research Fellow, Centre for Disability Studies and Centre for Disability Research and Policy, University of Sydney (Australia): sam.arnold@sydney.edu.au

Andrea Silvana Aznar—General Director, ITINERIS Foundation. Buenos Aires (Argentina): Itineris@fibertel.com.ar.

Andrea Baker—Provincial Quality Manager, Community Living British Columbia. Vancouver, BC (Canada): andrea.baker@gov.bc.ca

Alexandra Bonardi—Project Director, National Core Indicators, Human Services Research Institute, Boston, MA (USA): abonardi@hsri.org.

Valerie J. Bradley—President, Human Services Research Institute. Boston, MA (USA): vbradley@hsri.org.

Daniela Donna Breimeyer—Self-advocate. Gelsenkirchen (Germany).

Ivan Brown—Adjunct Professor, Centre for Disability Studies, Brock University (Canada) and Director, IASSID Academy on Education, Training, and Research: ivan.brown@utoronto.ca.

Roy I. Brown—Professor Emeritus, University of Calgary (Canada) and Flinders University (Australia): roybrown@shaw.ca.

Diego González Castañón—General Director, ITINERIS Foundation. Buenos Aires (Argentina): www.itineris.org.ar.

Claudia Claes—Dean, Faculty of Social Work and Welfare Studies, University College, Gent University (Belgium): claudia.claes@hogent.be.

Daniel Collins—Executive Director, Langley Association for Community Living, Langley, BC (Canada): dcollins@langleyacl.com

Luigi Croce—President, ANFFAS Scientific Committee (Italy) and Joint Professor, Child Neuropsychiatry, Catholic University, Brescia (Italy): luigi.croce@unicatt.it.

Laura E. Gómez—Assistant Professor, Department of Psychology, University of Oviedo (Spain): gómezlaura@uniovi.es.

Federico Oxley Guazzoni—Self-advocate, Paysander (Uruguay).

Dorothy Hiersteiner—Data Analysis Coordinator, Human Services Research Institute, Boston, MA (USA): dhiersteiner@hsri.org.

Karen Hoffman—Senior Trainer, Supports Intensity Scale (AAIDD, USA): karenhoffman@earthlink.net.

Heather E. Keith—Professor of Philosophy, Green Mountain College, VT (USA): keithh@greenmtn.edu.

Kenneth D. Keith—Professor Emeritus, Department of Psychological Sciences, University of San Diego (USA): kkeith@sandiego.edu.

Tim Lee—CEO, Qi Zhi Vocational Training Center, Taipei (Taiwan): tim.lee@vtcidd.org.

Marco Lombardi—Doctoral Student, University College Gent University (Belgium) and Catholic University of Sacred Heart (Italy): marco.lombardi@hogent.be.

Remco Mostert—Master Trainer, Arduin Foundation (The Netherlands): rmostert@arduin.nl.

Elias Mpofu—Professor, Rehabilitation Counseling, The University of Sydney (Australia), and Honorary Visiting Professor, University of the Limpopo (South Africa): elias.mpofu@sydney.edu.au.

G. Parthiban—Self-advocate, New Delhi (India).

Vivienne C. Riches—Center for Disability Studies, The University of Sydney (Australia): vivienne.riches@sydney.edu.au.

Brian Salisbury—Retired Former Director of Strategic Planning and Director of Individual, Family, and Volunteer Engagement, Community Living British Columbia, Vancouver, BC (Canada): bsalisbury@shaw.ca.

Robert L. Schalock—Professor Emeritus, Hastings College (USA): rschalock@ultraplix.com.

Xu Sheng—Professor of Special Education, Beijing Union University (People's Republic of China): xusheng1022@cqnu.edu.cn.

Karrie A. Shogren—Associate Professor, Department of Special Education; Co-Director, Kansas University Center on Developmental Disabilities, and Associate Director, Beach Center on Disability, University of Kansas (USA): shogren@ku.edu.

Roger Stancliffe—Professor of Intellectual Disability, Centre for Disability Research and Policy, The University of Sydney (Australia): roger.stancliffe@sydney.edu.au.

Jos van Loon—Director of Research, Arduin Foundation (The Netherlands): jloon@arduin.nl.

P. J. van Wijk—CEO, Arduin Foundation (The Netherlands): pwijk@arduin.nl.

Hanne Vandenbussche—Assistant Professor, Department of Social Work and Welfare Studies, University College-Gent University (Belgium): hanne.vandenbussche@hogent.be.

Miguel Ángel Verdugo—Director, Institute on Community Integration (INICO) and Professor of Psychology, University of Salamanca (Spain): verdugo@usal.es.

Mian Wang—Associate Professor of Special Education & Director, Pacific Rim Research Center on Special Education and Disability, University of California at Santa Barbara (USA) and Department of Special Education, Chongqing Normal University, Chongqing (China): mwang@education.ucsb.edu.

Nancy Ward—Self-advocate and Co-Director, National Technical Assistance Center on Voting and Cognitive Access. Oklahoma City, OK (USA): nancyward50@gmail.com.

Michael L. Wehmeyer—Director, Beach Center on Disability; Director, KU Center on Developmental Disabilities; Professor of Special Education, University of Kansas (USA): wehmeyer@ku.edu.

Leigh Worrall—Self-advocate, Sydney (Australia).

Youyu Xiang—Professor, Special Education College of Beijing Union University (People's Republic of China): Xiangyouyu3079@yahoo.com.cn.

Jiacheng Xu—President, Special Education College of Beijing Union University; Director, Education Institute of Beijing Union University; Professor of Special and Vocational Education, Beijing Union University (People's Republic of China): xujiacheng123@263.net.

Ziyato—Self-advocate, Beijing (People's Republic of China).

FOREWORD

We are both honored and pleased to be invited to write the foreword to this international book on quality of life. Like the book's editors, Robert L. Schalock and Kenneth D. Keith, we too have had quality of life as a dominant and enduring focus of our academic work for many years. It has been a delight for us to see how quality of life has progressed from being an almost unknown concept in the 1980s to now forming a central ideological and practical concept in intellectual disability policy and practice worldwide.

We have noticed, with interest, how quality of life as a concept has developed and been applied in so many countries over the years. During our quality-of-life workshops through the International Association for the Scientific Study of Intellectual and Developmental Disabilities (IASSIDD) and other travels, we have remarked on the breadth of interest shown in quality of life, not only throughout Europe, North America, and Australia, but also in countries such as China, Greece, India, Macedonia, Malaysia, Russia, Singapore, and South Africa. We have even been surprised at times, when in such countries, to find that interested researchers and practitioners were already familiar with the relevant quality-of-life literature.

Both of us were involved in foundational quality-of-life research in Canada. This early work, along with research in the United States, Australia, the United Kingdom, and elsewhere set the stage for the enormous burst of interest that followed throughout the world in researching and applying quality of life.

- Roy and colleagues obtained a 6-year grant in 1982 from Health and Welfare Canada to conduct a longitudinal study across the four western provinces of Canada. This resulted in several publications (e.g., Brown, Bayer & Macfarlane, 1989), much movement of people from institutions in the community, and families of others in the community offering to pay for services after the six years came to a conclusion.

- Ivan began work in 1991 with nine colleagues on research that sought to assess the quality of life of a random sample of adults with developmental disabilities in the Canadian province of Ontario who lived independently, with families, in group homes, or in institutions. This project, funded by the Ontario Ministry of Community and Social Services, followed 502 people over eight years, during which time many moved from institutions to communities (see Renwick, Brown, & Raphael, 2000, for a summary).

Each of these large research projects produced major assessment and application methodologies that are still being used today.

Much of the initial interest in quality of life emerged from the very practical problem of closing institutions and moving residents to the communities the rest of us live in. The central question, following the realization that life within over-crowded and underfunded institutions was never going to lead to "quality" living for residents, was whether life in communities was better, or could be better. It soon became apparent, as several chapters of this book note, that this was, and still is, indeed the case when opportunities and personal choice are provided, and when self-determination, personal strengths, and individual interests and objectives are pursued by policy, organizations, and both local and global cultures.

Knowledge in the field of intellectual and developmental disabilities (IDD) has expanded enormously over the past few decades. Genetics and other causes of disability, the interaction between genetics and environment, educational intervention, types of residential support, support for families, theoretical approaches, ethics, and lifespan issues are just some of the broad areas within which new information and perspectives are emerging. At the same time, a trend throughout the world has been that countries and cultures learn from one another, and try to understand best practices that emerge internationally. Within this context of rapidly increasing and sharing of knowledge, quality of life is a concept that has expanded its international reach by providing a steady ideological hand and an important guidepost for how our field should move forward. Simply put, the purpose of all work in our field is to improve the quality of life of people with IDD and their families.

This overall purpose of quality of life is especially important from a cross-cultural perspective. The quality-of-life approach provides a method to focus on individuals with intellectual disability and on their families, but it does so in a way that tailors that focus to individual and family needs and capacities within their personal and cultural environments. Cultural differences matter, but when the focus is on attaining person-specific or family-specific quality of life within one's culture, whatever it may be, the focus generates common goals and aspirations to a large degree. Moreover, this flexible methodology makes a quality-of-life approach appropriate for everyone, disabled and nondisabled alike, and thus it has generic application to the functioning of society as a whole (Brown & Faragher, 2014). In this way, the quality-of-life paradigm in intellectual disability works to support inclusion and equality for all members of cultures by making improved individual and family quality of life, in its myriad forms, the central rationale for undertaking most human activity in any culture.

But how is this purpose of quality of life to be attained in the field of IDD? Building on ideas offered by our Australian colleague Trevor Parmenter, and later expanded by him in 2014, effective work in quality of life takes a fundamental change in attitude and understanding, from thinking of people with intellectual disability as "others," incapable of participating fully in our cultures, to thinking of them as people with capabilities to offer, as valued members of our community life, and as individuals who are equally entitled to be fully included in the human experience, which is critical for any individual's identity. The continuing emphasis on quality of life as a general concept in cultures around the world works to strengthen the rationale for changing attitudes and increasing understanding in these ways. In addition, the international emphasis on human rights, inclusion, and equal treatment of all people goes a long way toward changing our attitudes and understanding; and specific practical methods of implementing such changes have been occurring.

The current book, divided into five major sections, represents a follow-up to the 2000 text *Cross-Cultural Perspectives on Quality of Life* (Keith & Schalock, 2000), which provided important descriptions of quality of life from the perspectives of leading scholars in numerous countries around the world. As noted in the first chapter, the second edition of this book is essentially concerned with developments in the first fifteen years of this century, and represents a much more integrated approach to understanding quality of life cross-culturally. This focus reflects—as the editors note in their overview and introduction—the large amount of new published literature in this field that has appeared since 2000 and represents both a significant expansion of thinking and a realization that quality of life may be viewed in a manner more similar than different in countries around the world (see, for example, comparisons of family quality of life in Samuel, Rillotta, & Brown, 2012).

The organization of the present book around the microsystem, mesosystem, and macrosystem levels appropriately emphasizes something with which most readers are familiar—namely, that quality of life is influenced by many aspects of life, and that these range in distance from, but not necessarily in importance to, the lived experience of people with disabilities. As the personal perspectives in Section II illustrate, and as the Section II overview states, "[t]he fulcrum of quality of life is the individual and his/her family", but as noted in the opening chapter of the 2000 edition, ". . . a full picture of quality of life includes the interrelationship among factors at various degrees of immediacy to individuals [and families]" (Renwick, Brown, & Raphael, 2000, p. 7). In keeping with this perspective, the overall emphasis of this book is that all factors ultimately need to be brought together and tailored to the individual or family unit.

This book has a number of features that make it particularly valuable and unique. Those that struck us as particularly relevant to a new understanding of quality of life include the following:

- There is something for every reader interested in supporting people with disabilities, including such areas as the nature of care environments (home or service agency).
- There is a recognition that quality of life emerges from a large body of conceptual and research work, primarily in psychology and sociology but also in other disciplines.
- Case histories featuring life stories illustrate how quality of life works in the lived experience of people with disabilities.
- Advocacy is recognized.
- The use of diagrams and tables throughout the book provides useful ways of illustrating interactions, which are at times complex.
- There is an interesting dialogue about the interaction between business and industry and human services (see Chapter 9 in particular). In view of the challenges facing adults with IDD in the community, and particularly in employment, the commentary and recommendations here are worth pursuing further.
- There are many examples of the practical skills needed by disability professionals and frontline workers (e.g., how to interview).
- The authors come from a wide variety of countries, and they represent policy makers, people with disabilities, family members, and service personnel.
- There is recognition that both objective and subjective (perceptual) views of quality of life are important.
- Various authors identify the challenges facing service development and practice (e.g., Chapter 6 on family quality of life in Argentina).
- It is noted that the principles of quality of life need to be put into practice, since the test of quality of life is whether its application works for the individual with disabilities, those who are employed in the system, and those who set policies.

The links between quality of life and human rights are important, and are clearly noted in this book. The challenge for our field, however, is how we ensure that international declarations—particularly those issued by the United Nations—are not only approved by all countries, but also translated into practice. Mittler (2015) saw this as an important challenge and one that has not yet been achieved in either the economically developed world or that of the low- and middle-income countries (LAMIC; see special issue of the *Journal of Policy and Practice in Intellectual Disabilities*, World Report and Disability; Cohen, Brown, & McVilly, 2015). The challenge of monetary policy impinging on the ability to run effective services in the economically developed world has become more obvious on a daily basis (see Jackson, 2015). Poor funding, restrictions in hiring inadequately trained and experienced personnel, and the incomplete application of independent monitoring strategies, need to be addressed when the quality-of-life model is being applied. Indeed, we see the need now to vigorously promulgate the application of a quality-of-life model as a platform to ensure effective services. Although this is a message for the field of intellectual and developmental disabilities, the need is even more systemic, as noted by Brown and Faragher (2014).

This book provides both a broad and an in-depth account of quality of life and well-being, and covers a wide range of its facets. Yet there is more to be done. We need to be aware when applying the concept of inclusion that in our haste to apply a concept, we may not fully understand that we can, and sometimes do, promote exclusion not just of the individual but also of the individual's family. We need to recognize more fully that quality of life is an individual process, whether we are considering community-living supports, health care, education, family participation, or other aspects of life. We need to understand the nature of family support, and, perhaps more importantly, we need to develop ways for quality of life to be adopted and applied at both the individual and group levels. Such needs do not represent a pessimistic view of the success of the quality-of-life approach to date, but rather identify additional areas to be worked on now that the foundations have been clearly laid. Fortunately for addressing such needs, the quality-of-life approach contains a wide range of principles for action (see Brown & Brown, 2003; Brown, Cobigo, & Taylor, 2014).

As indicated in the current book, the personal nature of quality of life means that needs and choices may differ considerably, and should be both respected and supported. But in practice, this is often no easy matter, as families may have views and concerns that do not match those of the person with the disability. It is here that our educational and applied organizations around the world need to educate, train, and support frontline disability practitioners as they learn how to use such a quality-of-life approach. In fact, we should recognize that we already rely to a great extent on disability practitioners and, consequently, ongoing and innovative methods for training disability practitioners in emerging quality-of-life approaches are essential. These methods must embrace the interesting complexity that emerges from the interaction of policy makers and disability practitioners (see Chapter 19).

The book represents a comprehensive account of quality of life. It is well-founded in theory and research, and discusses important implications for policy and support. The picture given is remarkably complete. It is a picture that further illustrates to our field the colors of dignity, rights, and quality in people's daily lives.

Roy Brown
Ivan Brown

PREFACE

When we published the first edition of this book, at the dawn of the 21st century, the concept of quality of life (QOL) had just begun to influence the field of IDD. By the year 2000, the concept had sensitized us to the importance of key principles reflected in the notion of QOL, and how values such as inclusion, equity, self-determination, and empowerment might be incorporated into best practices. In addition, by 2000, the QOL concept had become a social construct and a unifying theme around which disability-related policies and practices could potentially be developed and implemented. It was this promise that led us to ask a group of esteemed colleagues from throughout the world to share their understanding of the QOL concept from both cross-cultural and systems perspectives.

The 43 individuals from 19 countries who contributed to the 2000 volume addressed QOL from the perspective of the individual, the community and organization, and the larger culture. In the concluding chapter of that book we suggested, based on the material presented in the preceding 30 chapters, that four trends would significantly affect our future endeavors: (a) the search for core QOL domains, (b) the use of methodological pluralism to assess QOL indicators, (c) the use of the social-ecological model of human functioning as a basis for quality enhancement, and (d) the implementation of outcomes evaluation.

Since 2000, a lot has changed in the field of IDD, including our better understanding of the QOL concept, and the influence it has had on the field. The excitement and promise of this second edition is that the 34 contributors, representing 14 countries, capture in the book's 19 chapters the significant role the QOL concept has played in personal involvement and empowerment, self-advocacy, family-related QOL, supports planning, outcomes evaluation, continuous quality improvement, organization transformation, and systems-level change.

As with the first edition, we take a cross-cultural approach to QOL. *Cross-cultural* implies comparing and contrasting cultural and psychological phenomena from one country to another. In contrast, *multicultural* is a term that connotes the study of subcultural groups within a country. Like any cross-cultural effort, the work reported in this volume is limited to the particular cultures represented. Although the sample of cultures represented here is not exhaustive, and represents a somewhat different sample than that found in the first edition, the extensive reference list appearing at the end of the text presents a broader, more complete view of international QOL work. Additionally, we have made an effort to represent the developing world, and to recognize the significant challenges faced by many countries as they endeavor to implement policies and practices to enhance the QOL of persons with ID, and to conduct research investigating the results of these efforts.

In selecting the contributors to this second edition, we chose colleagues whose work is familiar and widely published, and who have influenced the field of QOL research and application. As in the first volume, we include the wisdom of those who best know the concept and the field: self-advocates who speak for themselves. We extend our thanks to the mentors of these six individuals who share their life experiences and viewpoints in Chapter 4.

To each contributor, we express our appreciation and admiration. To our wives, Susan and Connie, we express our love and thanks for a life of quality. And to Darlene Buschow, who provided technical assistance throughout the project, we say one more time, "We can't do it without you."

Bob Schalock and Ken Keith

SECTION I
THE CULTURE OF QUALITY OF LIFE

Section Overview

David Matsumoto and Hyi Sung Hwang (2013) discussed four perspectives on culture and the ways these perspectives occur cross-culturally in everyday language and discourse. The first perspective is that culture is a descriptive term that captures not only rules and meanings, but also patterns of behavior. Historically, disability has been described in terms of dependency, eternal childhood, segregation, and exclusion. More recent descriptions have emphasized empowerment, equity, self-determination, and inclusion. The second perspective is that culture provides guidelines or roadmaps on what to do, how to think, and what to feel. The more recent emphases on disability rights, disability pride, self-advocacy, and empowerment provide new guidelines and road maps for individuals with ID and their families regarding independence, productivity, and community inclusion. It is these two perspectives on culture that the reader will encounter in Chapter 1. In that chapter, we describe the evolution of the QOL concept as a descriptive term, and how over the last two decades the field has developed a better roadmap for its conceptualization, measurement, and application.

The third and fourth perspectives on culture are reflected in Chapter 2. Here the authors describe how culture reflects adaptational responses to contextual challenges and communicates a shared system of symbols that transcends individuals and reflects on the general group. Throughout history, people with intellectual disability (ID) and their families have had to adapt to both the condition of ID and society's attitudes and behaviors regarding the condition. Based on these two perspectives, Chapter 2 summarizes the emergence of a new moral community, reflecting how individuals and societies have adapted to persons with ID, and how societal attitudes and behaviors toward people with ID have changed in ways commensurate with the symbols and terms used to portray their identity, value, adaptability, and social role.

Across these four perspectives, which we suggest define the "culture of ID," the pursuit of a life of quality for persons with ID and their families has entailed a significant journey by multiple groups, including individuals with ID and their families, academics and researchers, and organization and systems-level personnel. Each has played a significant role in determining how the concept of a life of quality has been viewed and manifested. In Chapter 3 we provide an overview of these journeys, summarize briefly the journeys experienced by the chapter's three authors, and suggest that the journey is—and has been—the reward.

CHAPTER 1

THE EVOLUTION OF THE QUALITY-OF-LIFE CONCEPT

ROBERT L. SCHALOCK and KENNETH D. KEITH

Introduction and Overview

The evolution, or unfolding and advancement, of the quality-of-life (QOL) concept reflects a process of continuous growth in our understanding of its conceptualization, measurement, and application. This chapter describes that continuous growth and understanding from the perspective of two individuals (the chapter's authors) who have been involved in the process since the early 1980s. The chapter does not attempt to integrate the work of the hundreds of individuals who have contributed to our better understanding of individual and family-referenced QOL; instead, to describe the evolutionary process, we have selected key post-2000 events and publications with which we have been involved either directly or indirectly.

As we discussed in the first edition of this book (Keith & Schalock, 2000) and in Schalock (2000), by the year 2000 the field of intellectual and developmental disabilities (IDD) had already embraced the QOL concept as a sensitizing notion and an overarching principle for service delivery, due in large part to its capturing a changing vision of persons with IDD and its being consistent with the broader quality revolution. Leading up to 2000, four significant events/publications set the stage. The first was the publication of the book *Quality of Life: Perspectives and Issues* (Schalock, 1990b). In this edited volume early QOL thinkers, including David Goode, Nancy Ward, Steve Taylor, Bob Edgerton, Laird Heal, and Rud Turnbull, discussed the concept of QOL from personal, conceptual, policy, and assessment perspectives. This discussion integrated current thinking and provided a solid framework for subsequent developments.

As the decade of the 1990s progressed, three additional significant events occurred. The first was the establishment in Helsinki, Finland in 1996 of the IASSID (now

IASSIDD) Special Interest Research Group on Quality of Life. Its mission was (and is) to further work that enhances the QOL of individuals and families. The second event was the 2002 consensus document regarding the conceptualization, measurement, and application of the QOL concept (Schalock et al., 2002). The consensus group, comprising such QOL visionaries as Ivan Brown, Roy Brown, Bob Cummins, David Felce, Lena Matikka, and Trevor Parmenter, developed a set of principles that have stood the test of time (Brown et al., 2004; Schalock, 2007). These principles provide the overview to each section of this chapter. The final pre-2000 event was the publication of a number of significant QOL publications that also set the stage for the 21st century by sharing leading initial efforts to conceptualize, measure, and apply the QOL concept. Among others, these included publications by Brown (1997), Renwick, Brown, and Nagler (1996), Schalock (1996a; 1997), and The Council on Quality and Leadership (1997; Gardner, Nudler, & Chapman, 1997).

In the following sections, we focus on post-2000 events and publications that collectively describe how the conceptualization, measurement, and application of the QOL concept have unfolded and advanced over the last fifteen years. It's a fascinating narrative that reflects the power of stories. As Sanders (1997) observed, stories entertain us, they create community, they help us see through the eyes of other people, they show us the consequences of our actions, and they help us dwell in time.

Conceptualization

Conceptualization Principles

1. QOL is multidimensional and influenced by personal and environmental factors and their interaction.
2. QOL has the same components for all people.
3. QOL has both subjective and objective components.
4. QOL is enhanced by self-determination, resources, purpose in life, and a sense of belonging.

Although these four conceptualization principles incorporate measurement and application aspects, their major focus is on what constitutes a life of quality. To this end, work regarding the conceptualization of QOL has focused on both developing and validating a QOL conceptual model that incorporates core domains and domain indicators.

Developing the Conceptual Model

A conceptual QOL model is composed of core domains and domain indicators. *QOL domains* are the set of factors that constitute personal well-being and represent the range over which the QOL concept extends, and thus defines a life of quality. *QOL indicators* are QOL-related perceptions, behaviors, and conditions that give an indication of the person's well-being and are used as the basis for QOL assessment. Although there are several QOL conceptual models (See Schalock, Gardner, & Bradley, 2007, pp. 19–25, for a summary and comparison of these models), we focus here on what is frequently called the Schalock and Verdugo conceptual model.

Three significant events provided the data used to develop this conceptual model. The first was the extensive literature review and synthesis conducted by Carolyn Hughes and her colleagues (1995; 1996). Their work identified 44 definitions of QOL of persons with or without disabilities. Analysis of the definitions resulted in fifteen dimensions of QOL, with the most commonly identified dimensions relating to psychological well-being and personal satisfaction; social relations and interactions; employment; physical and material well-being; and self-determination, autonomy, and personal choice.

The second significant event was the cross-cultural measurement of critical QOL concepts by Keith, Heal, and Schalock (1996). In this study, a semantic differential technique was used across seven cultures to assess the meaning of ten QOL concepts (rights, relationships, satisfaction, empowerment, economic security, social inclusion, individual control, privacy, health, and growth and development). Respondents rated each concept on nine pairs of adjectives representing three dimensions (value, potency, or activity). Across seven countries, all ten of the QOL concepts received strong positive ratings on the value dimension, but lower positive ratings on the potency and activity dimension.

The third event used an eight-domain QOL conceptual model (see Table 1.1) that was based on the synthesis and integration of the Hughes et al. (1996) and Keith et al. (1996) work. Using this eight-domain model as an analytic framework, Schalock and Verdugo (2002) reviewed and analyzed 897 articles and book chapters published between 1985 and 1999 that were related to QOL in the areas of education/special education, mental and behavioral health, mental retardation/intellectual disability, and aging. In the *Handbook on Quality of Life for Human Service Practitioners* (Schalock & Verdugo, 2002), they summarized and discussed the relative use and associated indicators for each area. Based on this analysis, and collapsing across the four literature search areas, the most commonly referenced indicators associated with each domain were identified. These eight domains and exemplary indicators appear in Table 1.1.

Validating the Conceptual Model

The next evolutionary event involved two series of validation studies. The first evaluated the etic (universal) and emic (culture-based) properties of the eight domains and associated indicators (Schalock et al., 2005, for specific indicators). For each indicator, two sets of questions were asked related to the indicator's importance and use: (a) "how important is it (i.e. the indicator) for you (consumer), people with IDD (family), or people with IDD in your country (professional)?"; and (b) "to what degree do people at (the facility/service) take it (the core indicator) in mind (the consumer); how much

Table 1.1. *QOL Domains and Exemplary Indicators*

Domain	Exemplary Indicator
Personal Development	• Education status • Personal competence (cognitive, social, practical)
Self-Determination	• Autonomy/personal control • Goals and personal values • Choices
Interpersonal Relations	• Interactions (e.g. social networks) • Relationships (family, friends)
Social Inclusion	• Community integration • Community roles
Rights	• Human (respect, dignity, equality) • Legal (citizenship, access, due process)
Emotional Well-Being	• Contentment (satisfaction, enjoyment) • Lack of stress (predictability and control)
Physical Well-Being	• Health status • Activities of daily living (self-care, mobility)
Material Well-Being	• Employment status • Possessions

is it used in services/supports received (the family); or how much is it used in services/supports received or delivered (professional)?" Three respondent groups were surveyed (consumers, parents, and professionals) across five geographical groups (Schalock et al., 2005) and four European countries (Jenaro et al., 2005). The following results were obtained: (a) the etic (universal) properties of the domains were demonstrated by similar profiles for the respondent and geographical groups, (b) the indicators grouped into the respective QOL domain, and (c) the emic (culture-bound) properties of the indicators were demonstrated by the significant differences on scores across groups.

This etic/emic distinction is very important to both the conceptualization of QOL domains and associated indicators and the measurement of those domains/indicators. As we discuss in the following section, the eight domains provide the measurement framework, but the indicators used to assess the respective domain need to be culturally sensitive.

The second series of studies validated the factor structure of the QOL concept and suggested its hierarchical nature. There is general agreement based on factor analytic studies that the eight first-order domains listed in Table 1.1 are statistically the best fit to data from a number of cross-cultural QOL data sources (e.g. Gómez, Verdugo, Arias, & Arias, 2011; Wang, Schalock, Verdugo, & Jenaro, 2010). However, there is some debate about the hierarchical nature of the QOL construct as it relates to second-order factors.

Currently, there is empirical support for both the "Salamanca Model" (which proposes three second-order factors: personal well-being, empowerment, and physical and material well-being) and the "Schalock Model" (which proposes three second-order factors: independence, social participation, and personal well-being). A detailed discussion of these studies can be found in Gómez et al. (2011) and Wang et al. (2010).

Measurement

Measurement Principles

1. Measurement in QOL involves the degree to which people have life experiences that they value.
2. Measurement in QOL reflects the domains that contribute to a full and interconnected life.
3. Measurement in QOL considers the contexts of physical, social, and cultural environments that are important to people.
4. Measurement in QOL includes measures of experiences both common to all humans and those unique to individuals.

These four measurement principles challenged the field to rethink what QOL assessment instruments should encompass, how QOL-related measurement scales are developed, how persons with IDD are assessed on those scales, and what should be made of the assessment information. These challenges have been met over the last fifteen years through events and publications related to the measurement approach, the persons involved, and information use.

Measurement Approach

Best practices in measurement of QOL incorporate QOL domains as the measurement framework, domain-referenced indicators (i.e., perceptions, behaviors, or conditions) as the items assessed, and a 3–6 point Likert Scale as the measurement metric. Given the plethora of QOL assessment scales developed over the last fifteen years, it is important to implement this best practices measurement approach via scientifically sound measurement and test development guidelines. Table 1.2 presents these guidelines based on the work of Claes, van Hove, van Loon, Vandevelde, and Schalock (2009); Cummins (2004); Schalock and Verdugo (2012b); Stancliffe, Wilson, Bigby, Balandin, and Craig (2014); Townsend-White, Pham, and Vassos (2012); and Verdugo, Schalock, Keith, and Stancliffe (2005b).

Persons Involved

Traditionally, the quality of one's life was typically evaluated by others or on the basis of social indicators such as social-economic status or health. However, the quality and

8 The Evolution of the Quality-of-Life Concept

Table 1.2. *QOL Measurement and Test Development Guidelines*

Measurement Guidelines	Test Development Guidelines
Indicators Measured Should: 1. Be related to a QOL conceptual model 2. Include subjective and objective culturally sensitive indicators 3. Have demonstrated reliability and validity 4. Have a clearly articulated use 5. Be a guide for personal, service, or policy enhancement rather than a classification of individuals, services, organizations, or systems	Test Development Processes Should: 1. Collect items based on literature searches and expert panels and aggregate them into domains 2. Pretest items 3. Conduct pilot test (item analysis reliability, and validity check) 4. Develop final forms (self-report and report of others) 5. Publish administration and standardization manual

subjective well-being revolutions, the emergence of multidimensional models of QOL, and the reform movement in the field of IDD have changed the way we think about who should be involved in the assessment process. Hence, we have seen an emphasis on developing self-report formats for persons with IDD, and parallel versions used as the basis for reports of others. The parallel version uses the same indicators and measurement metric, but is worded to allow for a more "objective" assessment of the individual by persons who know him/her well. Concerning self-reporting, best assessment practices involve simplifying the wording of questions and responses, providing pictorial response alternatives, using interpreters, and utilizing augmentative communication.

Well-trained peer interviewers are also used as surveyors. It was a very significant event when the Ask Me! Project in the state of Maryland (Bonham et al., 2004) and investigators in the United Kingdom (Perry & Felce, 2004) implemented a peer-interviewer approach to QOL assessment. This approach has also been replicated in Alberta and British Columbia, Canada (see Chapter 14, this volume). As discussed by Bonham et al. (2004) and Verdugo et al. (2005b), the use of well-trained peer interviewers results in reliable and valid data. In addition, the analysis of response patterns among respondents indicates little if any acquiescence or response perseveration.

Information Use

The principle that has guided the use of QOL assessment information is that it is *not* used to compare persons, but as critical information that can be used at the individual, organization, and systems levels. At the individual level, the information can: (a) become the basis for a dialog regarding what is important to the person, and thus provide a communication platform for discussing with the individual and his/her family and significant others how each of the relevant and personally important QOL domains might be enhanced; (b) be used as an outcomes framework for developing an individual support plan (ISP); (c) be used to distinguish between what is important to the person (i.e. personal goals) and what is important for the person (e.g. assessed support needs); and (d) underscore that the ISP serves two purposes: what explicitly needs to stay as is, and changing those things for which a desire to change exists.

At the organizational level, QOL assessment information needs to be aggregated so that average domain scores are used for reporting, benchmarking, and quality improvement purposes. Specific examples of such use appear in Chapters 7–10 of this volume.

At the systems level, aggregated QOL assessment information is useful for reporting, benchmarking, technical assistance, and continuous quality improvement (see Chapters 9 and 14 this volume). One of the most significant events in this respect has been the development and use of Provider Profiles at the systems level to guide the development and implementation of systems-level policies and practices. Provider Profiles were implemented initially in the United States in 1998 by The ARC of Nebraska (2003). Since then, they have been implemented in Canada and Spain. As discussed by Gómez, Verdugo, Arias, Novas, and Schalock (2013), Provider Profiles contain key performance indicators for each organization within the system, including: (a) aggregated QOL-related personal outcomes of service recipients; and (b) organization-level data that may affect the QOL of service recipients, such as quality assurance activities, quality improvement activities, and specific, individualized support strategies.

Application

Application Principles

1. QOL application enhances well-being within cultural contexts.
2. QOL principles should be the basis for interventions and supports.
3. QOL applications should be evidence based.
4. QOL principles should take a prominent place in professional education and training.

The application of the QOL concept cannot occur in a vacuum. To date, successful applications have occurred because those involved understand two facts. First, we currently know something about the predictors of QOL outcomes, and second, application must be integrated with current contextual factors. The purpose of this section of the chapter is to discuss these two facts.

QOL Outcome Predictors

Based on the research to date (e.g. Brown, Hatton, & Erickson, 2013; Claes et al., 2012; Gómez, Pena, Arias, & Verdugo, in press; Reinders & Schalock, 2014; Schalock et al., 2007), we have an increasing understanding of the variables that significantly predict QOL-referenced outcomes. At the individual level, QOL outcomes are predicted by employment status, residential status, health status, adaptive behavior levels, and intellectual functioning levels. At the organization level, predictors include individualized support strategies, level of staff involvement with the client, type of organization services provided, availability of transportation, and the level of staff-reported job satisfaction. At the societal level, significant predictors (that are less well understood) include societal expectations, attitudes, and media impact.

Contextual Factors

The conditions that caused us to embrace the QOL concept in the 1980s are still with us: the changed vision of persons with IDD, the need for a common language, the emphasis on QOL principles, and the need for an overarching service delivery philosophy. However, the world has changed, and additional contextual factors have emerged: the approach to disability, the transformation of organizations and systems, professional education and staff development, and the approach we take to research. These four contextual factors are presented in Figure 1.1, which shows how they interface with the QOL concept. As depicted in Figure 1.1, the QOL concept can have an interactive role with each of the four contextual factors and one or more of the factor's components.

Approach to Disability
- Ecological Model of Disability
- Capacities Approach
- Supports Paradigm
- Person-Centered Planning

Organization Transformation and Systems Change
- High Performance Teams
- Continuous Quality Improvement
- Outcomes Evaluation
- Social Entrepreneurship

Quality-of-Life Concept

Research
- Participatory Action Research
- Evidence-Based Practices
- Methodological Pluralism
- Multivariate Research Designs

Professional Education and Staff Development
- Professional Standards
- Professional Ethics
- Critical Thinking Skills
- Best Practices

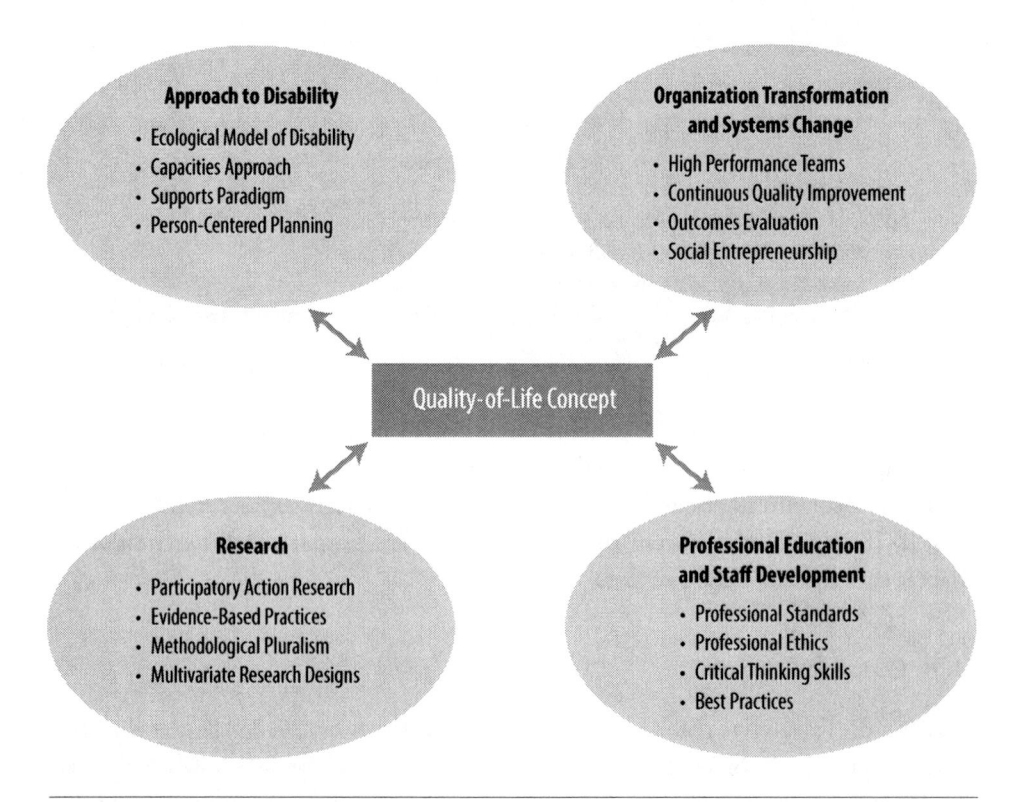

FIGURE 1.1. The context of QOL application

In Table 1.3 we expand Figure 1.1 to list, in reference to each contextual factor, the potential role the QOL concept can play in QOL-related applications. Column 1 lists the four contextual factors shown in Figure 1; column 2 lists those factor components listed within the respective factor oval in Figure 1.1; and column 3 indicates the potential roles the QOL concept can play in QOL-related application.

Conclusion

The evolution of the QOL concept is still unfolding and advancing. This chapter has focused on efforts over the last fifteen years to clarify its conceptualization, improve its measurement, and advance its application. In this chapter, we have discussed how the concept of quality of life has evolved into a validated multidimensional conceptual model composed of core domains and domain indicators; how best practices of QOL

Table 1.3. *Context-Based Application Strategies*

Contextual Factor	Factor Component	Application Strategies
Approach to Disability	• Ecological model of disability • Capacities approach • Supports paradigm • Person-centered planning	• Emphasize organization and environmental variables that enhance QOL outcomes • No threshold of capabilities is required to participate in life activities • Individualized support strategies that enhance personal goals • 'My Support Plan'; personal development opportunities
Organization Transformation and Systems Change	• High-performance teams • Continuous quality improvement • Outcomes evaluation • Social entrepreneurship	• Support Team; Quality Improvement Team • Outcomes-focused ISP • Focus on customer perspective • Individual and aggregated QOL-related outcomes • Partnerships with self-advocacy groups
Professional Education and Staff Development	• Professional standards • Professional ethics • Critical thinking skills • Best practices	• Assessing QOL domains • Justice • Beneficence • Autonomy • Alignment, synthesis, and systems thinking • Practices based on the principles of equity, inclusion, self-determination, and empowerment
Research	• Participatory action research • Evidence-based practices • Methodological pluralism • Multivariate research designs	• Involvement of service recipients • QOL outcomes used as evidence • Quantitative and qualitative methods • QOL domains/total scores used as dependent variable

measurement involve the assessment of domain-referenced indicators, the use of self-report and report of others, the active involvement of service recipients, and the multiple use of the assessment information for reporting, benchmarking, research, and quality improvement; and how application is based on an understanding of QOL-related outcome predictors and contextual factors.

This evolution in the conceptualization, measurement, and application of the QOL concept is reflected in each of the following chapters. In one way or another, the authors of these chapters have incorporated the QOL concept into their work, addressed the QOL-related contextual factors depicted in Figure 1.1 and Table 1.3, and explained the role that the QOL concept and QOL-related principles and actions can play to enhance a life of quality for people with IDD and their families.

Integral to the efforts described in subsequent chapters, however, is a conception of disability that is based on a new morality that re-defines intelligence and reason. This new morality is described in the following chapter.

CHAPTER 2

THE EMERGENCE OF A NEW MORAL COMMUNITY

HEATHER E. KEITH and KENNETH D. KEITH

Introduction and Overview

People have always pondered the meaning and quality of their lives. However, for much of our history society has limited individuals with ID to wretched lives in shameful conditions (e.g., Blatt & Kaplan, 1966; Wolfensberger, 1969), sometimes labeling them as subhuman (Vail, 1967; Wolfensberger, 1975) and for a time in the 19th century as freaks (Bogdan, 1988). Labels were not new in the 19th and 20th centuries—they date at least to the Greek and Roman eras (Evans, 1945; Whitney, 1949). The Hebrew language, for example, had terms for concepts like "imbecile" as early as the end of the 2nd century CE (Berkson, 2006). In Nazi Germany, people with a disability were seen as a menace to society, and their institutionalization and extermination were considered morally acceptable (Sofair & Kaldjian, 2000). The view that the lives of people with a disability were not worth living, and that euthanasia was acceptable, was prevalent in the 1930s and 1940s in both Germany and the United States (Dudley & Gale, 2002; Yount, 2000). Sadly, dehumanization has a long and unfortunate history.

In making assumptions about the QOL of those whom they may see as subhuman, the labels, conditions, and actions referenced above violated two of the fundamental premises of modern research in QOL (Keith, 2007):

- although the views of others may be important in understanding the QOL of an individual with ID, they are never an adequate substitute for the voice and perspective of the individual him/herself; and
- an individual's QOL need not always be compared to that of others.

We might ask then, whether there is an alternative philosophical view to that held in the past, whether we might construe differently the concept of humanity, and in so doing create a new moral community with the promise of enhancing QOL. This chapter addresses these questions.

What Does It Mean to be Human?

Philosophers have long debated the definition of humanity, often concluding that to be fully human one must have the capacity to reason logically and to make abstractions (Goodey, 2011). This view has powerful consequences, not only in determining who is human, but also in developing a theory of morality. In the early days of philosophy, Plato believed that reason governed the soul, that without reason a person could not be moral, and that without morality one *cannot* be fully human (see, for example, Keith & Keith, 2013). In Plato's view, reason and intelligence were innate and fixed, and to function as a member of society a person must have higher reasoning abilities. It followed then, that one's moral agency depended upon some level of intellect and rationality (Stainton, 2001), and that these were immutable individual traits. Aristotle (350 BCE/1988), for example, not only believed that humanity could not exist without reason, but also that babies with disabilities should be left to the elements because "no deformed child shall live" (p. 182).

As philosophy moved toward the modern era, René Descartes (1641/1952) believed that rational thought was essential to truly human existence—that without reason one can be little more than a nonhuman animal, and therefore incapable of morality. Immanuel Kant (1785/1983), too, viewed the capacity to act morally as dependent on ability to reason logically—a view that led naturally to the devaluing, by such contemporary philosophers as Singer (2010), of those who are "so profoundly mentally retarded that they lack self-consciousness or self-awareness" (p. 337).

In the tradition of utilitarian philosophy (e.g., Bentham, 1798; Mill 1861/2002), Kuhse and Singer (1985) attempted to couch disability in an approach that takes account not only of individuals, but also of others—including family members and the broader community—at times creating a dichotomous (and perhaps false) conflict between the interests of child and family. One might argue that the utilitarian view has made a humane effort to improve one's QOL and minimize suffering for parents and children, sometimes advocating withholding of treatment from infants with disability, selective abortion, and even euthanasia in the interest of family QOL. Singer (1993) asserted, for example, that there may be times when the interests of parents can be a reason for euthanasia. In its construal of what it means to be human, this utilitarian perspective makes assumptions about QOL—of individuals and of those around them—that may not take into account the possibilities of social structures to enhance life quality (Kittay, 2010).

The utilitarian approach has also fallen short in its tendency to treat people with disability as marginal, viewing their rights as akin to those of nonhuman animals (Carlson, 2010), and sometimes questioning whether there is anything particularly good or dignified about being human (Singer, 2010). Finally, critics have questioned whether an ethicist, no matter how well-intentioned, can pass judgment on the QOL of others (Johnson, 2003).

A New Moral Community

Can we define humanity, and thus morality, differently from traditional views of rationality, utilitarian philosophy, or static measures of intelligence? We believe the answer to this question is "yes," and that a new view, redefining intelligence and reason, is fundamental to enhancing the QOL of people with ID. Specifically, we envision a perspective that focuses on a humanity and morality based on relationships, with central roles for learning and emotion.

Intelligence

Sternberg (1986, 1996) observed that the intelligence we are accustomed to identifying via standardized tests, while perhaps being correlated with such measures as traditional school performance, is a lifeless, "inert" entity that does not encompass the range of behaviors underlying a successful life. We tend to think of inert intelligence as a fixed trait associated with the individual. An alternative according to Sternberg is *practical* intelligence, reflecting an ability to adapt to the environment and to achieve a fit between person and context. As pragmatist philosopher John Dewey (1957) argued, unlike the absolutism of historic rationalist views, "Intelligence is not something possessed once and for all. It is in constant process of forming . . ." (pp. 96–97).

Although Western cultural conceptions of intelligence generally value rapid cognitive processing and academic-related abilities, other cultures have construed intelligence as harmonious social relations (Azuma & Kashiwagi, 1987; Ruzgis & Grigorenko, 1994); participation in the activities of the family (Super & Harkness, 1982); friendliness (Wober, 1974); or cooperative, obedient, socially responsible behavior (Serpell, Marigan, & Harvey, 1993). Furthermore, the Western view of intelligence might be very different if, as Throne (1972) proposed, we were successful in making environments exceptional, rather than regarding individuals as exceptional.

Intelligence is a construct, the product of the psychosocial perspectives of people and their cultures. It can be a tool for dividing people into the in-group and the out-group (Goodey, 2011), prompting many to see people with ID as the "other" (Foucault, 2006), or as subhuman (Carlson, 2010). Such judgments may be based (erroneously) on traits as simple as facial appearance (e.g., Enea-Drapeau, Huguet, & Carlier, 2014). If Blatt

(1981) was correct in arguing that our traditional views have allowed us to fabricate a false story about people with ID, it follows that a different construction of intelligence might well contribute to a new, more enlightened story. One such story may be found in the writing of Ian Brown (2009), who related the struggle of his son, Walker, and his family to work out an individual-environmental fit that would allow Walker to adjust and grow despite significant disabilities. Walker became more successful only when those around him found new ways to conceive of intelligence and learning.

Some of the alternative ways we might conceive of ability include perception and expression of emotion (Mayer & Salovey, 1993); adaptation to, or shaping of, environments (Sternberg, 1996); or interpersonal skills (Gardner, 1983). A most encouraging development is the recognition that traditional intelligence measures might be replaced by assessment of the specific support needs of individuals in the context of their own particular environments (Arnold, Riches, & Stancliffe, 2011; Chapter 12, this volume)—perhaps moving the field away from the practice of defining people in reference to immutable inert intelligence, and toward a truly adaptive connection between the individual and his/her environment.

Relationality

We argue that the prevailing theories in the history of moral philosophy exclude people with ID, and that the moral community must expand to encompass the capacities of all people (Keith & Keith, 2013; see also Nussbaum, 2006, 2009, 2011). Stainton (2001) and Stainton and Claire (2012) also recognized the need to develop a moral philosophy that is not dependent upon a link between reason and personal value. An alternative exists in moral perspectives arising from the pragmatist philosophical tradition, offering the possibility of a pluralistic approach with an emphasis on helping people to live in rich, emotionally engaged ways (Fesmire, 2003). In addition to being pluralistic, pragmatism respects a science-based empirical view, and sees the self in its interdependent relationship with others, as opposed to an isolated autonomous entity (see, e.g., Markus & Kitayama, 1991).

Pragmatist John Dewey recast rationality as intelligence (Hickman, 1990), which for Dewey encompassed growth—toward richness in association with others, and toward social integration (Lekan, 2009). Such a viewpoint holds promise not only for individual well-being, but also for the ability of individuals to see themselves as contributing members of a community in which people of diverse capability are valued. In a similar vein, Nussbaum (2006) articulates a view of personhood and QOL predicated on recognition of each individual's unique capabilities, especially those that promote human association. A number of the capabilities enumerated by Nussbaum (e.g., control over environment) closely correspond to key dimensions of QOL studied by other researchers (e.g., Keith, 2007; Schalock et al., 2007). Defining people in terms of their capabilities has the added advantage of directing attention not to what they *cannot* do, but instead to what they *can* (Bérubé, 2010; Brown et al., 2013).

The socialization inherent in the association of people in community gives rise to important emotional possibilities, among them empathy and caring. Various authors have described empathy in different ways, including the notion that children learn their parents' response to the children (Hoffman 1979), that people take on the attitudes of others (Mead, 1964b), and that mirror neurons allow individuals to automatically respond to others as if they were those others (Gerdes, Lietz, & Segal, 2011). And it seems clear that this ability to respond emotionally to others is not dependent upon an immutable intelligence of the traditional sort; it occurs "not just by rational calculation" (Johnson, 1993, p. 200) and is consistent with the interpersonal, relational nature of emotional intelligence (Mayer & Salovey, 1993).

Thus, we see a sample of points of view that extend the meaning of "human" beyond inert intelligence and reason. Following Dewey (1922), we can conclude that all human conduct, even moral deliberation, is "*interaction* between elements of human nature and the environment, natural and social" (p. 10)—a notion consistent with contemporary recognition of ID as a social-ecological construct that includes person-environment interaction and deployment of environmental supports to maximize personal functioning (Schalock, 2011; Shogren, Luckasson, & Schalock, 2014). In a new moral community, the capacity for moral participation is much more widely construed (Keith & Keith, 2013) in that personhood is defined in relationships and expansion of goal-achieving opportunities (Danforth, 2008), and well-being and justice are dependent upon social integration that fosters individual capabilities (Lekan, 2009).

Conclusion

This chapter answered three questions basic to a forward-looking, positive conception of QOL for persons with ID. First, there is an alternative philosophical view of disability that is different from those held in the past. Second, we can construe differently the concept of humanity. And third, in doing the first and second, we can create a new moral community with the promise of enhancing the QOL of persons with ID and their families.

The challenge of life in the community for people with ID is in some measure a product of individual personal characteristics, whether cognitive, behavioral, or medical. But a major portion of the challenge may be found in the perceptual, social, and cultural obstacles arising from our views of what it means to be human, and the expectancies that follow from those views.

W. E. Fernald (1902), for example, thought that individuals with ID (known then as "feeble-mindedness") should be quite happy living in institutions and segregated from mainstream society. "What more," he wondered, "can a boy want!" (p. 489). It is significant that such views are psychosocial constructions, and that they are subject to revision if we choose to redefine them.

Individuals experiencing community life have generally enjoyed a better QOL than those residing in congregate facilities and programs (Chowdhury & Benson, 2011; Keith, Schalock, & Hoffman, 1986; Perry, Felce, Allen & Meek, 2011; Schalock, Keith & Hoffman, 1990). Yet we know that too many people *live in the community*, but not *in community*. Living in community implies that people belong to, and are interconnected with, other members (Rapley, 2000). Life *in community* is an aspiration that aligns with the Deweyan pragmatist aim of increased well-being possible for those whose lives are an ongoing adaptive, relational process. For happiness and satisfaction are found not in a fixed end or outcome, but in an active, forward-looking process (Dewey, 1957/1920).

As the international community moves toward individualized supports-based services, we must also move toward a new moral philosophy that encompasses growth, relationships, and the richness of community life. This movement will involve the personal journeys of consumers and their families, academics and researchers, and organizations and system-level personnel. Key aspects of these personal journeys are described next.

CHAPTER 3

THE JOURNEY IS THE REWARD

KENNETH D. KEITH, ROBERT L. SCHALOCK, and KAREN HOFFMAN

Introduction and Overview

In this chapter we characterize the quest for QOL as a journey. We have come a long way in that journey since our first joint QOL publication in 1986 and the subsequent appearance in 2000 of *Cross-Cultural Perspectives on Quality of Life*. Since these early publications we now: (a) have a better understanding of the QOL concept, including its domains and hierarchical structure; (b) assess QOL with instruments incorporating best practices of test development and consumer involvement; (c) apply the QOL concept to policy development, organization and systems transformation, professional education and staff development, and research; and (d) realize that context is critical to both understanding the factors influencing QOL at micro (individual or family), meso (community or organizational), and macro (cultural) levels, and to integrating systems of supports to enhance one's quality of life across these ecological systems.

Collaborative efforts have been key to the progress we have made. Common to these efforts has been an understanding of the desire of all people to experience a life of quality, the commitment among investigators to ensure the participation of consumers and their families, rigorous and principled research, and best practices in the collection and use of data. But even more fundamentally, the work reported in this volume represents the personal journeys, not only of the various authors and their colleagues around the world, but also of the many friends with ID and their family members who have made the work possible.

This chapter is an attempt to encapsulate the essence of those personal journeys from the perspective of consumers and their families, academics and researchers, organization and systems personnel, and the chapter's three authors. The journey has not always been easy; the practical and theoretical challenges are real. Change takes concerted effort over time, and the timing of change must be right. But at the end of the day, we are confident that each traveler will agree it has been a good journey, representing not the beginning of the end, but simply the end of the beginning of an ongoing search for enhanced life quality for people with ID.

The Journey of Consumers and Families

For individuals with ID and their families, the QOL concept emerged during a time of new hope and expectations, following on the heels of an era that was for many a time of abuse and neglect and a life lived in disgraceful institutional settings (e.g., Blatt & Kaplan, 1966; Race, 2002; Tagaya, 1985; Wolfensberger, 1975). New hope was reflected in the rise of the parent and self-advocacy movement, the passage of disability rights legislation, and in deinstitutionalization and mainstreaming.

Change began, at least in part, due to a growing recognition of the importance of normal life for all people (e.g., Nirje, 1969), basic cultural values (Wolfensberger, 2002), the ability of individuals with disability to find their own voices (Williams & Schoultz, 1982), and parental response to a lack of community support (Ferdinand & Marcus, 2002). Collectively, these events provided a significant impetus for changing where people lived and what they did, with a growing understanding that their rights to freedom and happiness should not require scientific "proof" (Blatt, 1987).

Concerns about QOL were implicit in the movement toward integration, normalization, and improved services, but the role of QOL as a key contributor to a better life remained to be articulated. As Schalock, Harper, and Genung (1981) noted, in reference to community integration of persons with ID in Nebraska, "we had accomplished our goal: we had brought people from the institution into the community and facilitated their living and working in more integrated and productive environments. But we had overlooked a significant factor: their quality of life" (p. 485).

Over time, and to address the above observation, the QOL concept has facilitated a journey among individuals with ID and their families, guided by a QOL-related language of thought and action. This language includes a *cast of basic concepts* such as equity, inclusion, empowerment, self-determination, and human and legal rights that have resulted in individuals being more a part of the mainstream of life and active participants in the change process. The language also includes a *set of relationships* that encompass interactions, social networks, community participation, valued roles, and positive experiences. Similarly, the language involves a *family of causal relationships* that foster autonomy/personal control, choices and decision making, self-advocacy, and emphasis on individualized systems of supports rather than general services. And finally, the language includes the *concept of a goal* reflected in the desire to experience personal outcomes, inclusive education, integrated employment, and community living.

The QOL language of thought and action, guided by the philosophic backdrop provided by such international advocates as Burton Blatt (Taylor & Blatt, 1999), Bengt Nirje (1969), Gunnar Dybwad (Allard, Howard, Vorderer, & Wells, 1999), Jack Tizard (1969), and Wolf Wolfensberger (1980), has provided a roadmap for many journeys. Of course the most important journeys have been those of individuals with ID—like those who, in Sweden in the 1960s, established their own clubs, culminating in the first national self-advocates' conference in 1968. Soon thereafter, conferences followed in Britain (1972), Canada (1973), and the American state of Oregon (1974), with the American movement quickly growing into the group that became known as People First (Williams & Shoultz, 1982).

Individuals have written the stories of their own journeys (e.g., Groulx, Doré, & Doré, 2000; Helle, 2000; Hunt, 1967; Ward, 2000; Webb, 2002), and others have told the stories of families who have both established and benefitted from such projects as the Pilot Parent Program, established in 1971 in the American state of Nebraska (Smith & Dean, 2002). Parents (e.g., Brown, 2009) have written moving, intimate accounts of their efforts to achieve improved life quality for their children. But progress has not been even. There have been individual, social, and cultural challenges, hurdles, roadblocks, and detours that have required legislative action, significant policy changes, attitudinal changes across multiple stakeholder groups, empirical support, and organizational transformation. Nevertheless, as the authors of Chapters 4–6 relate, the journey has also been both rewarding and increasingly successful.

The Journey of Academics and Researchers

Many of the contributors to this volume are academics and/or researchers. Their journeys have paralleled those of individuals and families, but their efforts have focused more on conceptual, measurement, application, and evaluation issues. These scholars have attempted to conceptualize, measure, and apply the QOL concept within the larger context of the international disability movement. As reflected in Sections III and IV of this volume, this larger context is characterized by an emphasis on civil and human rights, a social-ecological model of disability, the supports paradigm, the capacities approach to disability, evidence-based practices, and outcomes evaluation. To accommodate these contextual changes, education, advocacy, and research endeavors have incorporated best practices in test development, an empirical approach to theory construction, participatory action research, and multivariate research designs to determine the role of specific predictor variables on personal outcomes.

The journey for academics and researchers, like that of individuals and families, has been difficult at times, although sometimes for different reasons. Mental models and intellectual traditions are hard to change. For example, one of the authors remembers well the initial reservations and "scientific concerns" about using trained self-advocates as peer interviewers in QOL assessment, and the dismay ("you have got to be kidding!") of at least one reviewer of an early article on consumer-based QOL assessment (Bonham et al., 2004).

Some individuals questioned the wisdom of trying to assess QOL, due to the potential misuse of the obtained information (e.g, Luckasson, 1990; Taylor, 1994). Wolfensberger (1994), for example, considered the term "quality of life" so fraught with difficulty that it should simply be discarded.

There has been debate concerning research designs. These debates have centered around whether we should we use between-subjects designs, comparing peoples' QOL scores; multivariate designs, studying correlates of QOL and predictors of QOL-related outcomes; direct observation of behavior; discrepancy analysis of person/environment fit; or ethnographic studies of individuals' everyday lives (see Edgerton, 1996; Felce, 2000; Heal, Borthwick-Duffy, & Saunders, 1996; Keith, 2001; Schalock, Lemanowicz, Conroy, & Feinstein, 1994).

Researchers have also struggled with such fundamental issues as the relative importance of subjective and objective aspects of QOL (e.g., Cummins, 2002a; Cummins, 2002b). Hatton (1998) and Rapley (2004) raised key questions, not only about definition and measurement of QOL, but also about potential hazards that might exist in social construction of disability and OOL. Discussions regarding these and related issues have been, and are, productive, and have thus far led to the consensual approach appearing throughout this text related to the conceptualization, measurement, application, and evaluation of the QOL concept across cultures.

At the same time, however, researchers have continued to move away from simple reliance on instruments and definitions that could be prescriptive, limiting, or even "tyrannical" (Goode, 1997), and toward such person-centered approaches as active support (Chapter 12, this volume; Stancliffe, Jones, Mansell, & Lowe, 2008). Further, investigators have attempted to identify indicators of QOL that may be found and valued across cultures (Schalock et al., 2005), and to extend the use of QOL indicators to such groups as people with severely challenging behaviors (Perry, et al., 2011) and other diagnostic groups (Gómez et al., in press).

Across several cultures, research has suggested that better life quality is associated with living and working environments that more nearly approximate culturally typical settings (Keith et al., 1986; Otrębski, 2000; Schalock, Bonham, & Marchand, 2000; Verdugo, Canal, & Bermejo, 1997). Although people with ID sometimes report satisfaction with some aspects of their lives, they generally rate their QOL lower than individuals without disability (e.g., Bramston, Bruggerman, & Pretty, 2002; D'Eath, Walls, Hodgins, & Cronin, 2003; Hensel, Rose, Stenfert Kroese, & Banks-Smith, 2002; Keith & Ferdinand, 2000; Sands & Kozleski, 1994; Watson & Keith, 2002). Clearly, although researchers have long endeavored to understand QOL, well-being, happiness, and satisfaction (e.g., Campbell, Converse, & Rodgers, 1976; Thorndike, 1917, 1939), these concepts remain elusive targets for definition and measurement (e.g., Costanza et al.,

2007), and the journey toward their enhancement has miles to go for the academics and researchers who study them.

The Journey of Organizations and Systems-Level Personnel

Understanding the QOL concept has not resolved the challenges faced by service providers and service delivery systems. Across international jurisdictions, these challenges include dwindling or very limited resources combined with increased demands for services and supports, calls for organizations to be more effective and efficient, a focus on personal and organizational outcomes, an emphasis on consumer involvement and shared leadership, and an emphasis on using best practices that incorporate the social-ecological model of disability. What the QOL concept has done at the organizational level is to influence organizational policies and practices and allowed organizations to see their primary role differently. At the systems level, the QOL concept has sensitized personnel to the need for a conceptual and measurement framework to guide policy development and systems change (Schalock & Verdugo, 2008, 2012a). Most organizations and systems are going down this road, but their journeys are not yet complete and the challenges may be very different for organizations in developing countries.

Organizations

Many aspects of the QOL concept emerged from the quality revolution of the 1960s, and its emphasis on continuous quality improvement as a productive way to transform organizational policies and practices. Increasingly, the journeys of those organizations that want to incorporate the QOL concept into their culture are using a continuous quality improvement (CQI) framework to enhance their organization's effectiveness. This framework involves the following four components: assessment, planning, doing, and evaluating.

- *Assessment.* Assessment involves using the core QOL domains in two ways—both involving self-assessment. Many organizations, for example, use core QOL domains as a *conversation-based QOL planning guide* to determine what is important to the individual. This information then becomes a critical part of supports planning. A second way is for organizations to use a QOL assessment instrument to determine a baseline or benchmark pattern of QOL scores across the core domains. This information can then be aggregated at the organization level and used for staff development, program development, and/or resource allocation.
- *Planning.* A common procedure is for organizations to use the eight core domains as the framework for individual supports planning. Typical approaches include: (a) establishing for each core domain what is important *to* the person based on the QOL planning guide, and what is important *for* the person based on the

assessment of support needs; (b) aligning specific support strategies to each QOL-related domain; (c) establishing specific objectives that include an action verb, specific support strategy, and anticipated result; and (d) specifying how the anticipated result will be evaluated on the basis of the support objective or a standardized QOL assessment instrument.

- *Doing.* As organizations continue on their journeys and evaluate their effectiveness and efficiency, they re-evaluate how they develop, implement, monitor, and evaluate individual support plans. Two changes in these plans are increasingly apparent in QOL-oriented organizations. One change is that the plans become outcomes-focused and are developed by a Support Team that includes the individual and his/her family or advocate, direct support staff, a supports coordinator, and relevant professionals. The second change is that user-friendly formats are developed using one- or two-page support plans that include, for each member of the Support Team, those support objectives for which he/she is responsible.
- *Evaluating.* Two levels of evaluation are increasingly employed as part of the CQI process. At the micro-level, the status of the anticipated results stated in the respective support objective is used to determine the effectiveness of the related support strategy. At the macro-level, evaluation involves the use of a standardized QOL assessment instrument whose data can be used for reporting, benchmarking, evaluation, and research. Chapter 8 presents a more detailed discussion of this level of evaluation.

Systems

It is a different journey for systems-level personnel who are involved in policy development and systems change. As discussed in Chapters 11 and 14, policy development and systems change rest on the assumption that those involved have a clear understanding of their current service delivery system and how its components contribute to the system's effectiveness and efficiency.

The journey of systems-level personnel involves recognizing the value of the QOL concept as a conceptual and measurement framework. This framework can be used to guide policy development and systems change, and to move toward an understanding that: (a) the concepts of vertical and horizontal alignment provide the basis for policy development and systems change; (b) policy development is based on vertical alignment and focuses on enhancing congruence between systems-level processes and organization-level practices; (c) systems change is based on horizontal alignment and focuses on enhancing the logical sequence of the input, throughput, and outcome components; (d) program logic models can be used to articulate the relations among a system or program's input, throughput, and output/outcome components; (e) critical thinking skills involving systems thinking, alignment, and synthesis are essential in policy development and systems change; and (f) policy development and systems change are facilitated by taking a long-term perspective to ensure continuity and cumulative gain across administrations and administrators (Schalock & Verdugo, 2012a, b).

In summary, the QOL concept has generated four significant challenges in the journeys of organizations and systems. First, both entities have to overcome mental models related to the belief that the condition—including QOL—of persons with ID (and especially those with more significant limitations) cannot change. Second, they must incorporate multiple performance-based perspectives in planning and evaluation. Four essential perspectives are those related to the consumer, and the organization's growth, financial analyses, and internal processes. Third, CQI and transformation require cooperative self-assessment that is integrated into a quality-improvement loop that includes assessment, planning, doing, and evaluating. Fourth, effective and efficient organizations and systems need to implement outcome-oriented and user-friendly support plans that align support strategies to personal, QOL-related goals and assessed support needs (Schalock et al., 2014a; Schalock, Lee, Verdugo, & van Loon, 2014b).

Developing World

The focus on organizational and systemic journeys is not complete without recognizing the challenges that face those who work to enhance QOL in cultures in the developing world, where cultural priorities may work against the needs of people with disability (see Chapter 16, this volume), and where supports may be available to only a small proportion of people with ID (McConkey & O'Toole, 2000). Poverty is a significant factor in the well-being of individuals with ID and their families, not only in developing countries (Mitra 2004), but also in developed nations (Emerson, Hatton, Llewellyn, Blacher, & Graham, 2006; Emerson & Parish, 2010), and is a special concern for organizations working in the former (Mitra, 2004).

Until recently, such life-threatening challenges as malnutrition, infectious diseases, and infant mortality were the focus of attention of planners in developing countries (Christianson et al., 2002), with disabilities and QOL being lesser priorities. Little was known about the lives of people with ID (Fujiura, Park, & Rutkowski-Kmitta, 2005). Although various organizations and researchers have undertaken efforts to identify children with ID in low-income countries (see for example Kromberg et al., 2008), the status of service delivery efforts is influenced by both economic and cultural variables.

In Africa, for example, many people rely on metaphysical explanations for disability, and may seek their help from faith-based and traditional healers (Mpofu et al., 2007). Accordingly, service providers must have not only professional skills, but also cultural awareness, understanding of non-formal systems, and knowledge of program advocacy (Mpofu, 2006; Serpell et al., 1993).

Reflecting the concern that research and techniques developed in affluent nations may not find their way to implementation in lower-income countries, and that ninety percent of people with ID live in low- and middle-income countries (LAMIC), the

International Association for the Scientific Study of Intellectual Disabilities (IASSID) formed the IASSID Academy (Hassiotis et al., 2011). The aim of the Academy is to develop and deliver training for professionals, family members, and caregivers in less affluent countries where local customs, language, and resources might preclude access to typical published materials. Clearly, the journey is ongoing for those providing services in developing nations, and it is a journey more arduous than those of organizations and systems in more affluent societies.

Our Personal Journeys

More than three decades have passed since the authors of this chapter first collaborated in research and practice focused on the QOL of people with ID. Although our work paths over the years have intersected in various ways, our individual journeys are unique and personal. In this section we briefly recount how each of our lives became entwined with those of people with ID and of our colleagues.

Ken Keith

My interest in the lives of people with ID began when I was a young child, visiting the Glenwood (IA) State School, where my grandfather was a painter. I sometimes visited the paint shop, where my granddad and the other painters, some of them men with ID, would gather after work, talk, play horseshoes, and show me things they were making—birdhouses and other colorful projects. From an early age, therefore, I had friends and acquaintances with ID, and during my undergraduate days, I returned to the State School each summer as a student worker. Later, after undertaking graduate studies, I received an invitation to go to Nebraska, where the state institution, the Beatrice State Home, was under siege from media and citizens' groups, as a result of the dreadful conditions there. These were the late 1960s, change was afoot, and there was, in keeping with the times, the heady feeling of being part of an important social movement.

Before long, I had established contacts with people who were developing community services in the cities of Omaha and Lincoln, and I met advocates associated with the Nebraska Association for Retarded Citizens (NEBARC, now simply The Arc). The NEBARC executive directors, John Foley and then Dave Powell, provided leadership and inspiration to a powerful volunteer movement, and strong self-advocates like Tom Hoolihan, Ray Loomis, Nancy Ward, and Ollie Webb were irrepressible voices speaking out to better their lives and the lives of their friends. I was strongly influenced by my service on numerous NEBARC committees, some of them fundamental to the eventual directions of community services. And I was privileged in those days to meet some extraordinary professionals, including Shirley Dean, Frank Menolascino, Lyn Rucker, René Ferdinand, and, of course, Bob Schalock. Bob and I met in 1970, and before long we found reasons to begin a collaboration that has spanned the intervening 45 years.

Sometime in the early 1980s, Karen Hoffman, at Region V Services in Nebraska, came with a completed thesis that investigated QOL of people who had moved from the institution to community settings. She wanted help to do more research. As a consultant to Region V, my central interest at the time was the development of programs for people with challenging behaviors. The concept of QOL was, I thought, too soft, too squishy, to merit serious scientific study. But Karen was persistent, and my head finally followed my heart. She got the attention of Bob and me, and together we solicited ideas from many individuals, family members, and service providers, eventually field testing and publishing our first QOL questionnaire (Keith, Schalock, & Hoffman, 1986).

When Karen moved away, to the state of Washington, Bob and I found ourselves with a program of research that had become too interesting and, we thought, too important to abandon. The rest of the story, of course, is a tale of multiple revisions of instruments, an evolving view of the role of conceptual perspectives, measurement strategies, and applications of QOL, and a growing understanding of the centrality of self-determination, environmental context, and personal supports as critical foundations. I have also been lucky enough to live and work in Japan, the United Kingdom, and Mexico—experience that reinforced the significance of enhanced cultural understanding. In the process, I have been privileged to gain many friends—individuals with ID, their families, professionals, and scientists—across the United States and in many other countries.

The door to Grandpa's paint shop opened the way to a journey neither he nor I could have imagined in those long-ago days of my childhood. But it's been a delightful trip.

Bob Schalock

My personal QOL journey has been intrinsically linked to the journey of individuals and their families, academics and researchers, and organization- and systems-level personnel. Over these 40+ years, I have had the opportunity to interact and work with many individuals within each group.

I was very fortunate to be in the right place at the right time. During the 1970s, Mid-Nebraska Mental Retardation Services and the creative and dedicated people who worked there were grappling with a number of challenges related to the community placement of persons with ID. Collectively, during the 1970s and 1980s we established a forward thinking community-based service delivery system that focused on individualized support strategies and the value of personal outcomes. For over two decades, Mid-Nebraska was my "working lab."

During my formative years, I had the benefit of working with visionaries such as Wolf Wolfensberger and Frank Menolascino, who charted the course toward full citizenship, community inclusion, and enhanced QOL for persons with ID and their families. I also had the benefit of the leadership and wisdom of self-advocates like Ollie May Webb and Nancy Ward; parents such as Jack and Shirley Stark, and Patty Smith; human rights advocates like Bob Perske and Shirley Dean; and legislators such as Dan

Lynch. I also had the support of book editors like Mike Begab and Dave Braddock, who reached out and encouraged research and publication. It was that support and the insight I gained from my standing on the shoulders of giants, evaluating the results of the Mid-Nebraska Mental Retardation Services Program, and networking with national and international QOL researchers that led to the initial books I edited on quality of life in 1990 (b), 1996, and 1997. That encouragement and those experiences also resulted in probably my favorite edited book: *Out of the Darkness and Into the Light: Nebraska's Experience with Mental Retardation* (Schalock, 2002). That book, which was dedicated to "those giants who helped us out of darkness and into the light, including those who were visionaries, risk takers, and pioneers of the human spirit" (p. v), brought together self-advocates, parents, policy makers, service providers, and researchers who wrote the story about the people, places, philosophy, politics, advocacy, and just plain hard work that resulted in moving people from darkness into the light. That book also helped me greatly in understanding what QOL is all about.

Being in the right place at the right time meant that I could act on personal characteristics that reflected my proclivity to maximize opportunities, conduct practical, "real life" research, contribute to a changing social philosophy, foster collegiality and synergism, and be part of the lives of creative and well-meaning people. The net result has been—and continues to be—a very satisfying sense that I have been a part of a social movement that has brought—and will continue to bring—significant change in how people with disability and their families see themselves and become part of the mainstream of life; how academics and researchers approach a concept that has profound effects on each of us; and how organizations and systems can respond to the needs of people in a value-based and outcomes-oriented way. It continues to be a wonderful journey.

Karen Hoffman

I too found myself at the right place and the right time. As a college student, I happened to be wiping tables in the dorm cafeteria and asked another worker what she did over the summer. She had been a student in the SWEAT (Summer Work Experience and Training) program. It was a federal program designed to recruit young people into the field of mental retardation. When she described her summer, I knew I had to find a way to get into the program the next year. I was accepted and began my whirlwind education about the field from Wolf Wolfensberger and Frank Menolascino, who administered the program at the University of Nebraska Medical Center in Omaha. Over the summer, I also learned from Bob Perske, Linda Glenn, Brian Lensink, and a host of others. It was like stepping into a revolution. I learned more in those three months than in my previous college education. The following year, Wolf sent me to Sweden to study for a year. To me, it was like going to the mountaintop to learn about normalization.

When I started my career, I didn't understand the fuss about quality of community service versus institutional life. As people moved into the community, quality was defined in the rear-view mirror, simply as better than the previous service model. Location, size, and decor were common defining factors; the definition of quality centered around bricks and mortar.

Some (e.g. Bachrach, 1976; Santiestevan, 1976) viewed this trend with skepticism, suggesting that people would be lonely, homeless, and victims of those who would take advantage of them. Santiestevan (1976) called deinstitutionalization a "chronic ward of one," believing it was unfair to force people into the community, tantamount to "cruel and unusual punishment." Both sides argued about "quality of life," but no one defined what the words meant. Generally, the disability literature did not address broader issues related to the concept of QOL.

In 1978 I began my study of QOL with a master's thesis, wanting to conduct an ethnographic study; but my thesis committee would not approve it, nor were the committee members excited about the idea of QOL. However, I conducted an exploratory study, with the purpose of conceptualizing and identifying predictors of QOL. I was reminded of Wolfensberger's (1972) notion of the culturally-valued or "normal" analog—How was QOL measured for everyone else? Most conclusions about QOL were gleaned from the literature of human development, psychology, sociology, and social indicators, but persons with disabilities were specifically excluded (Neugarten, Havighurst & Tobin, 1961; Rosen, Clark, & Kivitz, 1977).

I became a devotee of Campbell (1976) and other authors on the concepts of QOL, loneliness, satisfaction, and choice. I constructed questions and interviewed people about their QOL. I asked friends, family members, and colleagues a simple question, "what does QOL mean to you?" I continue to this day to ask that question and I get the same answers: family, friends, enough money to make ends meet, job or purposeful activity, choice and control in life, safe housing, contribution and giving back. The order varies and other items are sometimes included, but the theme is consistent.

When my thesis was finished, I knew that I had some interesting data and concepts. I approached Ken Keith and Bob Schalock, asking them to read my thesis and help me get something published. It took several years before I was successful at getting an audience. We decided to collect more data using interviews conducted by numerous community providers in Nebraska. I remember the day in Ken's office when the first run of data came back. Bob looked at me and said the data were "looking very good and that we had isolated some core concepts."

When I left academia, my career evolved into being a service provider, hoping to direct change. I paired my two guiding principles of normalization and QOL. I used the normal analog as a benchmark for the quality of service design. I looked for jobs in the community that everyone aspired to, and residences tailored to reflect the people living there. Staff became proud of the homes and the work. Some even stated that the houses were better than theirs! Change didn't happen overnight, but over the course of several years, the services I managed in Nebraska City received the "Best Quality of Life" award from the state Association of Community Professionals.

Moving to the state of Washington in 1990, I was viewed as a country girl from Nebraska. How could I know anything about services, normalization, or QOL? What was QOL anyway? I used the early versions of our QOL instrument as a means to help staff have QOL conversations with people they worked with. But they were only interested in what the score meant. Depersonalization and "it is good enough for them" created low expectations, and engagement in many activities was "too risky." Again, I used the normal analog and benchmarking to organize services. This was a major departure from existing services, and was considered radical, challenging the system, and "scaring people." I persevered and eventually our services were viewed as innovative and progressive.

I now travel across the country, providing states with training on the *Supports Intensity Scale—Adult Version* (Thompson, et al., 2015). I enjoy conducting interviews with individuals with ID, families, and stakeholders. Individuals and families express a strong desire to have a more productive quality of life. And I see what Bigby, Knox, Beadle-Brown, Clement, and Mansell (2012) identified as the dimensions of culture that impede emergence of QOL in service provision. Caretaking may be viewed as the norm, with participation in the community seen as an add-on, taking too much time. Staff-centered practices result in lack of choice and participation by persons served. My journey has been long and winding, including some wrong turns and frequent speeding tickets!

So are we there yet? Undeniably, we have been able to conceptualize and measure QOL across a multitude of settings and cultures. However, there is a long way to go. Until there is passion and desire to achieve a good life for *all*, we will struggle. People, agencies, and systems must step forward to benchmark outcomes and align service values with the QOL of typical individuals and ask what we must do to achieve that. As Frank Menolascino (1977) observed, "The question of morality, then, is not 'us against them'. . . It is more a matter of the individual professional's perception of what we all, as human beings, deserve, and his assessment of his own knowledge, power, and vision to effect the necessary changes" (p. 339).

The Road Ahead

These brief snapshots of the various journeys of people concerned with QOL serve to illustrate that we have come from diverse places, and have taken different routes to reach this point in the early twenty-first century. Yet we are all bound for the same destination, a destination rooted in the universal desire for a better life. As David Matsumoto (2000) said in his foreword to the first edition of this book, "Whether African, European, or Asian, gay or straight, living with disabilities or not, the search and striving for a better quality of life is a goal for all of us. This striving separates us from our primate ancestors and all other animals. This striving is the most human of all strivings" (p. xxiii).

Perhaps, in the end, it is the striving, the journey, that makes our effort worthwhile. Thus, we try always to improve QOL for all people, understanding that there is no end, no stopping point; as Matsumoto noted, we are always striving for improvement. And there is a long way to go. Yet we have come a long way as reflected in the subsequent chapters. There is great satisfaction in the process, in trying to create change for the better. Maybe QOL is not an end, but simply the meaning of the experience, the process, of life. Maybe, in the words of the old Chinese proverb, "the journey is the reward."

SECTION II
QUALITY OF LIFE AT THE MICROSYSTEM LEVEL

Section Overview

We approach QOL and its enhancement from a systems perspective, integrating individual thoughts and actions with the three systems that affect human functioning and QOL: the microsystem (i.e., the individual and his/her immediate family), the mesosystem (i.e., organizations and the community), and macrosystem (i.e., larger society and culture). The QOL fulcrum, however, is the micro level: the individual and his/her family.

At the microsystem level, significant changes have occurred over the last four decades in how people with ID view themselves as individuals with personal interests, goals, and potential, and how they can build on these changed beliefs to enhance available opportunities to make decisions about their lives, to be valued members of society, and to be included in the mainstream of life. When people from six countries speak for themselves, as they do in Chapter 4, common QOL themes emerge. Those shared by the self-advocate contributors to Chapter 4 emphasize the importance of family, the desire for inclusive education and integrated employment, self-confidence and independence, choice and control, community access and regular community-based activities, safety and security, personal ownership, close friends and deep relationships, personal pride, and belief in a better, more interdependent future.

Organizations and systems-level personnel can facilitate people speaking for themselves by recognizing at the outset that personal involvement is a person's right, and that people differ, but rights don't. As we will see in Chapter 5, a number of conditions are part of any conversation or interview that can either facilitate or hinder personal involvement. Furthermore, there are empowerment-oriented interviewing skills and strategies that not only facilitate conversation and knowledge production, but also overcome many of the challenges that interviewers frequently encounter.

Although the major focus of this volume is on individual-referenced QOL, we would be remiss if we excluded the significant international work on family QOL. Chapter 6 provides an overview of that work, and shares with the reader a number of studies based in Argentina that describe the conceptual and measurement framework used to understand and assess family QOL in Argentina and the resulting profiles across multiple family QOL dimensions.

CHAPTER 4

PEOPLE SPEAKING FOR THEMSELVES

KENNETH D. KEITH and ROBERT L. SCHALOCK

Introduction and Overview

In Sweden in 1968, a group of young adults with ID convened to discuss the need for their voices to be heard in issues affecting their lives—such issues as job training, work, leisure, and their concerns about being grouped with children. In discussing this group, Nirje (1969) observed that "the choices, wishes, and desires of the mentally retarded themselves have to be taken into consideration as nearly as possible and respected" (p. 184). It followed that "people should be known by their names [and accomplishments], not by their disabilities" (Webb, 2002, p. 57). Pioneering American self-advocate Raymond Loomis famously encapsulated the aim of the self-advocacy movement in this way: "If you think you are handicapped, you might as well stay indoors. If you think you are a person, come out and tell the world" (Williams & Shoultz, 1982, p. 17).

In the first edition of this book (Keith & Schalock, 2000) we presented the perspectives of self-advocates from five countries, each discussing important personal views and aspects of life quality. For this second edition, we have once again assembled a cross-cultural panel of individual self-advocates, and, as we will see, their views illustrate important aspects of contemporary conceptual views of quality of life (QOL). Thus, they see the importance of personal and environmental facets of QOL as a complex, multidimensional part of experience; they seek the same things from life as any other person; they experience QOL in both subjective (e.g., relationships) and objective (e.g., availability of transportation) ways; and they value the role of self-determination and choice in their lives. We will also see in this chapter a picture of the evolution of self-advocacy in a culture—the People's Republic of China—where cultural and philosophical traditions have not typically encouraged self-determination.

Leigh's Journey of Life: Leigh Worrall[1], Australia

I am 32 years old and this is what's important to me. I was born at Paddington Women's Hospital, in Sydney, Australia. Later I went to mainstream primary schools near my home, which was at Coogee, a beach suburb of Sydney. When I was ten years old my brother, Tane, was born at the same hospital. When my brother was nine months old, my Mum, my Dad, my brother Tane, and I moved to Kalgoorlie, a gold mining town in Western Australia. There I went to Hannan's primary and Eastern Goldfield's Senior High School. These were mainstream schools which all students attended. I liked going to mainstream schools, because I could mix with all students.

Family is the most important thing in my life, but this wasn't always the case. When I was young there was only Mum and me. Then Mum met Rene and they got married. Then along came my 2 brothers. We didn't get along well due to our age difference. I am 10 years older than Tane and 12 years older than Kai, and I thought they were brats. At the time I felt jealous because I didn't have my father around and Tane and Kai did. And I was also jealous of the time Mum spent with my brothers, and I felt left out.

When I was 22 years old I moved back to Sydney to stay with my Grandma in Coogee, so I could get more treatment for my condition, called epilepsy. Due to the distance, I hardly ever saw my family and due to Mum and Granny clashing over many things I didn't speak much to Mum for the next nine years. Since Granny has died everything has changed. I have seen my Mum and we talk every couple of days on the phone. Mum and I have a special bond.

Last year I had the opportunity to go to Freemantle, which is near Perth in Western Australia, to present at a conference on inclusive research. While I was there I got to catch up with my brothers. It was very emotional and happy at the same time. I realized they had grown up and are now my big brothers, no longer little brats and now we get along well together. When it came time to leave them I was very emotional and cried. My relationship with my stepfather and brothers has grown. My stepfather and brothers are more important to me now than ever before. Soon Mum and Rene will be living in Newcastle, New South Wales, and I will be able to see them more often.

Having self-confidence, independence, and having a voice, choice, and control are really important to me, as for a long time I never got that chance. When I was young

---

1. Leigh would like to acknowledge the assistance she received from Megan Noveaux, one of her support staff, who typed many of her drafts. Dr. Trevor Parmenter also assisted Leigh over several visits to her home and cups of coffee at her favorite coffee shop, discussing her life's journey and the issues that helped give her a good life. However, this is entirely her story, without any additions from anyone else.

I had confidence through playing sports. While I was at school I represented Western Australia at the Special Olympics in both athletics and swimming. I did that for eight years. I was so proud of myself and I was good at it. I also played netball. When I got older I lost confidence due to shyness, wasn't sure of myself and being away from family. While I lived with Granny she was over-protective by not letting me make my own decisions and choices or have control. Every time I wanted to go out, I had to ring Granny to see if I was allowed to do things. Every time I went to birthday parties she had to come with me. I was 23 years old and I was not allowed to be on my own; she just didn't listen to me.

Over the past 18 months I slowly found myself. Slowly but surely I started to make decisions for myself. I felt scared at first as I was not used to having so much freedom. I speak to my Aunty and she gives me advice, but she does not make my decisions for me. Now I choose to go out when I want, and do what I want to do and at what time. Where I live now I have a residents' meeting once a week with my keyworker. These meetings are important to me and other people, because we can express our feelings and ideas.

In February, 2014 I was chosen to be involved with inclusive research at the Centre for Disability Studies. When I first started I was very quiet and shy, but over the year, with lots of encouragement, I was able to confidently present several times in front of groups of people. I felt proud, and I was shocked that I was able to do it, and have surprised myself by what I have achieved. I have even thought that in the future I would like to become an advocate for other people.

Over the past 32 years I have lived in Sydney, Kalgoorlie, back to Sydney, and then in Loftus. Finally, in January, 2014 I moved into my home at Taren Road. I feel safe and secure having a roof over my head and happy to have a space of my own. I can watch TV and listen to music whenever I want, and I can come and go as I please. I share with another lady called Tina, who uses a wheelchair and is nonspeaking. We get on great together, have jokes, laugh, and I help her when she needs it.

Friends are important, you socialize with them, sit down and have a chat and talk to them about things. You help them whenever they need it. They are someone you can trust and talk to. I met Todd out in the community when I was in trouble. We just didn't say goodbye. He found something special in me and I found something special in him. I know I can ring him anytime and he is there for me.

Having my circle of support makes me feel good inside, and I can always count on them for help and guidance. They have all helped me in different ways, such as taking the time to explain about different disabilities to me. I have become more accepting of other people. This has given me confidence and encouragement to always keep trying and it doesn't matter if I make a mistake (I still struggle with this but am getting better).

To close, I would like to sum up those things which give me a good life. These include my family, my friends, being independent, and being able to make my own decisions and choices. I also enjoy helping and supporting other people. I am now more mature, more confident, and can speak up for myself. I am very proud of myself and I have a life!

In the future I would like to go back to Perth, and also to Kalgoorlie, for a holiday and to see my brothers again and to see how much it's changed. I haven't been back since I left over 10 years ago. I would also like to travel out of Australia one day. At the moment I don't know where I would start, I just want to see new places and have new experiences.

For Me, Quality of Life Means a Life of Variety: Daniela Donna Breimeyer, Germany

I am 24 years old. I've lived in a residential group at Sozialwerk St. Georg for four years with eight to ten other people. Sozialwerk St. Georg is a social services company with differentiated services offered to people with mental disabilities, psychological illness or addiction. It is located in North Rhine-Westphalia, Germany. We get on well and sometimes go on trips together; for instance, we've been shopping in Cologne.

Self-Determination

I used to live in a children's home. I liked it there but I like it here too. I can live here like an independent adult. No one tells me that I must do this or do that, but if there are rules, then the staff explain them to me. I have my own room and can spend private time there whenever I want. It's decorated to my taste. I really like pink; it's definitely my color.

Self-Responsibility

I have a personal assistant who supports me when I need, or ask for, help. (In everyday life every client has a personal assistant at his side. The personal assistant supports the quality of life of clients through individual and appropriate service provision.)

But I don't usually need much. I do my own laundry, keep my room tidy, go shopping, and cook for myself. I did a two-year home economics course which taught me a lot. I also have my own bank account. I travel every day on my own to the day care center where I take part in a sport group and cookery group as well as painting pictures on canvas with the creativity group.

Hobbies and Free Time

On Thursdays I go to the Sozialwerk St. Georg theatre group, *Blitzlicht*, from 4:00 to 7:00 P.M. At the moment we're rehearsing a new play. I play the part of *Isabella*, which is one of the leading roles in *The Devil with Three Golden Hairs*. The play is due to be performed in front of an audience in spring 2015. There are ten or twelve other people in the theatre group.

I'm a Bollywood fan and know more than thirty Bollywood films. My favorite is *Always and Forever*, starring Shahid Kapoor. I like Shahrukh Khan a lot too. I also like the voice of the German actor who does the dubbing for him. I wrote a letter to the voice actor and he sent me his autograph. I was jumping for joy! I've got a lot of posters of those films on the walls in my room. I do Bollywood dancing myself. I'm actually in the St. Georg film, *Mittendrin*, and I perform at the St. Georg festivals.

Inclusion

At the weekend I like to have a DVD day or go into town with my friends, Vivien or Lars. Sometimes we go out for a meal or to the cinema. Lars and I are good friends—I got to know him at the day care center. I met Vivien on Facebook. She's an Aerzte (a German band) fan too. She contacted me on Facebook, we met up, and now we've been friends for over two years. I know all about Facebook and WhatsApp and find them easy to use. I've got lots of friends on there. I got to know Janine from Thueringen on Facebook. She's an Aerzte fan, too. We write to each other and sometimes we phone as well.

I've been to an Aerzte concert and I've also been to two Adel Tawil (a German musician) concerts this year with friends. I also like to watch television programs in my free time—for instance, the *Vampire Diaries* series and the *Twilight* films. I enjoy drawing, especially dolls and mandalas.

My mother, my uncle, and my aunt live in Essen. My mother visits me on Sundays once a month. We go for a coffee or an ice cream; sometimes we go for a walk or we'll stay in and watch television together.

Future Goals and Plans

My goals are, at some time, to move into my own place and to have a job at the sheltered workshop. I discussed this with my Teilhabebegleiter and my personal assistant at my conference on future developments. (A Teilhabebegleiter is an allocated "Social Participation Advisor" who works closely with the clients with the ultimate goal of helping them move toward full participation in society. He supports the clients in planning their personal development and future. In a joint conversation between the client, the Teilhabebegleiter, the personal assistant, and other persons the client would like to invite, a binding goal and action plan for the coming year is created.)

I have to practice at getting myself up on time in the mornings, going to the day care center, getting on with my neighbors, and cooking for myself. The others in my residential group eat together, but I have to learn to cook so that, at some time in the future, I can live on my own. What I wish for is to be able to carry on doing Bollywood dancing and be able to perform. My dream is to visit a Bollywood film studio.

In conclusion, I would like to thank the following people at St. Georg's Quality Department who helped me communicate my message. They are Frau Breimeyer, Manja Buchenau, Sandra Doerpinghans, and Frank Loebler. Danke.

Journey Toward Empowerment:
G. Parthiban, India

(Support Provided by Vijay Kant, Mentor, and S. K. Goel, Consultant)

The self-advocacy movement, in an organized manner, was promoted by our parent organization Parivaar (meaning Family) since 2008. The need for organizing a forum for persons with intellectual and developmental disabilities never dawned on the minds of rehabilitation professionals in the country. The value of our advocacy was realized only after the UN Convention on the Rights of Persons with Disabilities (CRPD) and the UN Economic and Social Commission for Asia and the Pacific (ESCAP) call for "Making Rights Real" for persons with disabilities.

We are also on the threshold of new legislation guaranteeing rights to people with disabilities in India. In recent times, support for us came especially from our parents' organizations. These developments are very good for us. Despite all these developments, we are still living in the shadow of our parents, professionals, and others. In 2008, Parivaar started to bring us together and to build self-advocacy organizations with support from CBM, which is an international organization, founded in 1908, that advocates for quality of life of people with disability. Since then, several active self-advocacy chapters have formed in the states of Andhra Pradesh, Karnataka, Kerala, Maharashtra, Odisha, West Bengal, and Tamilnadu. We have enrolled nearly 1,500 members across these states. In 2013, with support from The National Trust, CBM, and the South Asia Regional Office-India, we conducted the first National Convention in October 2013 at New Delhi with the participation of 150 self-advocates, mentors, family members, and other supporters from twelve states.

We have come a long way. We were able to demonstrate our capacity to speak for ourselves. We created the National Forum called SAFI (Self-Advocates Forum of India). We deliberated and issued a statement at the end of the National Convention indicating some of the key areas that need attention. These include self-respect, decision-making opportunity, public respect, employment opportunity in all sectors, free transportation at local areas, independence, equal citizenship, reservation in education and employment, right to raise our voice, right to choose who lives with us, right to privacy, right to know that our things are our things, right to know our money is our money, right to be safe in our own home, right to say no, right to plan for our future, and right to have freedom from abuse, negligence, and exploitation.

Our representatives from time to time have had the opportunity to address and participate in various public forums. We participated in the Inclusion International Asia Pacific Regional Forum held at Kathmandu, Nepal; an Indo-Irish Encounter on Legal Capacity organized by NALSAR University, Hyderabad; Global Action Week Conference on Education organized by National Coalition for Education at Delhi; and CBM National Consultation Workshop on the Rights of Persons with Disabilities Bill, 2014, at Bangalore. We regularly participate and address our issues at the annual Parivaar National Parents' Meets. Our representatives serve on the decision making bodies of state and central executive councils of Parivaar.

There was a time when no one trusted us and we were belittled. We are now emerging as strong advocates on our own behalf. We are raising our voice now, "*Yes, We can!*" SAFI needs capacity building for meaningful interventions when issues relating to us are discussed. We need professional guidance and support from our parents and professionals in realizing our dreams. We demand our right to be consulted. We want to make the changes for ourselves through the SAFI forum. In conclusion, no one should doubt our ability to make changes in our lives and the lives of our friends. We want the community to acknowledge the significant role we can play in drafting our agenda for tomorrow. We must be seen as allies rather than only viewed as sons, daughters, students, and dependents. We wish to be *partners* with everyone in the mission to help us in our transition.

Self-Determination of Children with Intellectual Disability: Journey of a 13-Year-Old Boy, Ziyato, and His Parents, People's Republic of China
(With Assistance from Jiacheng Xu and Mian Wang)

Ziyato, a 13-year-old boy with ID, has delays in language development. Despite a strong desire to communicate, he has limited language comprehension and expressive skills. With some assistance, he can maintain basic daily conversation, express his opinions, and speak out for himself.

Raised in a big family, Ziyato enjoyed his parents' less demanding parenting style (as compared to many Chinese parents) in nurturing his development. His parents keep Ziyato's requests and desires in mind and try their best to fulfill them. As a result, Ziyato takes initiative to make many new requests regularly despite frustration sometimes occurring due to unfulfilled desires.

Ziyato has numerous hobbies. He likes reading and listening to music. He reads comic books and newspapers during spare time to get more information, and his favorite hobby is playing computer games. Ziyato has been learning to play an electronic keyboard for nearly two years. When he meets other people, he likes to play music for them, and enjoys being listened to. Ziyato also has dreams—wanting to become a teacher or an astronaut. But he seems to lack goal-setting skills and self-control skills to execute a plan to reach his objectives. Therefore, he needs an Individualized Support Plan (ISP) and the key focus of his ISP is on his ability for self-determination.

Given that Ziyato has basic language and communication ability and a desire to speak out about his wants and wishes, the support team interviewed him. The team was very sensitive and respectful to his self-determination and his expression of desires and dreams during the interview process. Based on observations, a summary of Ziyato's opinions expressed in the interview, and his parents' expectations, the team worked together to identify his support needs. From Ziyato's expressed dreams, the team helped him choose music performance to be his main goal. By paying respect to his self-determination and encouraging his active participation in the decision-making of his ISP, the team (made up of Ziyato, his parents, school teachers, and relatives or acquaintances in the local community) created an ISP that comprises different strategies to meet his support needs. The ISP is based on self-determination, and specifies support needs, goals, strategies for achieving goals, Ziyato's self-determination skills, and the people and environments providing support for each goal. For example, for the goal of practicing to achieve fluency in piano playing, the natural support strategy includes supervision by parents in the family environment. Helping Ziyato to set goals and make an action plan to actualize his dreams and make stable self-decisions was the priority goal of the ISP.

A few months after the implementation of the ISP, Ziyato had successfully achieved his goals to his and his parents' satisfaction, with all the support needs being met. Ziyato had two opportunities to perform his music presentations at the New Student Orientation Party and the New Year's Party, and was very well received at both occasions.

The support team happily came to agreement that in this case study Ziyato had revealed improvements of his self-determination skills and was satisfied with his attainments. In the past, despite strong desires, he had a difficult time setting his goals and developing an action plan that he could stick to until it was realized. During the ISP implementation, the support team provided support to encourage him to attempt to achieve the goals by allowing flexibility of schedule and his own approach. For example, every afternoon Ziyato had some time allocated to practicing keyboard and rehearsing music performance. During this process, he was supported to learn how to set some small-step goals and develop an action plan to actualize it. In addition, he also found that in the ISP implementation process, the ability to control his emotions and mood had improved to help overcome some difficulties that he used to encounter before. More importantly, the team realized that Ziyato's support intensity varied over the course of this ISP process in the direction of lessening support needs.

Ziyato's case reveals that self-determination relates to a child's independence, emotional well-being, and self-advocacy. Through the planning and implementation of his ISP, the support team realized that the team's emphasis on his self-determination is critical, and has helped motivate Ziyato's active participation in the process while striving to accomplish his goals. He is now capable of making appropriate choices and decisions for himself. It also further improves the sustainability of his efforts toward achieving his personal goals and helps him become a more social and self-controlled person. The implementation of his ISP and the cooperation between Ziyato and the support team has helped him live an enhanced quality of life.

"I'm Happy and in Love."
Nancy Ward, United States

My name is Nancy Ward. I live in Oklahoma City. My job includes helping other people learn to speak for themselves. I love where I live because the bus terminal is right across the street. Since I don't drive, this makes it very convenient for me to catch any bus I want. I can also go anyplace I want to go and I do this by myself. It makes me feel very proud of myself that I can do this as independently as possible. These are just a couple of examples of what quality of life is to me. Now I'm going to share with you some other examples.

You need to think outside the box. What do I mean by this? You need to ask me what I want to have for dinner, not just tell me that we're going to have liver and onions. Also give me the chance to say what it is I'm trying to say. For example, when people make fun of you or label you.

I used to work in a workshop where the staff didn't believe in us. One of my friends asked me if I'd fix her hair because she was having a family reunion. I said yes, so that night I did it. The next day at work everyone complimented her on how nice she looked. People asked who did it. When she said I did it, no one would believe her. You know what we did? I did it again, and when people saw what I could do they apologized to me. I said thank you. But I was thinking that you really hurt my feelings and I hope you'll start believing in people. You know the saying that sticks and stones may break your bones but words will never hurt you. Well, I'm here to tell you it's not true that words don't hurt—they do and I hope you think next time before you don't believe in us. How are we supposed to believe in ourselves if the very people who are supposed to be teaching us how to be contributing members of our community don't believe!

My self-advocacy skills are very important to me. People First of Nebraska was one of the first self-advocacy organizations in the country, so when I joined I had no role models. It took me five years to learn how to speak out for myself. I don't want it to take anyone else five years; this is why I'm so passionate now about helping others learn how to speak out for themselves. I'd never thought I'd be helping people see the light bulb go on when someone learns they can tell their family what they're thinking and how they feel. You know what? I can say that I've got a disability, because it's what has given me the opportunity to go to seven different countries to help them learn about people with disabilities.

As you can see I didn't always have people in my life who believed in me, but now I do and I'm able to say with confidence that I've reached one of my dreams—teaching other people how to turn on the light bulb so they can dream and figure out what they want to do with their lives because they have people in their lives that believe in them. More importantly, they believe in themselves!

Next year I'll realize another dream of mine. I'm going to get married. Never give up on your dreams. I'll be 65, but it's still happening, and I'm so happy and in love!

Testimony From a Self-advocate from Uruguay: Federico Oxley Guazzoni

I was born on September 27, 1987 in Paysandú, Uruguay. When I was three years old, I started attending kindergarten at Instituto de Educación Integral (Institute for Integral Education) named Mafalda. In that same school I completed my primary education studies in 2002, at age fifteen.

It makes me happy and I really enjoy going out, traveling, listening to music, dancing and painting. When I was little, I learned percussion with a professional musician. Since the year 2000 I've been attending painting classes with a private teacher. In 2011 I started participating in art workshops in my community, with an artist that's very well known in my region. I have exhibited my paintings three times in several places in my city with my classmates. This year I participated in a painting competition organized by my city's chamber of commerce.

For me, having quality of life is being able to enjoy, be cheerful and happy with what I've got, without caring about money, and doing the things that make me happy. Having quality of life is eating well, dressing well, having friends, going to work, practicing sports, painting, and swimming. I have an intellectual disability and I follow a medical treatment for my epilepsy.

When I was 15 I started swimming in clubs and gyms in my city. Since 2009 I participate in the crossing of Rio Uruguay, between Paysandú and Colón, in Argentina; it's more than 5 kilometers long! I like *capoeira*, which is a martial art in the form of a dance, invented by slaves in Brazil in the seventeenth century. People gather in a circle to practice it and I'm a student in the Rueda del Sol (Sunwheel). I also practiced Sipalki-do and studied organic gardening.

I have fifteen co-workers with disabilities. In the workshop we make and sell ecologic paper bags. I get along with everyone, we work in a good mood; we have fun and celebrate birthdays. At home, I like to help my family to do house chores. In the future, what I would like is to change some things in the world. I want there to be no robberies and that violence against women also didn't exist: that men didn't hit women. I would like that people had more money. I would also like that there were less accidents and more bikes.

For people with disabilities I want more ramps in the city, so they can go out on their wheelchairs. We, as people with disabilities, have the same rights as everyone else; we are all human beings. I feel proud for practicing sports, working, having friends and choosing things in my life. I also appreciate the help I received in writing this from Estefani Oxley and Ricardo Fleitas Merello.

Evolution of Self-Determination and Self-Advocacy of Individuals with Intellectual Disability in the People's Republic of China: Jiacheng Xu, Mian Wang, Youru Xiang, & Sheng Xu

In the mid-1990s, the concept of QOL was introduced to the field of ID in China. In addition to our efforts to introduce the conceptual framework of QOL, we participated in a cross-cultural study to examine etic and emic aspects of QOL in the Chinese context (Schalock et al., 2005). We found that QOL is a multidimensional phenomenon composed of core domains and affected by both personal characteristics and environmental factors. Despite their variability in relative value and importance, these core domains seem to be universally true for all people. Self-determination and self-advocacy were introduced to China and gradually incorporated into intellectual disability (ID) research and practice, and over the last two decades understanding of these concepts by individuals with ID and their families has evolved dramatically (Xu, 2010).

In 2007, we surveyed 290 individuals with ID, 105 family members, and 146 professionals on their perception of eight QOL domains and 24 indicators (Xiang, Xu, & Wang, 2007). The findings suggested that Chinese individuals with ID perceive the domain structure of QOL very similarly to that of other countries, but that they rank the importance of QOL domains quite differently. In particular, they ranked the domains of self-determination and participation as least important. Parents and professionals reported similar views about the importance of self-determination. The main reasons for low ratings of the importance of self-determination include: (a) lack of a clear understanding of self-determination and how it differs from self-development; and (b) the influence of the traditional Chinese cultural emphasis on interdependence, and accompanying de-emphasis of independence and self-determination. For the latter, the cultural importance of patriarchal relations derived from Confucian teaching such as "loyalty of ministers to the emperor" and "loyalty of sons to the father" remains influential in social and familial relationships and impedes the embrace of self-determination.

In a semi-structured interview study of parents and teachers of Chinese youth with ID in Shanghai, Beijing, and Chongqing, Xu (2010) found that both parents and teachers emphasized the importance of academic life and vocational skills, rather than self-determination skills. Parents and teachers reported that students with ID had poor skills in self-efficacy, self-adjustment, self-advocacy, and psychological empowerment. The parents also noted a lack of social acceptance and family support for these students. Parents also reported a lack of employment opportunity and lack of governmental policy on protection and service provision to youth with ID (Xu, 2010).

Xu (2010) also found that different aspects of self-determination of youth with ID are correlated with severity of disability, family structure (e.g., one-child family vs. multiple-child family), and schooling experience. Youth with severe ID had a lower degree of self-determination skills than those with mild or moderate ID, and youth with ID from one-child families had poorer self-determination skills than those from other types of families. In addition, youth with ID who had only attended segregated special education schools had a lower degree of self-determination skills than those with different school experiences (e.g., regular school and/or vocational school).

However, over the last two decades, adoption of the QOL framework in research and practice for individuals with ID has given rise to emergence of a self-determination movement in China. Two important initiatives based on QOL work have gained increasing attention: a supportive education model and national curriculum and core standards for individuals with ID. The Beijing Municipal Government has adopted the QOL framework and has chosen supportive education as the core of inclusive education implementation in its five-year Inclusive Education Plan. As a result, more than 5,000 students with ID have received inclusive education placement in their regular neighborhood schools.

The supportive education model emphasizes three elements for students with ID: express your needs and hopes/dreams, internalize your needs and wishes for self-determination through goal setting and decision making, and enable your self-advocacy through an ISP based on self-determination. The emphasis on QOL-oriented supportive education has promoted school practices for improving self-determination, especially self-advocacy skills of students with ID. Such changes are manifest in the shift from a more professionally dominated individual education plan to the ISP, where students' self-determination is valued and respected, and is honored by having them participate in the process and in decision making.

The second initiative is related to development of a national curriculum and core standard system for all special education schools serving students with ID. The new curriculum reflects a shift of curricular focus from academic subject matters to functional skills, with one of the major educational objectives being promotion of self-determination skills of students with ID.

Self-determination and self-advocacy are about shifting the power for individuals with ID (Pennell, 2001). The gradual growth of the self-determination movement, along with the QOL movement has brought changes for Chinese individuals with ID. Self-determination motivates individuals with ID to lift up their internal desires and expectations, express their needs and wishes, and to advocate for their rights and the supports they need. Self-determination will change a person's learning, employment, and quality of life. Being more self-determined and taking action to advocate will support the campaign against discrimination and inequality in the social and cultural environment.

Conclusion

In the words of the individuals represented in this chapter, we can see a microcosm of the opinions, goals, and desires that we might find in nearly any group of people. In just a few pages, these individuals have shown us the full range of QOL domains. For example:

- *Emotional well-being* is evident in the satisfaction of helping others, in the desire for safety and security, and in the pleasure of meaningful leisure activities.
- *Physical well-being* is reflected in interest in participation in sporting activities, fitness, and treatment for such medical conditions as epilepsy.
- *Self-determination* is woven throughout, in repeated assertions about making one's own decisions, coming and going at will, and in personal choices (e.g., choosing room décor).
- *Interpersonal relations* are important to all these people, whether in mixing with all kinds of students, the importance of family, the use of social media to relate to friends, or falling in love.

- *Social inclusion* manifests itself in shopping with friends, associating with neighbors, and participating in the normal activities of the culture.
- *Rights* come to the fore in the desire of individuals to enjoy equal citizenship with all others, awareness of legislation and UN conventions, freedom from abuse, and the right to marry.
- *Personal development* appears in the universal will to learn meaningful skills, whether that be playing a musical instrument, painting, appearing in a theatrical performance, doing one's own laundry, or simply being a contributing member of the community.
- *Material well-being* is clear in the desire of individuals to have their own money, to have sufficient funds to do what they would like, and to engage in meaningful work.

Perhaps the most noteworthy characteristic of the aspirations described here is the fact that they are not really noteworthy at all. These are the ordinary perspectives of individuals who are simply striving to be themselves, ordinary. When Federico Oxley Guazzoni says he would like to change some things in the world, he has in mind the same things we might all want to change: violence, security, safety, and universal rights. Maybe, as Robert and Martha Perske (1980) suggested, "This is the way civilization betters itself. Change begins with highly visible revolutions but ends with unpretentious ones" (p. 72). Each of the voices in this chapter reflects an unpretentious effort to make life better.

CHAPTER 5

PERSONAL INVOLVEMENT AND EMPOWERMENT

REMCO MOSTERT

Introduction and Overview

Cross culturally, people with ID are speaking for themselves more frequently. As reflected in the previous chapter, the QOL-related principles of self-determination, equity, inclusion, and empowerment have significantly changed how people see themselves and live their lives. Additionally, research clearly shows that QOL is enhanced when people are accepted and integrated into the local society and when they participate actively in decision making.

Many decisions about people are made on the basis of interviews or conversations. During these times, individuals are asked to speak for themselves and share information about their personal interests, goals, and opinions. These interviews/conversations provide an opportunity for the interviewer to enhance the respondent's personal involvement and empowerment. Ways to maximize that enhancement are the focus of this chapter.

This is a very personal chapter written by an individual who has interviewed over 1,000 individuals using the Personal Outcomes Scale (POS; van Loon, van Hove, Schalock, & Claes, 2008), a widely used scale based on the eight core QOL domains described in Chapters 1 and 18. As an "advocate for self-advocates," the author shares his experiences and insight gained from these interviews or conversations. The first section of the chapter focuses on the realization that personal involvement is a right. The second section discusses important conditions in enhancing personal involvement, with the third section discussing a number of empowerment-oriented interviewing skills and strategies that not only facilitate conversation and knowledge production, but also overcome many of the difficulties that interviewers frequently encounter. The chapter concludes with comments from a number of interviewees about what it means to be personally involved and empowered.

Why Personal Involvement: People Differ, Rights Don't

The purpose of the United Nations Convention on the Rights of Persons with Disabilities (2006) is to promote, protect, and ensure the full and equal enjoyment of all human rights and fundamental freedoms by all persons with disabilities, and to promote respect for their inherent dignity. Knowing that people with disabilities have the same rights as all other people makes personal involvement not a question, but a fact. For example, I have a right to vote. You can disagree with my choice, but it makes no sense to discuss whether I am allowed to vote. It is my right. In the same way, I have many other rights that I use in everyday practice. Why? Because it is my right. Period. The same is true of personal involvement. When someone *wants* to be involved in anything that has to do with his personal situation, he *should* be involved. This should not be a question, in the same way that my right to vote isn't a question. It is my right. This knowledge is very important. We need to be absolutely convinced about equal rights. If not, we can forget personal involvement.

Involving persons should be the basic rule, not the exception. When someone is not involved, we should learn to see this as our limitation, not a result of the person's disability. Personal involvement should not be dependent on capability or knowledge; rather, we should make personal involvement happen. If people are not involved, it doesn't mean they can't be or won't be. Compare this with a bird in a cage: When the door is opened, the bird does not fly away immediately. Why not? Because he only knows his life in that cage. Now I ask you, does this mean a bird (any bird) belongs in a cage?

Important Conditions to Enhance Personal Involvement and Empowerment

As a person who interacts with someone with ID, you have a great influence on enhancing personal involvement and empowerment. I suggest three important conditions that enhance both. These involve separating system components, independent monitoring, and involving the person.

Separating System Components

A person-centered support system can be broadly divided into three parts: input (wishes and support needs), throughput (providing the supports in everyday practice) and output (evaluation of the result of the given supports). Many times these three parts are taken care of by one and the same party—the organization. My suggestion is that these three systems components be separated. For example, what is the position of the person when the people who are responsible for the input are the same as those responsible for the throughput, and even the output? In that situation the position of the person is weak. And from a weak position it is hard to become truly involved. If we want individuals to be personally involved, we should work on a strong position for each person. Therefore we need to work to separate the input, throughput, and output.

The focus on the input system component is different from the focus on throughput or output. The input should focus on investigating the wishes the person has and what his or her support needs are. We all know that there can be a discrepancy between what a person asks and what can be provided. The easiest thing is to say to the person that he should meet his wishes and support needs through the possibilities offered by the organization. But if that is the case, why should we ask the person about his wishes and his support needs? We could better tell him what his wishes and support needs are. No personal involvement. Investigating wishes and support needs should be done separately from the possibilities and limitations of the organization. Only when the person can freely talk about wishes and support needs can he or she be truly involved.

Separation between input and throughput gives the responsible people in each of the components the most freedom to use their skills, knowledge, experiences, and professionalism.

By being part of the input, you can focus on the real wishes and support needs, without being held back by the limitations of the throughput. Being part of the throughout, you can fully focus on providing the supports that address the person's wishes and support needs.

When it comes to the output it is important that this part is also separated. When I interview people about their quality of life I can focus completely on the output, because my role as an interviewer is an independent one. I do not support the person in everyday practice. I am simply connected to the person at the point of his or her outcomes. I don't have to understand why supports cannot be provided. I can just ask people about their situations. For example, no contact with neighbors means no contact with neighbors, whatever the reason might be.

Independent Monitoring

The supports provided should be a response to the person's individual goals and support needs. This process should be continuously monitored by a personal assistant who is independent of the process. When a person is not getting the needed support, he or she should be given the possibility to tell this. When the one to talk to is the same as the one who is responsible for providing the supports, it can be difficult for people to be sure that their voice is heard. If you want to place the person in the best position to give an opinion, an independent personal assistant is best equipped to assist the person in monitoring the supports process. A personal assistant who is engaged in the throughput, for example as a support worker in the living situation, can get stuck between the interests of the person, the support team, and the organization. Which to choose?

Being Involved

Nothing about us without us! The separation of the three parts of the person-centered support system and the independence of the personal assistant are important conditions. But these conditions alone are not enough to enhance the individual's personal involvement. The most important thing is that the person is actually involved. This means that, when speaking about personal goals and wishes, the interview should be done with the person. When talking about support needs, the person is there as well. And when it comes to monitoring the throughput, the person should be the one to do so. Finally, in regard to the output, the person should be the one to be interviewed.

Even when it might be very hard for people to express themselves, it is of high value for each person to be involved, anytime and in any part. For example, when someone is totally relying on others to give answers to the questions, you still will have a different interview when the person is in the same room where the interview is held. Once I had a POS interview using the "report of others" version. This version is used when the person is not able to answer for himself or herself. We then talk in one interview with at least two people from the social network of the person. During this report by others, the woman (Maria, age 78) whom the interview was about started singing a Christian song. Because of that I asked her if she went to church, but her answer was no. She thought it was not possible because she was in a wheelchair. The next question was if someone from the church ever visited her. The answer was no, but she would like the pastor to visit her. Because these interests weren't known by the others involved in the interview, we would never have fully understood Maria.

Therefore, again, nothing about us without us! When we search for this personal involvement we can create a true win-win situation. The win for the person is in the strengthening of self-esteem, experiencing influence in a personal situation, experiencing equality with others, and recognizing personal and positive qualities. The win for us is that we don't have to struggle about what is best for the person. The person will serve it for us on a silver platter.

Empowerment-Oriented Interviewing Skills and Strategies

Knowing that personal involvement is a right, and that it is important to create good conditions for the person, I now would like to discuss some practical skills regarding interviewing people. Although there are many different people with all kinds of different communication skills, I think there are some overall empowerment-oriented interviewing skills and strategies that can enhance personal involvement and empowerment.

Time

Time utilization to me is one of the main points. Use the time that is needed. Sometimes a conversation can take a lot of time. The amount of time spent on an interview is one of the main objections to involving people—It takes too much time. But does it? Let's make a simple calculation. In an average organization providing services to people with disabilities, it is common to have a regular team meeting. This can be once a month with a team of ten professionals. The meeting might take two hours, and the number of clients connected to the team is eight. This means twenty hours of team meetings per month (10 × 2). Let's say per year this is 10 (months) × 20 (hours), 200 hours. Or we could say an average of 25 hours per year is spent on talking about the person, without the person. Now I ask you, how much time is allowed to spend on interviewing the client? Additionally, one needs to ask two related questions: Who are our customers, and who is paying the bills?

Getting to Know Each Other

Getting to know one another is an investment for the rest of the interview. When you get to know each other, you establish trust. This means that you take some time before the interview starts. Do not just come into the room, shake hands, sit down, and start. When you meet, first talk a little about hobbies, about what the person has done yesterday, about movies, holidays, or whatever. To be the respondent in an interview can be exciting, but it can also make someone nervous. So invest in reducing these "nerves." It helps the person to understand that you have good intentions, and that you are not as "dangerous" as he or she might think. Investing in getting to know each other gives room for the rest of the interview. There will be a better understanding for the both of you.

Explain the Goal and Outcome of the Interview

Good explanation also improves the trust base. When the person understands why this interview is done, it will be easier to give the right information. The person needs to know in the best way what the topic of conversation is. When a person doesn't know the purpose or goal of the interview, it can lead to uncertainty, and uncertainty is a negative impulse for a good interview. Similarly, one needs to *explain what is done with the outcomes of the interview*. When an interview is finished something will be done with the outcomes, but what? The person has the right to know, before the interview starts, what the outcomes will be. Who is getting the results? What can be the effect of the outcomes? How can the person see the outcomes? Explain this very well, before the interview starts.

Time Schedule

Creating a good atmosphere for the interview also means the person has to know how much time the interview will take. One person is okay with "as long as it takes"; another may like to have a set time. If someone needs a break after a while, take a break. Don't push all the questions into a certain timeframe. Let the time involved be a servant, not a master. When the interview is underway, inform the person about the status. Are we halfway? Have we got only ten minutes left? Where are we and how much time is still needed? Is the person still comfortable with it? Do what the person prefers. Maybe even make a second appointment to finish the interview.

Sometimes I hear people say that a person with a disability is not able to spend too much time on an interview. My experiences have been different. When I ask people at the end of interviews how much time we have spent on the interview, many times they say half of the time we really spent. An hour and a half feels like 45 minutes. The secret here is attention—true and unconditional attention to the person.

Transparency

The person needs to know what is asked in the interview. Don't hide questions because you think they might be too difficult. Don't fill in answers based on your opinion, feelings, or attitude; when you do so and the person sees this, the trust base is gone. Be transparent about everything that is written down, about all the questions. When you think it is a difficult question, just let the person know.

The Interviewer Asks the Questions, the Person Provides the Answers

Having an interview doesn't mean that the person can be forced to give any information. Searching for true involvement goes hand in hand with respect. So respect the decision of a person who is not willing to talk about something. Forcing the person to talk about things will only make the person say even less. Also, ask yourself how important it is to know what you are asking. Are you trying to understand the person, or are you just curious? It is like walking on private property. You, as the interviewer, are the guest.

Don't Judge: There Are No Wrong Answers

If you want individuals to be involved, don't judge them on their answers. Too often people have negative experiences with interviews. When the person feels that involvement can lead to negative outcomes, the willingness to be involved is weakened. This doesn't mean that a person only wants to hear and see positive outcomes. It means that you respect the answers given by the person, in the same way as answers are given by others. Additionally, *don't hunt for answers*. A good conversation happens naturally. Hunting for answers doesn't fit in with that. Give the person all the room and time required to come to an answer. It is like tug of war: The harder you pull the more resistance you get.

Who is the "Problem" in the Communication?

When two people have a conversation and one of them has a (communicative) disability, who should invest more in understanding? My opinion is that the person with a disability knows what to say, it is clear for him. The problem is the understanding, and that is where the interviewer has a job to do. We shouldn't say that because of the lack of expressing oneself we have a difficult conversation. Turn it around: Is it because of our lack of understanding that we have a difficult conversation? When I see myself as the able person in the interview, it means that I have the responsibility to move toward the one with the disability. So action is necessary. Don't just sit and wait for the person to do all the work.

Analogously, don't behave differently in an interview with a person who is being assisted by others and for whom a report of others is sought. Keep the focus on the person instead of focusing on the information provider. It might be easy to talk with the supporter or personal assistant, but whom do we really want to get involved? If the person prefers to have a supporter or an assistant available during the interview, that is fine. But before starting the interview, explain clearly what the role of each person is. The supporter or assistant should assist the person in giving answers, not be the one who is answering. When the role of each person is clear right from the beginning, you can then provide reminders of this during the interview when needed.

Unclear Answers

It can happen that you, as an interviewer, don't understand the given answer. If so, don't pretend that you do understand. Ask the person to repeat the answer. For example, I once had a great, long, and intense interview with someone who was using a very specific communication system. For me as an interviewer it was sometimes hard to understand what it was that she wanted to tell me (although it was absolutely clear for the person herself). The interview was held in the dining room and the personal assistant was sitting in the living room. At a certain time, when I really didn't understand, I asked the person if it was okay for me to ask the assistant for help. The person didn't allow me to do so! Although this wasn't easy for me, it was a big, big lesson. This example showed me that people prefer to have a difficult, direct involvement, step by step, instead of having an indirect smooth conversation involving someone else!

Offer Your Help in a Respectful Way and Be Patient

As an interviewer it may be that you want to help the person with the interview. You might fill in the words for the person. Be aware: Don't help the person without his or her permission. For example, not everyone who stutters likes to be helped to finish sentences. Agree, before the interview starts, on what help is expected and what not. Also, *be patient*. Don't push the person. Sometimes a person needs a bit more time to give answers. Allow the time the person needs. Counting to ten can do miracles here. Many times communication can be a hard thing to do. We need many different tools to get communication to happen. One of the easiest and most important tools is to be patient, and it is better to make another appointment with the person than to put high pressure on the interview to finish everything in a set time.

Speak Clearly and Use Communication Tools

Make sure the person understands you well. Speak clearly, adapting your speed and volume of speaking. When necessary, use the communication tools that the person already uses. Another option to meet the person's limitations in communication can be to simplify the interview form.

All Information is Relevant

When a list of questions is used in an interview, it can be hard to fit the person's answer into the question you just asked. Sometimes the answer is close, but not exactly about what you asked. Does this mean the information is useless? No. To get the people involved means they need to have the possibility to talk about anything they want. If this happens, the interviewer can learn a lot about the vocabulary of the person. This can be helpful in the rest of the interview. It is the interviewer's job to connect all the information to the right question. Not that the answer is wrong; it was simply the wrong question for that moment.

Asking Questions is Easy

How are you doing? Do you worry about something? Are you happy? How is your health? Pretty easy questions to ask, but sometimes they are very hard to answer. Place yourself in the person's position. What would your answers be? Be aware of the load a question can have for the person.

The Person is the Expert

When you look in the mirror, you see things about yourself that you didn't know before. Interviewing can be like that. Each question is like a part of a mirror. This is what an interview can do to a person. People know a lot about themselves, and through questioning this information may be provided. Recognize and appreciate this self-knowledge. It will improve the individual's self-esteem and help the person to participate even more because you recognize his or her role as an expert.

Attention

Involving a person is not possible without giving him or her full attention. This can be a tough thing to do, depending on the moment. An interview conducted at the end of the day can be more taxing than one conducted first thing in the morning. The person should not suffer the negative consequences of your fatigue. Personal attention leads to personal involvement.

Location

It is preferable to conduct the interview at the location preferred by the person. Some like the interview to be done at home; others prefer the office. Either is fine.

In summary, there is a difference between an interview and a conversation. For the best involvement, I would say that you should work on moving from an interview toward a conversation. An interview might be a bit more like a list of questions you have to go through; a conversation is more about meeting each other. As many readers have experienced, interviewing frequently involves many difficulties and challenges, such as concealing a stigma, wanting to be liked, and echolalia. Yes, interviewing can be tough, exhausting, and painful, but it can also be fun and highly rewarding. It is learning every time. It is a privilege. It is a pleasure. It is like digging for gold. Enjoy!

Conclusion: What It Means for a Person to Be Involved and Empowered

In preparing this chapter I asked several people about their experiences and what personal involvement means to them. Denise (age 18) said, "When I am not involved, I don't know what has been said about me." This was also echoed by Christian (age 38). Wilco (age 17) said, "It is a good thing that I am asked about my opinion. I don't like it when too many people are involved in the interview. Then I feel a bit uncertain. I want to choose who is involved in the interview."

When we train people about interviewing with the POS, we ask co-trainers to be part of this. Co-trainers are people with a disability. For the practical part, they are interviewed by the trainee. Afterward, the co-trainers give their feedback. This is the most important part of the training. Each time we see that the co-trainers are the first (I would even say naturally) to understand what personal involvement is all about. In one training session, a co-trainer stood up at the end of the training and proclaimed to all in attendance the importance of being heard. She finished her positive and heartbreaking speech with tears, and all of us were silent . . . and we understood. As a co-trainer, Chantal (age 37) told me some very important things. About involvement, she told me that her experience has been that when two people have the same opinion and one of them has a disability, that person needs to do more to be heard than someone without a disability. The disability label puts you two steps behind. When it comes to supports, she told me that support workers should also support people in communication. Chantal realized more empowerment from the moment she decided to make her own decisions instead of doing what she was told.

Collectively, these people provide a final message: Do everything you can to get people involved. Use custom-made supports. Don't say someone is not able; if you do, it will not become possible for the person. If you want something to happen, you have to be positive and challenge, motivate, involve, and empower the person.

CHAPTER 6
FAMILY QUALITY OF LIFE IN ARGENTINA

ANDREA SILVANA AZNAR and DIEGO GONZÁLEZ CASTAÑÓN

Introduction and Overview

The concept of family QOL emphasizes that all members of the family group are interrelated, that what affects one affects all, and that therefore the challenges facing a member with a disability influence the overall functioning of the family unit. Family QOL, which has enjoyed a surge in interest and study since the beginning of the 21st century, is cross-cultural in nature, and has its foundation in the extensive work on individual QOL and the supports paradigm (Burton-Smith et al., 2009; Samuel, Rillotta, & Brown, 2012; Svraka, Loga, & Brown, 2011; Wang & Kober, 2011).

Researchers recognize that characteristics of individuals and family dynamics are among the predictors of family QOL (Zuna, Summers Turnbull, Hu, & Xu, 2011). And, like researchers studying individual QOL, those interested in family QOL assume that all people deserve lives of quality—a perspective leading naturally to efforts to assess the QOL of families having a member with a disability.

Measures of family QOL, like those used for individual QOL, should be muiltidimensional, both subjective and objective, capable of assessing environment at multiple levels, and inclusive of individuals with ID in their design and implementation (Samuel et al., 2012). A variety of instruments has arisen from the broad area of family QOL research, some of them primarily health-related, and others aimed toward nondisability groups (see, for example, Hu, Summers, Turnbull, & Zuna, 2011). However, when psychometric properties, a focus on ID, and peer-reviewed research reports are considered, two instruments emerge as the major measures of family QOL: the Beach Center Family Quality of Life Scale (Beach Center on Disability, 2005) and the Family Quality of Life Survey (FQOLS-2006; Isaacs et al., 2007; Brown et al., 2006).

Considered together, these instruments assess the following family QOL domains: family interaction, parenting, emotional well-being, personal development, physical well-being, financial well-being, community involvement, and disability-related supports.

This chapter focuses on an in-depth study of family QOL in one country, Argentina. The authors begin with an overview of the Latin American perspective, and then present and analyze the results of studies assessing family QOL in Argentina on the basis of indicators related to emotional well-being, personal strengths and development, rules of convenience (i.e., rights), family life, physical/material well-being, and interpersonal and community relations. The chapter concludes with a discussion of the need to be sensitive to the contextual and cultural differences in families, and how a family unit is viewed.

Latin American Perspective

The authors started working in the disabilities field as psychotherapists, and acquired experience as employees and trainers of more than 4,000 workers in 180 organizations. Currently the authors work with developers of public policies. This chapter is based on that history, on the recognition that cultural conditions in Latin America (e.g., poverty and high rates of unemployment) may influence the importance of family QOL domains (Aznar & González Castañón, 2005), and on the understanding that the rights of people with disabilities may be perceived differently in different cultures (Aznar, González Castañón, & Olate, 2012).

In Latin America, the lack of articulation between the actors and stakeholders in the disabilities field is a general problem. Although their respective discourses recognize the importance of the rights of people with disabilities to personal development and social inclusion, if the different components of the system are not articulated and person- and family-centered, their achievements have fairly predictable "ceilings" and "fences."

The context in Argentina is in some ways the exception to that of Latin America in general with regard to disabilities. The country has developed a huge free system that covers all possible services during the person's lifetime. The data for this chapter come from that context.

The relation between poverty and disability still exists. However, people with disabilities get subsidies, exemptions, and a wide array of services more efficiently than those in poverty. Interventions in health, social welfare, and education are positive aspects of inclusion, because they are universal and free, although not centered on the person. Diverse services superimpose on each other with no social agent promoting the necessary adjustments. The services that people with disabilities receive are provided by professionals with college education and by undergraduate students or workers who stay in the same organization for decades. As services are not adjusted to individual requirements, they are frequently ineffective and lack demonstrable results.

The state finances thousands of health and education organizations. The subsidies that individuals or families receive are numerous, albeit small in amount. Transportation within and between cities in the whole country is free, as are many cultural events. Despite this wealth of resources, neither the providers nor the governments or educators have an obligation to show results. The provision of services consists of routine activities that are standardized, segregated, and arranged according to organizational criteria. In most cases, they do not produce meaningful changes in the QOL of people with disabilities, although they can be beneficial. Without systematic evaluation, the state bureaucratically regulates the infrastructural and formal levels of the system. This way of functioning reinforces professional hegemony, silences families, and postpones the emergence of people with disabilities as the main foci.

Because organizations do not evaluate the results of the services they provide, they are like ships adrift, navigating without a compass or a map. Their treatment plans are technically and politically correct. They guarantee minimal risks and maximum security, without "stretching" to use community resources and maximize social involvement. The use of all available resources is not planned in reference to results that are relevant to people with ID and their families. As far as we know, no state in Latin America monitors the evolution of QOL among people with disabilities. Without that input, it seems improbable that they will make the collective adjustments needed to actively approach the goal of full inclusion.

The international conception of QOL in ID started to spread in Argentina near the beginning of the new millennium. Nevertheless, very few organizations that provide services, public servants, or professionals learned to implement that conceptual view. The excellent scales developed in other social-economic-cultural contexts were deemed inappropriate to account for the Latin American reality. Thus our approach has been to assess family QOL from the perspective of both the individual with ID and his/her family member(s). Our rationale is that because all members of the family group are interrelated, what affects one affects all, and therefore, the challenges facing a member with a disability influence the overall functioning of the family.

The Latin American Scale of Quality of Life

The context we described previously drove us to develop our own conceptual and measurement framework, based on the premises that a family QOL scale should: (a) be meaningful to people with ID and their families; (b) be useful for health and education professionals; (c) utilize a multidimensional perspective on QOL; and (d) provide indicators written in plain Spanish, with an accessible protocol and a simple way to visualize the results. The development of the Latin American Scale of Quality of Life (the scale) was based on these premises. The Scale evaluates six QOL areas through assessment of 42 indicators phrased as desired situations in everyday life (see Aznar &González Castañón, 2005). Individuals respond as to how frequently each indicator is true in their lives (almost always, sometimes, almost never); scores are obtained using this metric.

Table 6.1. *Description of the Latin American Scale of QOL*

Area	Definition	Comparable Individual-Referenced QOL Domains
Emotional well-being (EWB)	Feeling stable and serene with oneself and with others; with what one has and with what one does.	Emotional Well-Being
Personal strength and development (PSD)	Knowing and projecting oneself. Having goals and developing as a person.	Self-Determination Personal Development
Rules of convenience (RC)	Being part of different groups. Being considered an equal. Being respected and respectful of freedom and intimacy of everyone.	Rights
Family Life (FL)	Participating in convivial activities. Sharing both good and bad times. Includes the interaction between family members and objective aspects of the family in its context.	Interpersonal Relations
Physical/material well-being (PMWB)	Having basic needs satisfied and the resources to feel good.	Physical Well-Being Material Well-Being
Interpersonal and community relations (ICR)	Interacting and having relationships with people outside the family. Using and enjoying community's resources and public spaces with others. Fulfilling a role in the community.	Social Inclusion Interpersonal relations

To acquire a license to use this scale, users must be trained in its use. Completing it requires interviews with people with disabilities and their families. This allows respondents to reflect in first person, assuming a personal knowledge about the quality of their life, without depending exclusively on the evaluation of professionals. A brief description of QOL areas and their relation with the individual-referenced QOL domains described in Chapters 1 and 18 appear in Table 6.1. These abbreviations are also used in Figures 6.1 and 6.2.

Composite Data from the Latin American Scale of Quality of Life

Over the last ten years we have collected QOL data using the scale. To date, we have collected and analyzed data from a group of 348 people with ID who live with their families and attend some organization within the community, and another group of 190 people with ID who live in care homes. A care home is a house with a centralized infirmary, housekeeping, and food services provided 24/7 by an organization. Typically, 15 to 30 residents (average age 30) share rooms for three, divided by gender. Most residents do not have a family and have severe or multiple disabilities. All of them take part

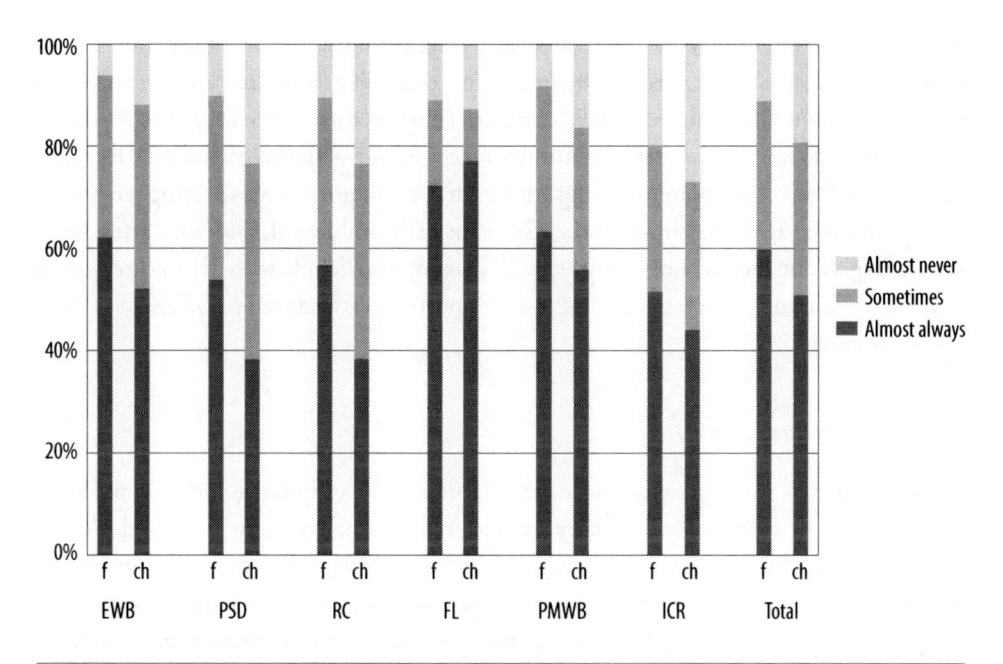

FIGURE 6.1. QOL data from PWID who live with their families or in a care home

in programmed activities, coordinated by professionals, during six to eight hours per day, from Monday to Friday. During weekends they can receive visitors, go out, or, if the family agrees, go back to their place of origin. These data are summarized in Figure 6.1.

Figure 6.1 summarizes the percentage of item responses for individuals who live with their families (N = 348), compared to those who live in a care home (N = 190). Factors related to both the scores summarized in Figure 6.1 and broader contextual factors are discussed below and on subsequent pages.

Emotional well-being (EWB)

In most cases, families, friends, and organizations contribute favorably to providing safety and security. People with ID often circulate in protected environments which are not exposed to social violence or delinquency. Abuses and mistreatment motivated by their disabilities are infrequent in the community. However, within families and organizations that act as families, there are frequent subtle abuses of power.

Personal strength and development (PSD)

Self-determination is a key concept to the full development of people with ID. The concept is replacing autonomy as social actors understand its transcendent meaning. It is not enough to just do things unsupervised; it is necessary that people with ID choose what they want to do with advocacy, responsibility, and freedom, and articulated within their social context. Organizations keep allocating time and resources to achieve autonomy through skills development. They see their inclusive goals frustrated because they do not develop self-determination conjointly with their families. The highest scores in PSD correspond to young adults with low requirements for support, whose families enabled them to circulate socially from early childhood, and who attended a school (regular or special) until they were 25 years of age. People who live in care homes have higher support requirements and fewer opportunities to develop and exercise their self-determination.

Rules of convenience (RC)

In Latin America, some citizens ignore their rights and live submissive and resigned lives; furthermore, the extent to which they exercise rights is not directly measured (Aznar et al., 2012). Rights awareness encourages protest and formal demands. In countries in which the state does not provide services to people with disabilities and everything is done by charity, it is unlikely that an individual will sue someone because of the lack of fulfillment of the United Nations Convention on the Rights of Persons with Disabilities (2006). In Argentina, where health and education services are universal, some families pursue legal proceedings with success. Nevertheless, faults in the system persist. Services do not guarantee full inclusion because they maintain the functional isolation of people with ID within the organizations. During the last few years, different sorts of observational strategies have been constituted to monitor fulfillment of the UN Convention, which Argentina has ratified and incorporated into the National Constitution. The Civil Code has also been modified to limit guardianships and the suspension of rights based solely on the existence of a disability. These are recent breakthroughs and their effects on QOL will be more fully appreciated in the future.

Family life (FL)

In our country, parents' associations have a strong presence in the disabilities field. Many of them have become service providers, trainers for human resources, or public policy advocates. The vast majority of families are satisfied just by obtaining services for their children, and do not keep struggling for their employment and social inclusion. This prolongs their dependency and maintains over-protection. When older parents get sick or die, the person with ID who is not capable of living as an adult becomes a burden for siblings and they all may enter a period of social conflict in their family life. Eventually, they are referred to care homes, which is not a popular solution.

Nevertheless, Figure 6.1 shows a high level of satisfaction among those who live in care homes. In our culture, convenience and daily routines awake genuine and intense bonds and feelings. Thus, the cultural sense of family is wide and not confined to immediate kinship. Staff who work in care homes (or in any organization in the ID field) are qualified workers who often hold their positions for many years. Naturally, they consider themselves foster family members. Reciprocally, residents turn to staff with the trust they would have in their own relatives.

Physical/material well-being (PMWB)

There are pronounced inequalities in the life conditions of citizens in Latin America. In big cities, families living below the poverty line share the city and public services with a large middle class. Poverty is real and is present, despite free access to health and education. In Argentina, the certification of disability may open a flow of resources and allow a family to leave the condition of indigence. However, comparison with indicators from other QOL scales should illustrate what poverty can mean, contextually and culturally.

Interpersonal and community relations (ICR)

States, in general, are involved in health care and education of children, although not always in an inclusive way. They have a hard time, though, regulating the placement of people with disabilities as valued members of their communities. For example, the jobs quota imposed by law does not require private companies to hire persons with a disability. In fact, governmental agencies seldom reach that quota. In big cities, any cognitive delay of an individual tends to marginalize him/her from peers. This does not happen in smaller cities or towns that are oriented to agricultural production, where technology and speed do not yet create a substantial difference. On the other hand, these communities present few niches for people with disabilities and may be overtly prejudicial toward them. For example, a few years ago we compared the QOL of people with ID who were employed with that of their unemployed peers. Significant differences were evident, especially in the areas of personal strengths and development, rules of convenience (i.e., rights), and interpersonal and community relations.

QOL of Relatives of People with Intellectual Disability

In a separate study, we worked with Martin Sapag, who interviewed 280 relatives (mostly parents and siblings) of children and teenagers with multiple and severe disabilities who live in Cutral-Có in the province of Neuquén. He visited them in their homes and evaluated every member of each family on the Scale. Figure 6.2 presents a summary.

This study found that in some areas, for example, EWB, MPWB and FL, family members, including the person with ID (PSDD), have relatively similar profiles. But in other areas (PSD, RC and ICR), the levels of QOL are different, especially for people with ID. The consideration of global scores dilutes these differences, which is why we recommend reviewing each indicator independently.

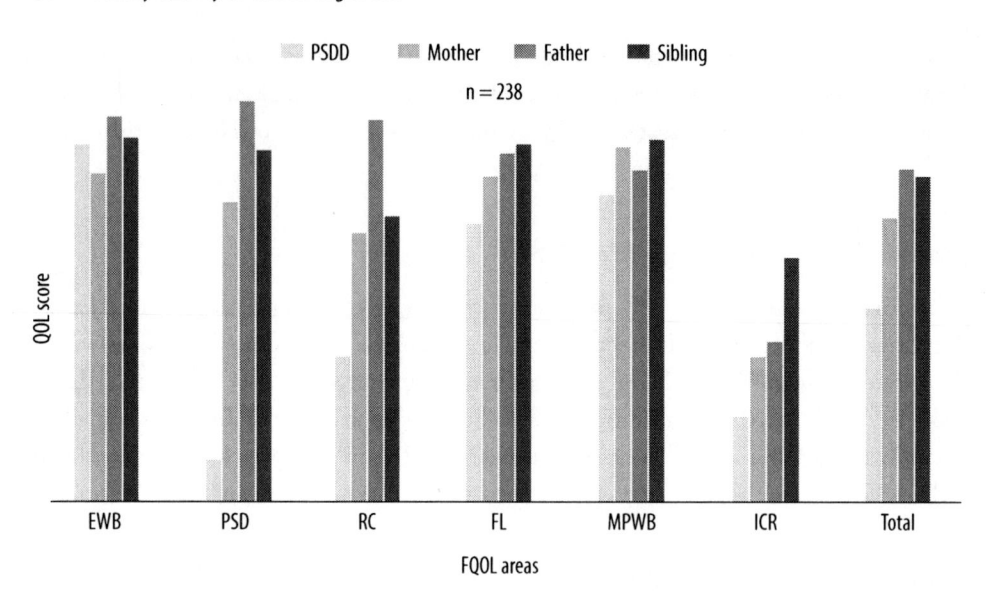

FIGURE 6.2. QOL of whole families

Responses to a subset of items from the Scale appear in Figure 6.3. In some respects, these scores surprised us. More specifically, in the past we used to think that an individual with a disability could not expect a QOL higher than that of other citizens; we believed that the environment was the limit. But reflective of the data presented in Figure 6.3, and additional data regarding the fulfillment of rights of persons with disabilities, we found that they had a better level of satisfaction in education, health care, and assistance with inclusion in the community than a control group of college students. The fulfillment of rights was lower in items that concerned independence and self-determination. These findings led us to refine our previous beliefs. Some aspects of the QOL of people with disabilities are guaranteed through the organizations that serve them. This provides a better situation than their peers, even in the same family, who have to obtain similar levels of satisfaction through personal efforts.

Conclusion

The concept of family QOL is based on the premise that all members of the family group are interrelated and that what affects one affects all. Therefore the challenges facing a member with a disability influence not only the functioning of the family, but also how family members perceive the life conditions and circumstances assessed by the 42 indicators comprising the Latin America Scale of Quality of Life. The data summarized in both Figures 6.1 and 6.2 underscore the above premise and the need to be sensitive

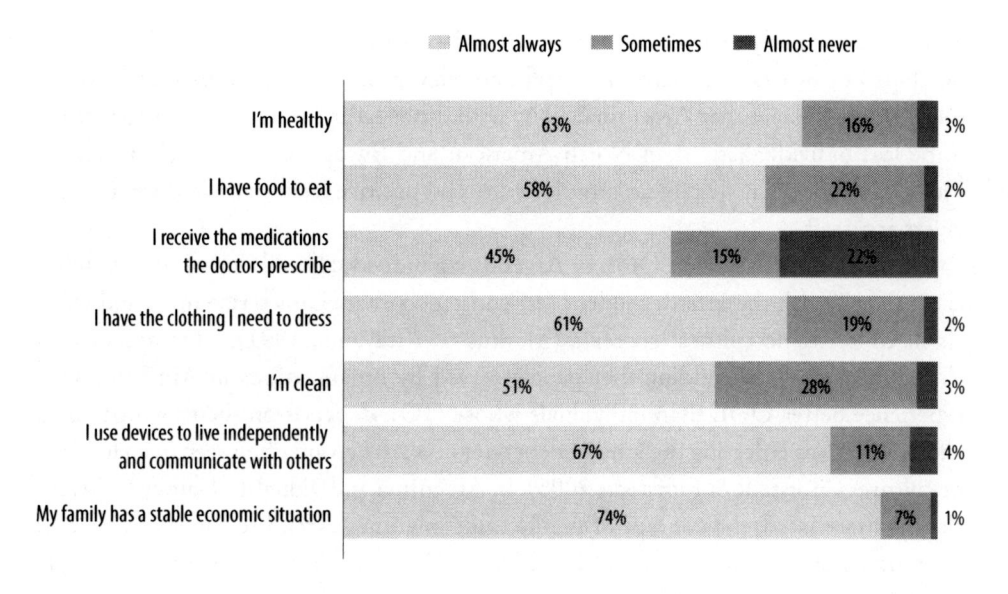

FIGURE 6.3. QOL of relatives of PWID (n = 280)

Categories: Almost always | Sometimes | Almost never

- I'm healthy: 63% | 16% | 3%
- I have food to eat: 58% | 22% | 2%
- I receive the medications the doctors prescribe: 45% | 15% | 22%
- I have the clothing I need to dress: 61% | 19% | 2%
- I'm clean: 51% | 28% | 3%
- I use devices to live independently and communicate with others: 67% | 11% | 4%
- My family has a stable economic situation: 74% | 7% | 1%

to contextual and cultural differences in families, and how a family unit is viewed. For example, in reference to Figure 6.1, although there are differences between the family and care home, many of the differences are insignificant. This may be due to the fact that as mentioned previously, workers within the care homes consider themselves foster family members, and that (reciprocally) residents turn to staff with the trust they would have in their own relatives. This is not to say, however, that there are no differences between the family and the care homes. There are, and the largest differences relate to personal strengths and development, and rights.

The data presented in Figure 6.2 indicate that all members of the same family can evaluate their own QOL differently. This is apparent in people with ID who score significantly lower in the areas of personal strengths and development, rules of convenience (rights), and interpersonal and community relations.

The importance of the concept of family QOL in Argentina and elsewhere cannot be over-emphasized. For example, as part of the study summarized in Figure 6.2, one interview occurred in a home where the house's roof had huge holes through which snow was coming in. The mother answered plainly that the family had enough food and that their life condition was good. However, the interview and the detailed dialog about the 42 items in the Scale motivated her to ask her neighbors for help. They accommodated the family and collaborated with the repairs. Afterward, they also received assistance from the government.

This chapter illustrates the importance in Latin America in general, and Argentina in particular, of cultural context as a key determinant of perceptions of QOL, whether individual or family. Thus, while there is overlap between the family QOL domains developed by others and those we have found relevant in Argentina, there are also key differences. The fact that Argentina, along with other Latin American countries, tends to be less individualistic than North American and European cultures (Hofstede & Hofstede, 2005) may help to account for trust and positive feelings toward service providers and staff.

The relation between the QOL of Argentinian individuals and that of their families is consistent with the interdependent self-constructs that characterize many individuals in collectivistic cultural contexts (Markus & Kitayama, 1991). This observation also accords with the finding that people served by organizations in Argentina may experience better QOL than individuals whose QOL depends on their own personal effort—perhaps reflecting the kind of dependence on the group often seen in collectivistic cultures (Hofstede & Hofstede, 2005). In Argentina, individual and family QOL are closely interrelated, the concept of family can sometimes extend to caregivers beyond the bounds of the biological family, and family QOL is influenced by some uniquely Latin American characteristics.

SECTION III
QUALITY OF LIFE AT THE MESOSYSTEM LEVEL

Section Overview

Based on current research, the most significant predictors for service recipients' assessed QOL are related to the culture of the organization providing services and supports, and the specific services and supports they provide. Embedded within this culture and the services/supports are the values of personal development, inclusion, self-determination, and empowerment, and best practices related to outcomes evaluation, right-to-left thinking, aligning individual support strategies to personal goals and assessed support needs, and continuous quality improvement. Incorporating these values and best practices into an organization's policies and practices not only transforms organizations, but also allows them to fulfill accountability requirements, performance management needs, and stakeholder expectations.

The four chapters presented in this section discuss this tranformative process from an international perspective. We begin with a discussion of outcomes evaluation and how QOL-related outcomes can be used as a basis for clinical, managerial, and policy decisions, but also allow organizations to develop evidence-based practices that enhance personal well-being. The authors of Chapter 7 provide guidelines for assessing QOL-related personal outcomes, and review current QOL assessment instruments based on the eight-domain QOL conceptual model.

Alignment is the focus of Chapter 8. In this chapter, the authors describe a major innovation project in Italy that aligns supports planning to a QOL-outcomes framework. Essential to the process is the embrace of a number of organizing concepts that allow organizations in Italy to avoid being overwhelmed by the plethora of theories, models, instruments, and data and becoming "data-rich but information-poor." The authors describe the use of an ecological matrix and a supports matrix that facilitate understanding, data organization, and effective and efficient implementation.

As organizations transform their policies and practices to become more person-centered, accountable, and horizontally structured, they turn to continuous quality improvement (CQI) as the change mechanism. CQI is an internal, collaborative, and transformative process that involves a plan-do-check-act cycle. A significant cross-cultural contribution of Chapter 9 is the approach by which CQI is operationalized as a parallel process at the level of the individual, team, and organization.

Organizational transformation does not end with deinstitutionalization and the development of community-based programs. Rather, transformation is a continuous process. Building on the successful deinstitutionalization of a large program in the Netherlands, the authors of Chapter 10 describe how they have implemented a quality management framework that is based on the concept of QOL, the supports paradigm, and evidence-based outcomes. This framework has allowed Arduin, the program in question, to adapt more successfully to new developments affecting ID-related organizations and service delivery systems around the world. These new developments are universal rights of persons with disabilities, integrating the supports paradigm with individualized supports planning, using evidence-based outcomes, and employing a collaborative approach to organizational self-assessment.

Collectively, the material presented in these four chapters underscores the importance of beginning with the end in mind, aligning supports planning within a QOL outcomes framework, engaging in continuous quality improvement, and adapting to new developments. These chapters also reflect important conceptual skills related to alignment, systems thinking, synthesis, and the transformative process.

CHAPTER 7
OUTCOMES EVALUATION
LAURA E. GÓMEZ and MIGUEL ÁNGEL VERDUGO

Introduction and Overview

Evaluations based on assessment of personal, QOL-related outcomes allow organizations to develop evidence-based practices that enhance personal well-being. These practices are based on current best evidence, obtained from credible sources, and grounded in the use of reliable and valid methods and a clearly articulated and empirically supported theory or rationale (Schalock et al., 2011, p. 274). They are increasingly used as a basis for: (a) clinical decisions about interventions, services, and supports provided to clients; (b) managerial decisions about the strategies used by organizations and agencies to increase their effectiveness, efficiency, and sustainability; and (c) policy decisions regarding strategies for enhancing QOL and the implementation of protections for the human rights of citizens with disabilities (Gómez et al., 2013; Navas, Gómez, Verdugo, & Schalock, 2012; van Loon et al, 2013; Verdugo et al., 2012).

This chapter discusses outcomes evaluation as an important first step in developing evidence-based practices that enhance the QOL of people with ID. We begin by discussing five guidelines for assessing QOL-related personal outcomes, including guidelines related to the development of QOL assessment instruments. Next, we provide an overview of recently developed QOL assessment instruments based on the eight domains of the QOL conceptual and measurement model described in Chapters 1 and 18. We conclude the chapter by illustrating how evidence-based outcomes can be used at the micro, meso, and macrosystem levels.

Guidelines for Assessing QOL-Related Personal Outcomes

The current approach to the measurement of QOL-related personal outcomes is characterized by its multidimensional nature, the coexistence of universal and culture-bound properties, the use of methodological pluralism involving self-reports and report of other significant persons, and the importance of the involvement of people with ID in the design and implementation of their person-centered planning (Schalock, Verdugo, Gómez, & Reinders, 2016). Although the eight core domains comprising individual QOL (Schalock & Verdugo, 2002) are the same for all people (universal properties), their assessment is based on culturally sensitive indicators (Gómez et al., 2011; Jenaro et al., 2005; Schalock et al., 2005; Wang et al., 2010) whose quantitative measurement results in QOL-related personal outcomes at the organization or systems level (mesosystem), and are reported in normative ways (e.g., prevalence, percentage) at the societal (macrosystem) level (i.e., regional, state, country).

The assessment of QOL has high stakes for both consumers and organizations. Therefore, assessment must conform to a number of best practices in test development and assessment. Guidelines reflecting these best practices are discussed next.

Well-Formulated and Validated Conceptual Model

The first step in developing or choosing a QOL assessment instrument is to ensure that it is based on a well-formulated and validated conceptual model that clearly defines QOL. This includes enumerating domain-referenced, observable conditions, behaviors, or perceptions that are assessed, and specifying the relations expected among them. In this sense, if we want to work with the eight-factor model (Schalock & Verdugo, 2002), we must expect that the instrument to evaluate QOL-related personal outcomes needs to be composed of eight subscales (one per domain), each comprising a representative number of items to assess the domain-related indicators. In the same way, given that the model postulates that the eight domains are interrelated, we must expect that if there are changes in the scores obtained on one subscale, there will also be changes in other domains. Therefore, scales to assess QOL should be structured with subscales and should provide scores for every domain. They should also allow for aggregating the scores obtained in the eight domains to get a total QOL score.

Culturally Sensitive Indicators

Domains should be well-represented by relevant, culturally sensitive indicators. Thus, the pool of indicators (or their translation into specific items assessing specific QOL-related personal outcomes) should be reviewed by a committee of experts, focus groups, or both to assure that they are suitable, important, and sensitive. These panels of experts and focus groups should ideally be composed of key agents (such as people with ID, family members, academics and researchers in the field, other professionals, and direct care staff) because it is important that instruments have a consumer perspective and encourage dialogue between providers and clients (Gómez, Verdugo, & Arias, 2010). Interrater agreement or concordance among experts, such as kappa coefficients, should be provided (i.e., validity evidence based on the content of the scale).

A second reason why it is essential that items be reviewed is to guarantee they represent a good sample of operationalizing each domain, and that no relevant aspects have been omitted. Given that a domain should never be assessed with fewer than four items, an instrument assessing the eight domains should never comprise fewer than 32. Ideally, each domain should have between six and twelve items. Therefore, instruments should be brief—but long enough to adequately represent each domain—and simple to administer and score.

Scoring Metric

Another key aspect of QOL scales concerns the response options. The preferred system is a Likert scale (e.g., *totally disagree, disagree, agree,* and *totally agree*) that use the same options with all the domains assessed. (Frequency options—e.g., *never, sometimes, often,* and *always*—are also commonly used.) Although Likert-type scales require the complex task of distinguishing subtle differences in attitudes or behaviors and are more vulnerable to low response rates than yes/no questions, they are preferred, given their potential to capture a wider response variance and their greater reliability for people with high levels of functioning and communication skills (Hartley & MacLean, 2006).

The optimal number of response alternatives for people with ID ranges between three and five. To avoid central tendency bias that occurs when respondents consistently choose the middle option—e.g., "neither agree nor disagree"—we prefer four scale anchors to force a non-neutral response. Special care and attention must similarly be taken to avoid other biases, such as acquiescence or the tendency to choose the most positive response alternative, and a bias that arises when responders choose the prior alternative (Hartley & MacLean, 2006; Schalock et al., 2000; Verdugo et al., 2005b).

Psychometric Properties

Another important aspect of personal outcomes assessment is the importance of the instruments' psychometric properties. There are many instruments to assess the QOL of people with ID; however, many are not as psychometrically sound and robust as they should be—due to significant limitations of attempts to validate them, or because they are not related to a clearly articulated theory (Li et al., 2013; Townsend-White et al., 2012; Verdugo, Arias, Gómez, Navas, & Schalock, 2014). Thus, rigorous study designs are required to demonstrate the reliability and validity of instruments.

Reliability—understood as the overall consistency of a measure—is usually measured with Cronbach's alpha, a statistic calculated from pairwise correlations between items that range between negative infinite and one. However, providing Cronbach's alpha for the overall scale is not enough when we are using instruments that assess several domains. The reliability coefficients for each domain are absolutely essential, and values lower than .50 are not acceptable. Those domains with internal consistencies between .50 and .70 are poor and questionable, while only those greater than .70 are considered adequate.

Validity is demonstrated by providing evidence based not only on content, but also based on relations with measures of other variables (i.e., convergent and discriminant evidence) and on the internal structure of the scale. While other evidence of validity is frequently provided (e.g., criterion, convergent, and discriminant validity), this is not the case with evidence related to the internal structure of instruments, which requires use of exploratory factor analysis and, especially, principal component analysis (PCA). Three methods have been used broadly to date: a particular combination of PCA for extraction, the Kaiser criterion to determine the number of factors, and orthogonal rotation (Varimax).

Given that we begin with the assumption that we are using instruments based on a clear factor structure of a set of observed variables, structural equation modeling and confirmatory factor analysis (CFA) should be the statistical techniques used to verify such structure and provide the best evidence of validity. In this sense, for conducting preliminary descriptive analysis (e.g., missing data, collinearity, and outliers), the estimation of parameters and assessing the model fit are mandatory steps. Moreover, when conducting a CFA, it is also absolutely necessary to establish convergent and discriminant validity and reliability (e.g., composite reliability with average variance extracted).

Administrative Procedures

QOL assessment instruments should be administered by a qualified interviewer. The interviewer could be a professional who administers the scale and is familiar with the QOL conceptual framework and definition. As discussed more fully in Chapter 5, it is essential for the interviewer to spend time initially getting to know the person and to conduct the interview in a conversational manner that allows the interviewer to expand on the original question, simplify its meaning, and provide concrete examples. During the interview, the interviewer should remind the respondent that he or she must think about "what is true generally," and also stress that the information obtained will not be used to evaluate his or her abilities or eligibility for support services, but rather to provide information.

Self-Report vs. Report of Others

In developing or choosing a scale, one needs to determine whether the potential user is interested in assessing the individual's perception of the quality of his or her life, or the perception of another person who knows the individual well (e.g., friends, professionals, family members, direct support staff), or both. To date, the distinction between "objective" and "subjective" instruments in the scientific literature related to QOL has often been based on the use of the term *subjective* to mean the individual's own perspective, and the use of *objective* for the perspective of a third party. We advocate replacing this terminology, as it is confusing (both perspectives reflect the perspective of a person, and therefore, both are subjective) and recommend more specific and exact terms, such as "self-report" and "report of others." However, the instruments should offer only one version (i.e., same domains and indicators) but different assessment formats.

The self-report format assesses the individual's perception of his or her status on the respective indicator (e.g., "I state my preferences when I am allowed to choose" or "I am worried or nervous"). Self-reporting underscores the right that people with ID have to express their own feelings about their QOL and to receive feedback about the assessment's results. Our challenge is to increase the percentage of self-reports, which challenge test developers and test administrators to become more involved in consumer-based focus groups, to develop more simplistic phrasing for items, orient more conversation toward item assessment, and implement more sophisticated use of augmentative devices (e.g., visual icons), user-friendly approaches (e.g., trained peer interviewers and conversation formats), and response elicitation strategies (e.g., joy sticks).

If the person cannot or does not self-report, then interviews should be conducted with two individuals who have known the person for a period of at least six months. The interviewees should have had face-to-face contact with the person, and have observed the person in different environments. These respondents can be a parent, relative, guardian, direct support staff, teacher, other professional, or any other individual who works or lives with the person. Each respondent should be asked to assess the person's status on the respective indicator item and encouraged to give a response based on how they think the person with ID might respond to the item (i.e., they should avoid expressing their *own* opinion or perspective, which would bias the report). Respondent ratings for each item might be averaged, or they could be encouraged to reach a consensus.

The form for the report of others assesses the respondent's perception of the person's status on the respective indicator (e.g., "the person states his or her preferences, verbally or by gesturing, when allowed to choose" or "the person shows signs of anxiety"). We prefer the term *report of others* rather than the term *proxies*, given that the latter implies that the proxy has authority or power over the person in question, and this implication is inconsistent with the values underlying the QOL concept and the principles underlying the disability rights movement.

There are differences found when the concordance between self-reports and reports of others is analyzed. Although some researchers find very little or no agreement (e.g., Claes et al., 2012; Zimmermann & Endermann, 2008), others provide evidence for moderate to strong concordance (e.g., Schmidt et al., 2013). Actually, when both perspectives are compared, researchers find that people with ID rate themselves significantly higher then do caregivers or staff working with them. (e.g., Balbon, Coscarelli, Giuntia, & Schalock, 2013).

These discrepancies between self-reports and reports of others make both kinds of data useful and necessary; they might be comparable but are not interchangeable. The significant advantage of using a one-version/two-formats approach to the measurement of QOL is to provide a holistic framework for assessment that defines QOL in terms of its multidimensionality and assesses it via common domain-referenced indicators. In general terms, it is preferable to use the perception of persons with ID themselves because numerous studies have shown that these do not have a high correlation with the perceptions of others, even others who know them well. There are times, however, when the perceptions of others need to be used as measures, especially when it is not possible to obtain reliable responses from people, such as those with severe or profound impairments. Another reason why measures based on the report of others might be important is that others who are close to people with severe disabilities often make major life decisions on their behalf, and thus it is important to know what these people's perceptions are, keeping in mind that they will most likely be different from what would be gathered from the person.

In addition, the goal of the assessment is also relevant whether we opt for one format or the other. If the goal of the assessment is related to program evaluation or quality improvement strategy implementation, applying the reports of others might be more useful because they are based on observations and might be more sensitive to changes and interventions. In contrast, when the goal is to develop person-centered planning to reflect what people think about and want in their lives, self-reports are essential. Comprehensive measures involving both forms are recommended when the focus is enhancing QOL (Gómez, Verdugo, & Arias, 2015).

Some Recent Instruments to Assess Quality of Life-Related Personal Outcomes

In this section of the chapter we provide a selection of instruments recently developed that are consistent with the aforementioned guidelines to assess QOL-related personal outcomes. Each of these instruments provides direct scores for each of the eight QOL domains that are then either converted to standard scores and percentiles or transposed onto a QOL profile that allows easy interpretation. Each of these instruments was developed using the eight-domain QOL conceptual model. Many are available in multiple languages and collectively they are used widely throughout Europe, North America, Asia, and South America.

Inico-Feaps Scale

The Inico-Feaps Scale assesses QOL-related personal outcomes from the perspective of an adult with ID having expressive and receptive skills sufficient to complete the self-report format or from the perspective of a third party who knows the person well (e.g., family member, professional, direct-care staff, friends, or guardians). It comprises both self-report and the report of others. Both formats are composed of 72 parallel items and the answer format is a frequency scale with four options (*never, sometimes, often,* and *always*). In the self-report, picture symbols are provided to facilitate the assessment. Moreover, in case using this answer format is difficult, a four-point Likert scale (*totally disagree, disagree, agree,* and *totally agree*) can be used instead. The scale was validated with 1,624 participants from Spain, but an English version is also available. Internal consistency, interrater reliability, and confirmatory factor analysis are available (Gómez et al., 2015).

Gencat Scale

The Gencat Scale is a self-administered questionnaire for professionals to answer about clients' QOL based on direct observation. It addresses the situations of social service recipients (among them, people with ID, physical disabilities, sensory disabilities, elderly persons, people with HIV/AIDS, people with drug dependency, or people with mental health issues). The advantage of this instrument is that it allows score comparisons across diagnostic groups. It is composed of eight subscales and 69 items that are formulated as third-person declarative statements. The answer format is a frequency scale with four options (*never or hardly ever, sometimes, often, always,* or *almost always*). However, in case using this answer format is difficult, a four-point Likert scale (totally disagree, disagree, agree, and totally agree) can be used instead. The scale was validated with a representative sample of 3,029 clients from Catalonia (Spain). Catalonian, Spanish, English, Italian, Japanese, and Portuguese versions are available. Psychometric properties have been broadly studied through classical test theory and item response theory (Gómez, 2010; Verdugo, Arias, Gómez, & Schalock, 2010).

San Martin Scale

This San Martin Scale is a self-administered questionnaire for a third-party respondent to answer questions about the person's QOL. It is composed of 95 items formulated as third-person declarative statements. The answer format is a frequency scale with four options (*never, sometimes, often,* and *always*). It is addressed to people with ID and extensive or pervasive support needs (e.g., due to a profound or severe ID, very significant limitations in adaptive behavior, multiple disabilities, motor dysfunctions, chronic and pain-related medical conditions, sensory impairments, or mental health problems) who are receiving support services at an organization, who are sixteen years of age or older but not currently engaged in the education system. The scale was validated with a sample of 1,770 persons from Spain, but English, Italian, and French versions are available. A Dutch version will also be available soon. Both reliability and validity evidence based on the internal structure of the scale have been provided (internal consistency and CFA; Gómez et al., 2015a; Verdugo et al., 2014).

KidsLife Scale

The KidsLife Scale (Gómez et al., 2014) is a self-administered questionnaire that assesses QOL-related personal outcomes in children and adolescents with significant disabilities (under 21 years of age) who are recipients of educational or other social services. A third party who knows the study subject well and has the opportunity to observe the person completes the assessment. It is currently being validated with a sample of more than 1,000 people from Spain. The field-test version contained 156 items, but it will be shortened to 96 items following selection of the most reliable items. The scale is available in Spanish and English, and internal consistency and AFC are available (Gómez et al., 2015b).

Personal Outcomes Scales

The Personal Outcomes Scale for Adults (POS-A) and the Personal Outcomes Scale for Children (POS-C) are based on the eight-domain and three-factor QOL conceptual model described in Chapters 1 and 18. The POS-A was developed and standardized with individuals sixteen years and older; the POS-C for children and adolescents 6–18. Both versions (A and C) contain six items per domain, and both use two assessment formats: self-report and report of others, although for the POS-C the report of others is recommended for children between the ages of six and twelve years. The POS-A is available in Dutch, English, Spanish, Italian, and Complex Chinese. For the POS-A, reliability data are reported, including internal consistency coefficients (Cronbach's Alphas), interrespondent coefficients, and concordance rates between self-report and report of others. Data are reported for content, construct, and concurrent validity (van Loon et al., 2008; www.poswebsite.org). Comparable psychometric studies are currently underway for the POS-C (www.poswebsite.org). The POS-C is available in Dutch, English, Spanish, and Italian.

My Life Scale

The My Life Scale is a peer-to-peer administered QOL assessment instrument used with adults with developmental disabilities who receive supports for community inclusion, employment, and residential living in Alberta, Canada (the Scale is also used in British Columbia; see Chapter 14 of this volume). The Scale is administered by adults with DD who have been trained to administer the Scale to other adults with DD (self-report), or to others when the individual is unable to answer on his/her own behalf (i.e. report of others). To ensure answers remain confidential, all Scale completions are done with only the surveyor and the respondent in the room. The Scale is composed of 50 questions, six questions per QOL domain. The answer format is a frequency scale with one of the following scoring metrics used: *most of the time, sometimes, rarely or never;*

often, sometimes, rarely or never; yes, somewhat, no; lots of choice, some choice, little or no choice; lots of control, some control, little or no control. Facial icons are also used and an app is available for IPAD use. The Scale was validated with a sample of 415 adults with DD. Both reliability and validity evidence based on the internal structure of the Scale have been provided, resulting in a range of .60–.75 across the eight QOL domains. The Scale was developed by Alberta, Canada PDD and is available in English only (personal communication, Gloria Wesley, Gloria.wesley@gov.ab.ca).

Uses of Personal and Organizational Outcomes for Evidence-Based Practices

QOL-related outcomes can be used for multiple purposes that include reporting, evaluation, research, benchmarking, and continuous quality improvement. Additionally, they can be used to inform decision making and recommendations regarding clinical activities, program management, and public policy. In this section of the chapter, we focus on their uses at the micro, meso, and macrosystem levels.

Microsystem Uses

At the individual level (microsystem), we advocate that QOL scores should be used to provide feedback to individuals regarding their status on the domains composing a life of quality. Such feedback establishes an expectation that change can possibly occur in the eight domains (and shows how changes in one domain produce consequences in other domains, as all are related), confirms that the organization serving the individual is committed to a holistic approach to the person, and evaluates whether personal and organizational-level quality improvement strategies have made a difference in their lives. For these purposes, scores from self-reports and reports by others can be used and might be reported separately, giving special attention to similarities and discrepancies, and giving special relevance to the personal goals, opinions, and preferences of the person with ID to develop person-centered planning. A good illustration of the use of personal outcomes at this level can be found in van Loon et al. (2013).

Mesosystem Level

Evidence-based outcomes may be used not only to improve clinical and individual decisions (personal outcomes) but can also be aggregated to inform managerial decisions and program strategies. At the organization level (mesosystem), they can be used to develop provider profiles for the purposes of: (a) helping consumers and families choose services and identify successful practices (see Gómez et al., 2013, for examples); (b) determining which individual, organizational, and community factors predict outcomes scores (see Gómez et al., in press, for examples); and (c) using information about

QOL-related outcomes and their significant predictors as a basis for strategic planning, training, and continuous quality improvement (International Research Consortium on Evidence-Based Practices, 2013; Schalock et al., 2014). For these purposes, self-reports and reports of others should also be reported separately.

Macrosystem Level

When using the provider profiles at the macrosystem level, analyses of aggregated QOL-related personal outcomes can help guide the development and implementation of social policies to enhance QOL of social service recipients. For example, in a recent study carried out in Catalonia (Gómez, 2014; Gómez et al., 2013), the results obtained after assessing QOL-related personal outcomes at the macrosystem level emphasized the need for public and social policies to focus on improving personal outcomes related to social inclusion and self-determination. Similarly, QOL-related personal and organization outcomes can be used for determining public and, especially, social policy. A good illustration of how to use these QOL-related personal outcomes to operationalize and assess the articles of the Convention on the Rights of Persons with Disabilities (United Nations, 2006) can be found in Gómez et al. (2011), Verdugo et al. (2012), and in Chapter 15 of this volume.

Conclusion

In conclusion, an organization's services and supports significantly influence the QOL of service recipients; conversely, the assessed QOL of service recipients can significantly influence how an organization sees itself and how it fulfills accountability requirements, program management needs, and stakeholder expectations. What is common to both individuals and organizations is the assessment of personal, QOL-related outcomes. In this chapter, we have discussed outcomes evaluation as an important first step in developing evidence-based practices, and that QOL-related personal outcomes obtained from a reliable and valid instrument provide useful evidence that can be used for multiple purposes across ecosystems. To be credible, relevant, and useful, however, a QOL assessment instrument must be developed based on a validated QOL conceptual model, best practice test development and assessment techniques, and must have demonstrated reliability and validity.

As we will see in the following chapter on aligning supports planning within a QOL outcomes framework, QOL-related outcomes provide both a validation proof of the influence of an organization's services and supports and a basis for right-to-left thinking. From this perspective, outcomes evaluation is at the center of person-centered planning, individualized supports, continuous quality improvement, and organization transformation.

CHAPTER 8

ALIGNING SUPPORTS PLANNING WITHIN A QUALITY-OF-LIFE OUTCOMES FRAMEWORK

MARCO LOMBARDI and LUIGI CROCE

Introduction and Overview

Organizations in Italy and elsewhere face a common challenge: With all of the theories, models, instruments, and data about people with ID and service delivery practices, how can organizations avoid getting lost in the process of service provision and becoming "data rich but information poor" (Gleick, 2011)? Fulfilling one's professional responsibilities in the field of ID involves understanding and applying best practices based on relevant conceptual models of human functioning and disability. The QOL concept and the supports paradigm play an important role in promoting best and outcome-oriented practices that are based on the ecological model of human functioning and the operational and constitutive definitions of ID. These models have led to instruments and procedures, key performance indicators, evidence-based practices, assistive technology, and a focus on environmental accommodation (Buntinx & Schalock, 2010; Schalock et al., 2010; WHO, 2001).

This chapter addresses the challenges presented by these models and describes an approach used in Italy to align supports planning within a QOL outcomes framework. The chapter begins with a description of four organizing concepts that reflect current best practices and provide a framework to fulfill one's professional responsibilities. Thereafter, we outline the four steps involved in organizing supports planning and delivery across ecological systems. The final section of the chapter describes how a program logic model can be used to align personal goals and assessed support needs (the input) to individualized support strategies (the throughput), to QOL-related personal outcomes (the output). We present two matrices that facilitate this alignment.

Organizing Concepts

Alignment

Alignment involves logically connecting a service delivery system's input with its throughput and anticipated or desired output (Schalock & Verdugo, 2012b). The process of alignment starts with the individual expressing his/her own desires and expectations. An individual, as Dante said, should be "Nel mezzo del cammin di nostra vita" (in the middle of the journey of his/her life) and very often, to paraphrase Dante, the destination and the route of our process of support delivery "era smarrita" (becomes lost). Support professionals and support systems behave as Virgilo, Dante's guide, did to actively accompany the person to a successful and satisfactory destination. Identifying such a destination is the key criterion and the motivational engine. Dreaming to fly to Bora Bora instead of climbing Mount Everest means a set of skills, clothes, tools, attitudes, and garments specific and appropriate to the targeted goal.

How to ensure entitlement to a life of quality for people with ID is challenging. Yet, emphasis on finding uniquely individual solutions to presenting problems suggests that QOL conceptualization and operationalization might be the right approach to use in developing individualized support strategies. But how? We begin with these two premises: (a) no planning is really QOL-oriented if it excludes the person's values, preferences and priorities; and (b) focusing only on personal priorities and preferences without thoughtfully considering using individualized supports to address the gaps between a person's competence and his or her environmental demands will be misleading (Thompson et al., 2009). This leads to our second organizing concept: a system of supports.

A System of Supports

As recommended by Schalock & Luckasson (2013, 2014), a system of supports should: (a) express a society's commitment to enhance the functioning of individuals with ID and their families; (b) address personal goals and assessed support needs; (c) use support strategies that involve natural supports, technology, education and new skills learning, environmental accommodation, incentives, personal strengths, and professional services; and (d) involve support teams composed of the individual and family members who work with direct support staff and other organization personnel to align needs, resources, and desired outcomes. The QOL approach tries, overall, to help people to be satisfied with their own lives in ways that are customary to them and valued by them, while a system of supports focuses primarily on restoring structural and functional integrity to aspects of people that have been affected by their condition.

Planning an individualized system of supports begins with professionals understanding what is important to and valued by each individual, and what aspects of life or the environment contribute positively to life quality or detract from it. This approach makes every effort to respect the right of the individual to choose the course of action that best suits him or her. Consequently it is possible to select appropriate endeavors and provide supports required to assist the person to live an effective life, uniquely shaped by individual characteristics and circumstances (Brown & Brown, 2003). These changes are bringing new challenges to social, health, and mental health services, suggesting the use of positive interventions that incorporate a more holistic and integrated perspective. The QOL concept and a system of supports are ideally suited to be used in tandem. Successfully doing so involves our third organizing concept: An individualized support planning process.

Individualized Support Planning Process

Service systems are committed to identify personal objectives, plan and deliver supports, provide opportunities, and display outcomes in terms of better functioning and QOL. The starting point of an individual support planning process should always focus on aspects of life that are unique and important to individuals and result in an Individual Supports Plan that is functional (useful, implemented, and evaluated), relevant (to the person's goals and assessed support needs), and outcome oriented (directed to personal outcomes and a desired future).

Individual supports planning is the formalization and documentation of the process. A support system organizes and manages support provision and focuses on bridging the gap between support needs and environmental demands. In addition to personal goals and assessed support needs, two additional factors should be integrated into the individual supports planning process: The United Nations Convention on the Rights of Persons with Disabilities (CRPD) and the concept of capabilities.

The ratification of the CRPD has begun to generate a cultural change in service support provision in Italy. Beyond the general and particular assumptions declared in the Convention, an attentive look at the literature has revealed the commonalities and the rational connections between the CRPD and the domains of QOL for individuals with disabilities (Verdugo et al., 2012; see also Chapters 11 and 15 of this volume). This means that implementation of the rights declared in the Convention passes through a QOL-oriented support system, according to a link between rights and domains (Shogren & Turnbull, 2014). The declaration also introduces reasonable accommodation and universal design as useful principles to manage service provision. Reasonable accommodation requires the legal principle of fairness, proportionality, and appropriate investment of community resources, to ensure that persons with disabilities experience rights, non-discrimination, and individualized, specific supports (Croce, Cosimo, & Lambardi, in press).

The human capability approach, as expressed by Nussbaum (2011) and Brown et al. (2013), introduces an important perspective to a supports planning process. Conceptually, capability refers not only to the abilities residing within a person, but also integrates the degree of freedom and opportunity created by a combination of personal abilities and the political, social, and economic environment. In a synthetic way, supporting people with ID toward a life of quality reflects the responsibility and the civility of a community to emancipate those citizens by offering supports and opportunities according to natural and personal assets. Capabilities, in this view, are a collection of skills facilitated and selected by formal and informal co-citizens, sometimes organized as service resources. Capabilities emerge from a managed educational process, and reflect the combination of individual, psychosocial, economic, and community skills and environmental opportunities necessary to live, learn, work, and develop in the human common. Focusing on a person's capabilities and involvement results not only in increased motivation and a sense of accomplishment, but also the enhancement of personal outcomes (Brown & Brown, 2003). Thus, the relevance of our fourth organizing concept: outcomes evaluation.

Outcomes Evaluation

As discussed in the previous chapter, the assessment of personal, QOL-related outcomes allows organizations to focus clearly on their mission and to develop evidence-based practices that enhance personal well-being. These outcomes can also be used for multiple purposes across ecological systems. Furthermore, as Brown et al. (2013) noted, to successfully measure individual development and the results of the individual support plan process, objective and subjective indicators should be considered. QOL indicators of aspects of life unique to individual people with ID are probably most useful for enhancing individual development and for applying person-centered supports. QOL indicators that are common to all people are also useful for subjective purposes but, in addition, have been applied to both policy and service practice evaluation.

Four Steps to a Quality of Life-Focused Support Plan Delivery

Four essential critical thinking skills are relevant to applying the concepts noted above and to implementing a QOL-focused support plan: alignment, system thinking, synthesis, and transformational thinking (Schalock & Luckasson, 2014; Schalock & Verdugo, 2012b). An organization facing the challenge of arraying its support delivery under a QOL construct should consider using these essential skills to increase the effectiveness and efficiency of their service delivery systems. The integration begins by employing the concept of alignment, which we discussed previously, and recognizing the important role played by the three ecological systems that affect human functioning and personal outcomes: the individual and the family (the microsystem), the organization and community (the mesosystem), and the larger society and culture (the macrosystem). By incorporating these ecosystems into the organization's service delivery system through alignment and systems thinking, the service provider will create an organization empowered to influence the different levels of the societal system and will be oriented to QOL promotion. The following four steps are involved in this process.

1. Begin with the end in mind. Service delivery starts with the will of the organization to produce QOL outcomes. An organization oriented to promote QOL declares it in its mission, vision, and values. This commitment must be an essential part of the organization's culture.
2. Understand the organization's context. An organization also has to face the normative setting that defines its field of interest and support provision. Connecting and mediating between norms and supports provision implies that the organization is able to offer ethically and economically sustainable person-centered systems of supports that build on opportunities and the individual's capabilities.
3. Make use of transformational thinking. Shared knowledge and an empowered team can make the difference in implementation of the process to align functioning, supports, and QOL. The team shares the mission and the vision of the service provider agency and understands the QOL concept and support provision. The team must be informed about the effectiveness of support teams in planning and implementing individualized supports and in understanding the effectiveness and efficiency of user-friendly ISP formats. Support teams receive training about the concept of QOL, human potential, social inclusion, empowerment, equity, self-determination, and community inclusion. Furthermore, support teams employ the concept of evidence-based practices and use it as the basis of support delivery choices.
4. Use synthesis. Synthesis involves integrating information obtained from multiple sources into an ISP that is functional, relevant, and outcome oriented. This synthesis is facilitated by the use of a framework that organizes decision making about planning supports and implementation. As we will see in the following section, commonly used components include an organizing framework, support area, support strategy, support objective, and personal outcomes.

The Process of Aligning Supports Planning within a QOL Outcomes Framework

Over the last few years we have developed and field-tested two matrices to align supports planning and delivery within a QOL outcomes framework. These matrices are the *Ecological Matrix* that integrates important input and throughput information, and the *Supports Matrix* that aligns support objectives and support activities to each of the eight

QOL domains. These matrices have allowed organizations throughout Italy to organize information and develop a computerized real-time approach to align supports planning within a QOL outcomes framework. In addition, the matrices have made information visible and outcome oriented, facilitated the sharing of information with different support providers, coordinated information collection and analysis, and clarified communication among key stakeholders.

Input: The Ecological Matrix

The Ecological Matrix appears in Figure 8.1. The first two columns of the figure delineate what is important *to* the person, what is important *for* the person, and the factors composing a multidimensional understanding of human behavior. The remaining columns denote each of the QOL domains. Each cell at the cross point between a specific QoL domain (abbreviated) and an ecological variable, identifies classified information. That is the value of the specific ecological variable relevant and to be integrated to define specific support objectives. An extended version of the Support Matrix is observable in software "Matrici"® (MBS, s.r.l, Bologna, Italy, 2015).

The ecological matrix planning format allows organization staff to get a complete picture of the person to use as a basis for developing a system of supports. An overview of each of the first two columns in Figure 8.1 is presented next.

Important to the person. Determining what is important *to* the person is the starting point of person-centered planning (PCP) and the most relevant part of the assessment. A hallmark of PCP is the focus is on the individual's dreams, personal preferences, and interests. The primary purpose of a PCP process is to find what is important to a person, and it is essential that discussions are not constrained by available services or perceived barriers such as fiscal restrictions or limitations in a person's skills (O'Brien & O'Brien, 2000). In this part of the process, an interview, in a conversational format, is conducted with the client and focuses on his or her perceived support needs.

The areas explored in the conversation include global goals, relationships, home living, community living, education/training, employment, health and safety, behavioral, social and protection, and advocacy. A QOL assessment instrument could also be useful to extract important information to the desires of the individual (van Loon, van Hove, Schalock, & Claes, 2008). An interview and a conversation regarding the QOL of the person could be a great moment to provide important and integrative information. The use of a QOL instrument at the beginning of the planning process has three advantages: (a) it gives important information in the first phase of the assessment; (b) it orients people to a personalized and tailored individualized support plan (ISP); and (c) it provides a picture of the overall QOL profile of the individual before the definition of the Support Goals and Activities. QOL assessment instruments useful for these purposes were described in the previous chapter.

Determining what is important to the person can also be accomplished through an assessment of the person's preferences. Assessment of preferences gives dignity to the

	Ecological Variables	Quality-of-Life Domains							
		PWB	MWB	EWB	SD	PD	SI	IR	RE
What is important *to* the Person?	Personal Goals and Preferences general								
	Personal Goals and Preferences specific								
What is important *for* the Person?	1. Home living								
	2. Community living								
	3. Lifelong Learning								
	4. Occupancy								
Support Needs Items	5. Health and Safety								
	6. Social								
	7. Protection and Advocacy								
	8. Medical excp.								
	9. Behavioral excp.								
Adaptive Behavior Particip. incl.	Functioning strengths								
	Functioning limitations								
Health	Physical Health								
	Mental Health								
Context	Facilitators								
	Barriers								
QoL level	QoL profile								
	Support Objectives								

FIGURE 8.1. Ecological matrix

aspects of life that are important to the person, and different modalities and instruments exist for this purpose (Cavagnola, Corti, Fioriti, Leoni, & Lombardi, 2015). The relevant persons present in the life of the subject, or at least those who know the person best (and for at least six months) can give meaningful information in this process, outlining and integrating what is important to the user. In the Italian context, the family is the key provider of this information.

The best source of information for determining what is important *for* the person is a standardized assessment of support needs across major life activities and exceptional medical and behavioral support need areas. As described in more detail in Chapter 12 of this volume and in Thompson et al. (2004, 2009), major life activities are those involving home living, community living, life-long learning, employment, health and safety, social activities, and protection and advocacy.

Description of functioning. In order to have a more complete understanding of the person's ecological context, a description of the individual's functioning is a relevant component on the pathway toward QOL outcomes. Developing a picture of the different components and their composition is an important process, asking which supports are needed to bridge the gap between the person's level of functioning and the requirements of the environment. To fulfill this task, different instruments can be used to assess individual functioning, including intellectual abilities and adaptive skills (Schalock et al., 2010). This information provides insight into the person's strengths and limitations.

Health. Physical and psychological aspects of health must be considered, both in terms of strengths and limitations and in reference to supports provision. In the Ecological Matrix, health conditions are related to the effect they have (or might have) on a specific QOL domain (e.g. seizures: what are the domains and their indicators affected by the presence of seizures?).

Context. On the basis of observation, interviews, and reports from relevant support providers (in the micro, meso and macro system), the context is described in terms of limitations or strengths (or barriers and facilitators as in ICF; WHO, 2001) regarding education, life environment, job, free time and leisure, safety, material well-being, finances, and civil and spiritual life. Each contextual barrier or facilitator is referenced to the QOL domain where it has a relevant influence. This highlighting focuses on all the formal and informal support providers present in the person's natural network, and defines their contribution in terms of QOL-related activities and outcomes.

Throughput: The Supports Matrix

The Supports Matrix presented in Figure 8.2 outlines how supports are classified and managed in order to increase functioning and improve QOL of service recipients. The Domain (abbreviation) columns give a topographic criterion to embed specific categorized supports along the rows below. Any column accommodates the coordinated series of supports invested to improve QOL in that specific Domain. An extended version of

QOL Domains	PWB	MWB	EWB	SD	PD	IR	SI	RE
Support Objectives								
Indicators								
Monitoring instruments								
Support Activities (Schalock categories)								
1. Natural Support								
2. Cognitive Support								
3. Prosthetics								
4. Skills and competencies								
5. Environmental modifications								
6. Incentives and reinforcers								
7. Personal characteristics development								
8. Professional services								
9. Positive behavioral support								
10. Politics and practices (organizational)								
11. Politics and practices (System)								
Functioning Outcomes								
QOL Outcomes								

Time

FIGURE 8.2. Supports matrix

the Support Matrix is observable in the software "Matrici."® The activities involved in the process of classifying and managing supports to increase functioning and improve quality of life are described below.

Ecological balancing and definition of the support area. This is a synthesis phase. The relevant values of variables investigated and reported during the assessment step are categorized in the Ecological Matrix (Figure 8.1). The ISP development process starts with analyzing what is important to the person and integrating this information with what is important for the person. The number of variables present in the specific QOL domain highlights the importance of that specific area in the life of the person. Priority is given to those outcome areas best reflecting the person's goals and relevant supports for inclusive participation in the environment. At the end of this process, the Supports Matrix (see Figure 8.2) shows areas of intervention, categorized in cells of the table, where potentially modifiable functioning variables and personal characteristics are sorted according to their relevance for each of the QOL domains.

Long-term goal definition. Definition of long-term QOL goals is a crucial step. The case manager uses the QOL domains and support areas to aggregate the information in a clear and outcome-oriented framework. The specific QOL domain defines, through alignment of the data collected from the support areas, which goals are most meaningful. The goals are demarcated on the basis of the *importance* of the information filed in the previous step.. At the end of this phase, life goals related to specific QOL domains will be clearly understood.

Choice of appropriate support strategies. Possible support strategies are based on a system of supports: natural, technology, prosthetics, education, environmental accommodation, incentives, personal strengths, and professional services (Claes, Van Hove, Vandevelde, van Loon, & Schalock, 2012). The dimension that drives the process of choosing appropriate support strategies is the presence of opportunities. The organization or the case manager who defined the long-term objectives, will need to address the facilitators and the barriers present in the community and in the relevant environment of the person. Based on the defined goals and the present opportunities, the case manager will choose the appropriate support strategies available from the formal and informal support provider(s). The effect of this process is to have different support strategies associated with different QOL domains and defined for each long-term goal proposed, as well as a support provider responsible for the future implementation of the outcome.

Definition of the support objective. At this step the case manager will define the objective of the intervention and the intended result. Here there is a shift from the future to the present moment. It is important that an optimistic and realistic plan of action is designed and implemented. This process is developed through integration of the specific strategy chosen in the previous phase, an action verb, and the intended result of that strategy. The definition must as operational as possible, to increase the chances of having an objective that can be evaluated and a clear intervention strategy for all the support providers. At the final step of this process, the support objective will be defined and related to a specific QOL domain. This step reflects a completed Support Matrix. The result of using the Support Matrix is an unambiguous, individualized plan that specifies (a) the settings for and activities in which a person is likely to engage during a typical week, and (b) the types and intensity of support that will be provided (and by whom). "Whom" is composed of the different support providers (formal and informal), the case manager/support coordinator, the direct support staff, family members, and natural supports from the community.

Output: The Validation Proof

The output process is systematically and progressively disclosed by monitoring the process of support implementation and determining its efficacy in producing personal, QOL-related outcomes.

Monitoring. The monitoring process involves periodic analysis of the status of support objectives, determining which have been accomplished and which have not, and is fundamental. Evaluation of the plan includes regular verification of modifications in functioning conditions and updates regarding all major changes in individual goals. Whenever a substantial modification of the support needs of the person occurs, the care manager verifies the effect of the modification in the ISP, updating the system and determining new outcomes.

Outcomes evaluation. The evaluation of outcomes is determined by the organizing framework the organization chooses to implement in its system of support provision (e.g. life activities areas, functioning areas, or QOL domains). The determination of the measure should be driven by the nature of the outcome: Personal, Functional, Environmental, or Clinical. In reference to QOL-related outcomes a reliable and valid QOL assessment instrument can be used. As summarized in the preceding chapter and according to current literature on psychometrically sound instruments for adults with ID (Townsend-White et al., 2012), evidence supports the use of POS and GENCAT for "persons with mild to severe levels of ID, the San Martin Scale for people with profound disabilities (Verdugo et al., 2014), and the POSCA for children and adolescents (Croce, Lombardi, Claes, & Vandevelde, 2014)."

The use of these instruments greatly influences quality of service provision and allows evaluation of the efficacy of the support strategies in enhancing QOL levels (Gardner & Carran, 2005). Routine administration of a QOL instrument, at least every two years, can orient and direct support provision. If improved QOL levels are verified, they should be identified with the support strategies that were implemented in the relevant domains (Claes et al., 2012; Gómez et al., in press). If desired QOL levels are not present, it is necessary to modify the support strategy and/or objective. For this reason it is important to update the program of support at least once a year (or every time a significant event happens) to maintain a constant alignment of the input data with the QOL outcomes promoted.

Conclusion

We have described in this chapter how many organizations in Italy are currently aligning support planning within a QQL outcomes framework using best practices in the field. Alignment is at the center of this process, for without alignment, support provision is "empty" and meaningless for the person and the community, resources are wasted, and QOL outcomes for individuals, their families, and their community become more or less random occurrences. Moreover, alignment has allowed these organizations to: (a) consolidate the scientific approach to QOL profiling and measurement, (b) widen the outcome vision from the values, human rights, and legal perspectives, sharing the connections between QOL domains and CRPD articles; (c) integrate the human capability approach to characterize individual and system support provision as an opportunity-rich means to personal and community QOL; and (d) develop a growing human capital, with an increasing number of capable individuals and environments, in which each step of the aligned ISP moves toward a valued, participatory QOL.

At the implementation level, the ecological and support matrices described in the chapter are implemented as metacognitive devices. They represent a way to align personal characteristics and QOL domains and to manage QOL-related variables.

At this point, we have collected data on more than 1,700 cases, with 3,400 matrices, with alignment as the guiding architectural principle for the ISP process. The two matrices, beyond framing and organizing the ISP process at the level of the person, also show at the organizational level the environmental assets that help to better increase specific components of a life of quality.

CHAPTER 9
CONTINUOUS QUALITY IMPROVEMENT

TIM LEE

Introduction and Overview

Throughout the world, organizations providing services and supports to persons with ID are undergoing significant change and transformation (Schalock & Verdugo, 2013; Schalock et al., 2014). This chapter focuses on two of those changes: (a) the person as central to provisions of services and supports and (b) organizations becoming more streamlined. Accompanying the change toward person-centeredness is the shift from general services to individualized supports, and the alignment of person-centered values with service delivery practices. These person-centered values relate to QOL, self-determination, inclusion, empowerment, and equity; service delivery practices related to assessment of personal goals and person-referenced support needs, provision of an individualized system of supports, and evaluation of personal outcomes. As organizations become more streamlined, there is a corresponding movement from vertical to horizontal structure that is accompanied by the increasing use of collaborative approaches to organization self-assessment, leadership and management strategies, and high-performance teams.

Continuous quality improvement (CQI) is increasingly viewed as central to these changes. The approach to CQI presented in this chapter incorporates the following CQI-related premises:

- CQI is an internal, collaborative, and transformative process that involves a plan-do-check-act cycle.
- CQI focuses on enhancing personal outcomes and increasing an organization's effectiveness and efficiency.

- CQI combines the emphasis on effectiveness and efficiency of a business mindset with the values and mission of not-for-profit organizations.
- CQI is a parallel process at the individual, team, and organization level.
- CQI incorporates best practices based on current best evidence obtained from credible sources that used reliable and valid methods and/or information based on a clearly articulated and empirically supported theory or rationale.

The chapter begins with a brief overview of CQI in business and industry, including a description of the Plan-Do-Check-Act (PDCA) quality improvement cycle. Thereafter, I discuss how the CQI process operationalized by the PDCA cycle can be applied at the level of the individual, team, or organization. The chapter concludes by sharing with the reader specific tables summarizing how the PDCA cycle can be applied to improving an individual's QOL, organization-based team performance, and an organization's overall effectiveness and efficiency.

CQI in Business and Industry

Background

CQI and related concepts are influencing management in all industries in significant ways. CQI is a system of thinking, of principles and approaches that can be used to transform organizations and how they operate so they can bring greater value to their customers.

CQI principles and approaches can be traced back to three key individuals, Taiichi Ohno and Kiichiro Toyoda of Toyota Motor Company (Ohno, 1988) and Edwards Deming (Rafael, 1991, 1996). Deming and his ideas, such as the PDCA cycle and statistical process control, transformed Japanese manufacturing and businesses after World War II, and CQI was at the heart of that transformation. The Toyota production system, envisioned and realized by Taiichi Ohno and Kiichiro Toyoda, is a great example of CQI at work (Liker, 2004).

PDCA Cycle

The PDCA Cycle, perhaps Deming's most famous idea, is the core of much of the CQI process. The *plan* stage involves identifying gap to goal, analyzing root issues and barriers, and formulating countermeasures and strategies. It is the analysis and strategy formulation stage. The *do* stage involves developing executable implementation processes, communicating the plan, and executing the plan. It is the implementation stage. The *check* stage involves monitoring the progress of plan implementation and measuring results. It is the impact evaluation stage. The *act* (or *adjust*) stage involves standardizing effective strategies or countermeasures, identifying further improvement possibilities, spreading best practices, and starting the PDCA cycle again (Liker & Franz, 2011). Key components of each cycle step are shown in Figure 9.1.

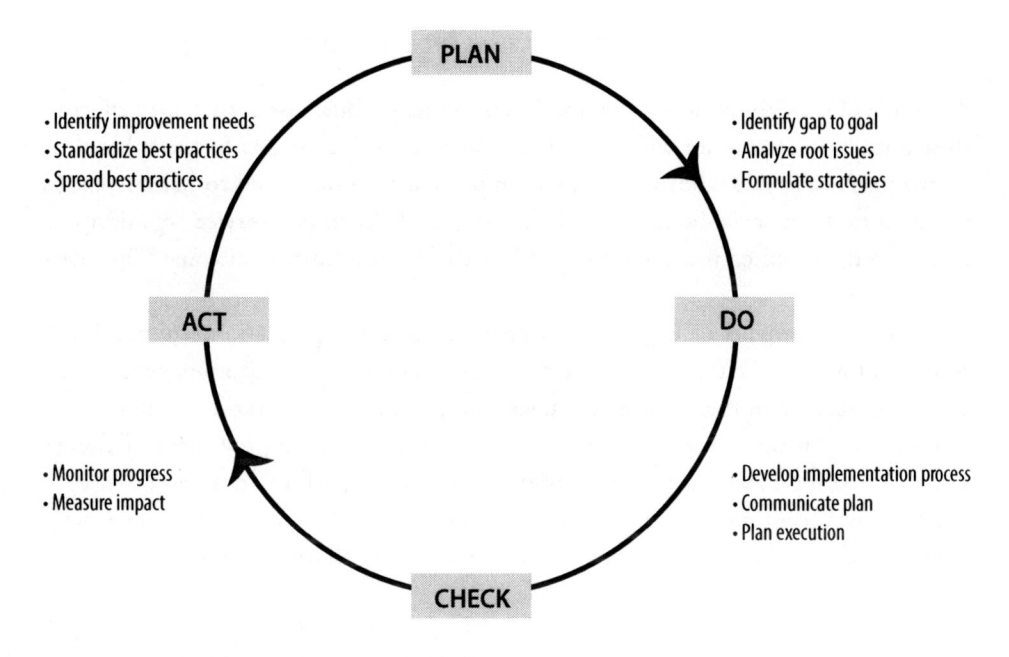

```
                          PLAN
   • Identify improvement needs              • Identify gap to goal
   • Standardize best practices              • Analyze root issues
   • Spread best practices                   • Formulate strategies


            ACT                                    DO


   • Monitor progress                        • Develop implementation process
   • Measure impact                          • Communicate plan
                                             • Plan execution

                          CHECK
```

FIGURE 9.1. The PDCA cycle and its components

Business and Industry Application

Increasing efficiency by eliminating waste is one of the key values of CQI. In the thinking behind the Toyota production system, there are three kinds of waste: muri (waste through unreasonableness or overburden), mura (waste through inconsistency or unevenness), and muda (waste through bad outcome; Ohno, 1988). The PDCA cycle addresses the three types of waste and improves quality and efficiency. The *plan* stage seeks to avoid muri through analysis and strategic planning. The *do* stage seeks to avoid mura through thorough and consistent plan implementation. The *check* stage seeks to avoid muda through outcome evaluation. The *act* stage allows teams to make improvements and spread them throughout the organization (Sutherland, 2014).

Today, CQI is no longer limited to the Japanese manufacturing industry. The U.S. automobile industry has long since adopted many key elements of CQI found in the Toyota production system (Liker & Franz, 2011). CQI is now taking root in other industries, such as medical services, food services, and information technology (Reis, 2011). It is having a great influence on the field of management. An example is the SCRUM agile project management and product development methodology developed by Sutherland and Schwaber. This is an approach that incorporates many of the foundational CQI principles such as PDCA cycle, customer centricity, cross-functional teams, and openness (Sutherland, 2014).

CQI in Human Services Organizations

The value of CQI thinking and approaches is immense. Businesses see CQI's effect in their bottom lines and are willing to do all they can to harness its financial benefits. Human service organizations, with more important missions, need to harness CQI's potential for their social benefits. CQI thinking can help human service organizations maximize their limited resources and produce the greatest human outcome. The question is "How?"

To reap the benefits of CQI, it must be a part of the organization's culture. For a system of thinking, values, and approaches to take root in an organization, people need to be transformed in their thinking, values, and practices. Such transformation needs to take place on three levels: the customer level (continuous improvement of client's QOL), the team level (continuous improvement of team performance), and the organization level (continuous improvement of organization effectiveness and efficiency). Figure 9.2 depicts how the PDCA cycle can be applied at all three levels.

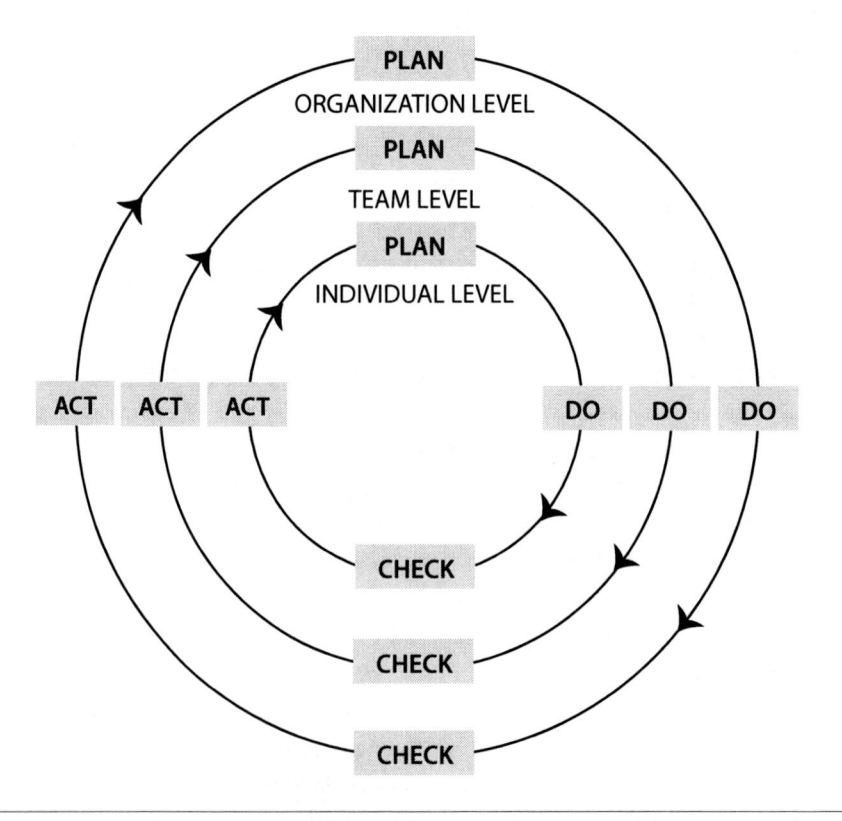

FIGURE 9.2. PDCA cycle for continuous quality improvement on different levels

The Continuous Quality Improvement Process

The process of CQI on the client level, team level, and organization level is built on the same core concepts. Because the scope of the chapter is limited and cannot cover all aspects of CQI, we will focus on three foundational ideas: the PDCA cycle, cross-functional teams, and openness.

PDCA Cycle

As shown in Figure 9.2, the power of the PDCA cycle is that it can take place on all levels of an organization's operation to improve both processes and outcomes. On the macro level, it can be used to continuously improve the middle- and long-term strategies and goal-oriented outcomes of the organization. The PDCA cycle turns more slowly at this level. For example, an organization's long-term goals and strategies may be formulated, implemented, assessed, and adjusted on an annual basis. A team's performance may be evaluated, and improvement strategies formulated and implemented, once a year. On the micro level, the PDCA cycle turns more rapidly and can be implemented to continuously improve an organization's day-to-day processes and operations. For example, a team can run weekly or bi-weekly PDCA cycles to micro-adjust the implementation of a project based on changing circumstances or new obstacles. A support team of direct service staff and a client can implement, monitor, and adjust the client's individual supports plan as frequently as necessary to better meet the client's support needs. Figure 9.3 shows how the PDCA cycle can be such an integral process on the macro and micro levels.

The iteration of the PDCA cycle can vary in speed, depending on the speed of change of conditions or goals. For example, an organization's long term goal of establishing services in a new city may take 18 to 24 months to realize. The PDCA cycle would be appropriately longer. However, there are small incremental targets along the way. The quicker iterations that range from weekly to monthly would be the appropriate approach to meet the targets and find potentials for improvements and adjustments. Whether fast or slow, one key idea to keep in mind is that the iterations are for the purposes of learning and improvement, not control.

Cross-Functional Teams

For the mindset of CQI to take root in an organization, it must be thoroughly engrained in the minds and working habits of teams of people. Liker (2004) formulated Toyota's approach to CPI into a 4P model, including philosophy (long-term thinking), process (eliminate waste), people and partners (respect, challenge, and grow them), and problem solving (continuous improvement and learning). Growing people is a fundamental value to Toyota's approach in continuous improvement.

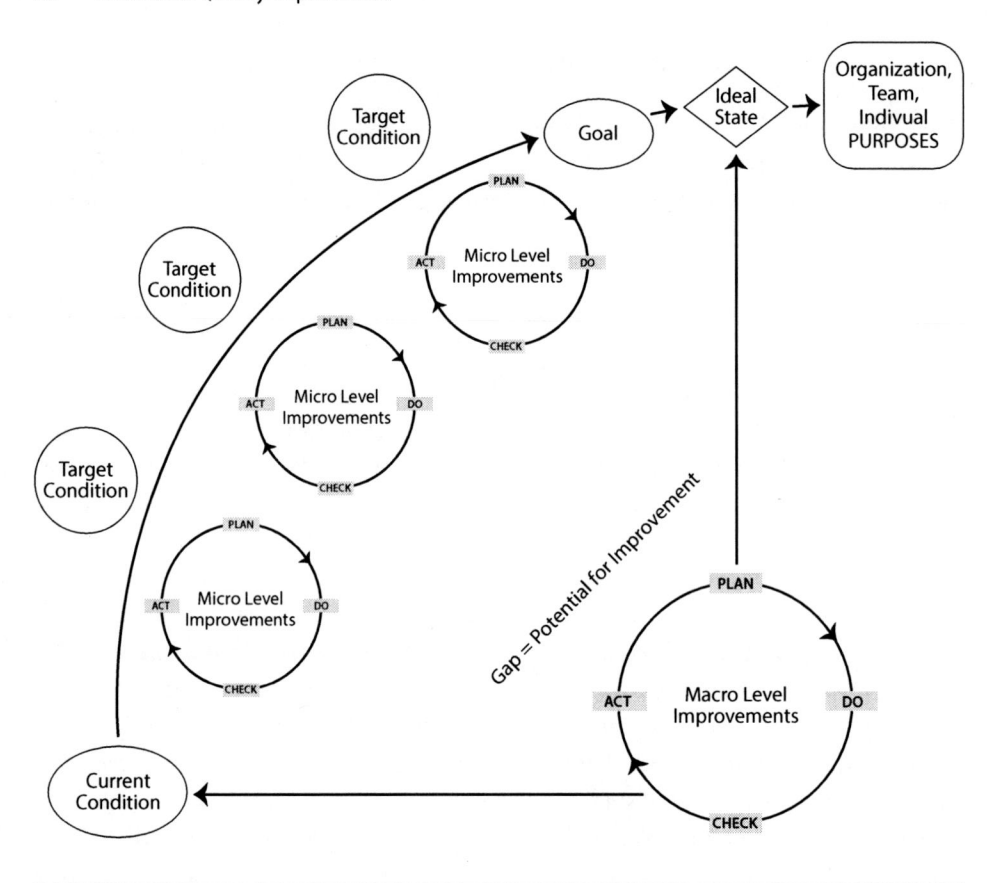

FIGURE 9.3. The PDCA cycle as a CQI process on macro and micro levels

For social service organizations, developing individuals and teams is critical to continuous improvement of clients' QOL and for enhanced overall organizational outcomes. Though teams are composed of individuals, the effect of developing teams as a whole may be much greater than focusing only on individuals' growth. Performance differences between individuals may differ by factors of ten or even twenty. Performance gaps between best and worst teams may vary by factors of as much as 2,000 (Sutherland, 2014).

In order for teams to perform at the highest level, they need to grow in these three ways: transcendence (a sense of purpose beyond the ordinary), autonomy (empowered to self-organize and self-manage), and cross-functionality (have all the skills needed to complete their work). A strong sense of purpose beyond the ordinary plus autonomy in how they work toward their goal, whom they work with, and when they work, will foster strong internal motivation (Pink, 2011). A cross-functional team with all the necessary skills will enable the team to achieve its goal. A team with high internal motivation and a comprehensive skill set, when given clear goals with objective indicators and a fluid CQI process with minimal bureaucracy, can continue to grow in performance and capacity. Because an organization is ultimately a collection of individuals and teams, high performance cross-functional teams that continue to increase in performance and capacity then become the change agent that can potentially transform an organization into one with a mindset and culture of continuous improvement.

Openness

It is a natural human tendency to cover up problems and weaknesses. Project delays and cost overruns are often discovered late due to unaddressed hidden issues. Departmental challenges are dealt with in-house, instead of being shared with others, creating unnecessary silo effects. The tendency to cover up issues is a great hindrance to continuous improvement. Therefore, many of the CQI processes and methodologies, such as Kanban (visual boards), heijunka boxes (pigeon-holes boxes), and SCRUM task boards, are designed to create openness so as to uncover problems. SCRUM is a framework for a rapid and iterative development process that allows the team to meet the actual project needs in the fastest way possible. These visual tools and processes clearly and openly present goals, plans, tasks, assigned responsibilities and progress, allowing teams and other stakeholders to monitor performance status in real-time and quickly identify any problems and issues.

For CQI to take root in the culture of an organization, openness needs to be a foundational value that is lived out by individuals and teams through processes and tools that promote authenticity and transparency. When a culture of openness and transparency is realized through tools such as SCRUM and Toyota's A3 reports, teams and organizations will experience the following effects that promote continuous improvement:

- Open communication of clear and concrete goals, tasks, assignment of responsibilities, and progress
- Increased common understanding by teams and other stakeholders
- Quicker discovery of problems, setbacks, and delays
- Timelier attention to improvement needs
- Increased accountability, collaboration, and mutual support

Applying CQI Processes in Human Services Organizations

As shown in Figures 9.2 and 9.3, the PDCA cycle and the CQI process can be applied to improve an individual's QOL, a team's performance, and an organization's effectiveness and efficiency. The CQI process has two types of iterative PDCA cycles, a slower cycle addressing longer-term goals and a faster cycle addressing shorter-term targets and ongoing status changes. These iterative cycles allow teams to close the gap between the current conditions and the desired outcomes of individuals, teams, and organizations.

At the end of this chapter, the reader will find six tables that show how the CQI process can be applied to enhance an individual's QOL, a team's performance, and/or an organization's effectiveness and efficiency. Each table contains suggested processes, tools, timing/frequency, and participants, one for the slower PDCA cycle (Tables 9.1, 9.3, and 9.5), one for macro-level goals, and one for the faster PDCA cycle for micro-level targets (Tables 9.2, 9.4, and 9.6).

Four assessment instruments are used in reference to the slower PDCA cycle (see Plan, Tools, and Processes in the respective tables). A brief overview of these instruments is provided below.

- Personal Outcomes Scale-Adult (POS-A; Table 9.1). As described in Chapter 7, the POS-A is based on the eight-domain QOL model and provides domain and factor scores based on a self-report or report of others.
- Supports Intensity Scale-Adults (SIS-A; Table 9.1). The SIS-A (Thompson et al., 2009; Thompson, et al. 2015) is used to determine the pattern and intensity of support needs across seven major life activity areas (home living, community living, life-long learning, employment, health and safety, social, and protection and advocacy) and exceptional medical and behavioral support need areas.
- Championship Formula Inventory (CFI-360; Table 9.3). The CFI-360 assesses the five factors and associated dimensions characteristic of high performance teams. The five factors are professionalism, leadership, emotional stability, interpersonal skills, and resourcefulness. Scores are aggregated into dimension and factor scores and presented for either individual team members or a full team. The instrument is available on line at www.CFI-360.com.
- Organization Effectiveness and Efficiency Scale (Table 9.5). The Organization Effectiveness and Efficiency Scale (www.oeesonline.org) was developed by the International Research Consortium on Evidence-Based Practices (2013) and measures best practice indicators related to four performance-based perspectives: the customer, and the organization's growth, financial analyses, and internal processes. Assessment results are presented in profiles summarizing scores for each of these perspectives and three evidence-based indices: an effectiveness index based on measures related to the customer and organization's growth, an efficiency index based on the organization's financial analyses and internal processes, and a sustainability index, which is the sum of the effectiveness and efficiency indices.

CQI Process Applied to Individual's Quality-of-Life Improvement

Table 9.1. *Slower PDCA Cycle for Continuous QOL Improvement*

		Continuous Quality-of-Life Improvement Slower PDCA cycle for macro level goals		
	Tools and Processes	**Timing & Frequency**	**Participants**	**Purpose**
Plan	Personal Outcome Scale	Annually	Client and interviewer	Assessment of individual's current quality of life.
	Supports Intensity Scale	Every 3 years or major life change	Client and interviewer	Assessment of individual's support needs.
	Goals and Dreams Interview	Annually	Client and interviewer	Identify personal goals and dreams that are important to him/her
	Individual Supports Plan	Annually	Client, personal manager, support team	Formulating supports strategies based on assessed needs and personal goals
Do	Develop support procedures	Annually	Client and support team	Initial formulation of specific supports procedures
	Visually communicate supports plan	As needed	Client and support team	Use clear and easy to understand charts and pictures to communicate supports plan to all relevant stakeholders
	Implement supports	As needed	Client and support team	Implement supports strategies and procedures
	Track support plan implementation	As needed	Client and support team	Track and record support plan implementation progress
Check	Monitor support implementation	As needed	Client and support team	Monitor whether support is provided according to plan
	Personal Outcome Scale	Annually	Client and interviewer	Assessment of individual's quality of life after receiving support services.
	Evaluate support strategies	Annually and as needed	Client and support team	Evaluate effectiveness of support strategies
Act	Identify major improvement needs	Annually	Client and support team	Identify major quality of life improvement needs based on quality of life domains
	Share effective strategies	Annually	Support team	Enter effective strategies and procedures in to organization knowledge base
	Start PDCA cycle again	Annually	Client and support team	Go to the Plan stage of the PDCA cycle and start the process again.

Table 9.2. *Faster PDCA Cycle for Continuous QOL Improvement*

		Continuous Quality-of-Life Improvement Faster PDCA cycle for micro level targets		
	Tools and Processes	**Timing & Frequency**	**Participants**	**Purpose**
Plan	Identify desired short term outcome	Monthly, quarterly, as needed	Client and support team	Identify client's desired short term goals and outcome through regular interactions
	Identify ineffective support procedures	Monthly, quarterly, as needed	Client and support team	Identify and analyze root issues of ineffective support strategies and procedures
	Develop support procedures	Monthly, quarterly, as needed	Client and support team	Develop specific support procedures based on support strategies in the ISP
Do	Visually communicate supports plan	Weekly, monthly, as needed	Client and support team	Use clear and easy to understand charts and pictures to communicate supports plan to all relevant stakeholders
	Implement supports	As needed	Client and support team	Implement supports strategies and procedures
	Track support plan implementation	As needed	Client and support team	Track and record support plan implementation progress
Check	Monitor support implementation	As needed	Client and support team	Monitor whether support is provided according to plan
	Evaluate support strategies and procedures	Monthly, quarterly, as needed	Client and support team	Evaluate whether particular support strategies and related procedures are effective in reaching client's short term goals and targets
Act	Identify ineffective strategy and procedure	Monthly, quarterly, as needed	Client and support team	Identify ineffective support strategies and procedures that needs immediate adjustment.
	Start the PDCA cycle again	Monthly, quarterly, as needed	Client and support team	Go to the Plan stage of the PDCA cycle and start the process again.

CQI Process Applied to Team Performance Improvement

Table 9.3. *Slower PDCA Cycle for Continuous Team Performance Improvement*

		Continuous Team Performance Improvement Slower PDCA cycle for macro level goals		
	Tools and Processes	**Timing & Frequency**	**Participants**	**Purpose**
Plan	Championship Formula Inventory	Annually	HR Interviewer, team leader, team members	Initial assessment of individual and team performance
	Initial staff member review	Annually	Team leader and team members	Annual personal performance review
	Initial team review	Annually	Team leader and team members	Annual team performance review
	Team goal and growth plan	Annually	Team leader and team members	Formulate growth strategies based on assessed team goals and performance growth needs
Do	Develop personal goal and growth action plan	Annually	Team leader and team members	Initial formulation of specific personal goal and growth action steps
	Develop team goal and growth action plan	Annually	Team leader and team members	Initial formulation of specific team goal and growth action steps
	Visually communicate action plans	As needed	Team leader and team members	Use clear and easy to understand charts and pictures to communicate action plans with team members and foster mutual support and accountability
	Implement action plans	As needed	Team leader and team members	Implement personal and team goal and growth action steps
	Track plan implementation	As needed	Team leader and team members	Track and record goal and growth action steps implementation progress
Check	Monitor goal and growth plan implementation	As needed	Team leader and team members	Monitor whether plans are being implemented and supported
	Championship Formula Inventory	Annually	HR Interviewer, team leader, team members	Assessment of individual and team performance after implementation of personal and team goal and growth action steps
	Staff member review	Annually	Team leader and team members	Annual personal performance assessment after implementation of goal and growth plans
	Team review	Annually	Team leader and team members	Annual team performance assessment after implementation of goal and growth plans
	Evaluate growth strategies and actions	Annually and as needed	HR Interviewer, team leader, team members	Evaluate effectiveness of growth strategies and action steps
Act	Identify major growth needs	Annually	Team leader and team members	Identify major team performance growth needs based on key performance indicators
	Share effective strategies	Annually	Team leader and team members	Enter effective growth strategies and action steps into organization knowledge base
	Start PDCA cycle again	Annually	Team leader and team members	Go to the Plan stage of the PDCA cycle and start the process again

Table 9.4. *Faster PDCA Cycle for Continuous Team Performance Improvement*

		Continuous Team Performance Improvement Faster PDCA cycle for micro level targets		
	Tools and Processes	**Timing & Frequency**	**Participants**	**Purpose**
Plan	Identify short term team targets	Weekly to quarterly	Team leader and team members	Identify team's short term goals and targets as the team members tackle their work responsibilities
	Identify ineffective action steps or barriers to targets	Weekly to quarterly	Team leader and team members	Identify and analyze root causes of ineffective action steps and barriers to team goals
	Develop specific action plans	Weekly to quarterly	Team leader and team members	Develop specific action steps and tasks based on strategies in goal and growth plans
Do	Visually communicate action plans	Weekly to quarterly	Team leader and team members	Use clear and easy to understand charts and pictures to communicate action plans with team members and foster mutual support and accountability
	Implement action plans	Weekly to quarterly	Team leader and team members	Implement personal and team goal and growth action steps
	Track plan implementation	As needed	Team leader and team members	Track and record goal and growth action steps implementation progress
Check	Monitor goal and growth plan implementation	Weekly to quarterly	Team leader and team members	Monitor whether plans are implemented and supported
	Evaluate strategies and action steps	Weekly to quarterly	Team leader and team members	Evaluate whether particular strategy and/or action is effective in reaching personal and team goals and targets
Act	Identify ineffective strategies, processes, and barriers to goals	Weekly to quarterly	Team leader and team members	Identify ineffective strategies, processes, and barriers to goals that requires immediate adjustment
	Start the PDCA cycle again	Weekly to quarterly	Team leader and team members	Go to the Plan stage of the PDCA cycle and start the process again

CQI Process Applied to Organization Effectiveness and Efficiency Improvement

Table 9.5. *Slower PDCA Cycle for Continuous Organization Effectiveness and Efficiency Improvement*

Continuous Organization Effectiveness and Efficiency Improvement
Slower PDCA cycle for macro level goals

	Tools and Processes	Timing & Frequency	Participants	Purpose
Plan	Organization Effectiveness and Efficiency Scale	Annually	Interviewer and key leaders	Assessment of organization's current level of effectiveness and efficiency
	Review of organization's long term goals	Annually	Core leadership team/team leaders	Identify and verify organization's larger goals and purposes
	Review of organization's annual plan and budget	Annually	Core leadership team/team leaders	Assessment of organization's current status and potential issues
	Develop organization strategic and improvement plan Strategic Action Map (Porter) Business Model Canvas (Osterwalder) Playbook (Lencioni)	Annually	Core leadership team/team leaders	Synthesize various assessment information with organization goals and formulate an organization strategic and improvement plan
Do	Develop detailed operations plan One Page Project (Campbell) SCRUM (Sutherland)	As needed	Team leaders and team members	Develop actionable implementation plans based on overall strategy and improvement plan.
	Visually communicate operations plan	As needed	Team leaders and team members	Use clear and easy to understand charts and graphs to communicate implementation plan to all relevant teams and team members. (i.e. SCRUM charts, Playbook, One Page Project Plan, A3 Report)
	Implement operations plan	As needed	Team leaders and team members	Implement operations plans, completing tasks and action items, using processes such as SCRUM and One Page Project Management
	Track operations plan implementation	As needed	Team leaders and team members	Track and record operations plan implementation progress using processes such as SCRUM, One Page Project Management and Playbook
Check	Monitor plan implementation	Monthly, quarterly, annually	Core leadership team/team leaders	Monitor whether strategic, improvement, and operations plans are being carried out
	Organization Effectiveness and Efficiency Scale	Annually	Interviewer and key leaders	Assessment of organization effectiveness and efficiency after implementation of strategic and improvement plans
	Evaluate improvement strategies	Annually	Core leadership team/team leaders	Evaluate effectiveness of improvement strategies
Act	Identify key improvement needs	Annually	Core leadership team/team leaders	Identify major organization improvement needs based on performance perspectives and key indicators
	Standardize and spread best practices	As needed	Team leaders and team members	Develop and spread standard operating procedures and policies based on improvements.
	Start PDCA cycle again	Annually	Core leadership team/team leaders	Go to the Plan stage of the PDCA cycle and start the process again

Table 9.6. *Faster PDCA Cycle for Continuous Organization Effectiveness and Efficiency Improvement*

		Continuous Organization Effectiveness and Efficiency Improvement **Faster PDCA cycle for micro level goals**		
	Tools and Processes	**Timing & Frequency**	**Participants**	**Purpose**
Plan	Identify short term targets	Weekly to quarterly	Team leaders and team members	Identify short term targets within organizational strategic and improvement plan
	Identify problems and/or barriers	Weekly to quarterly	Team leaders and team members	Identify and analyze root issues and/or problems hindering performance or progress.
	Develop task list/ action items	Weekly to quarterly	Team leaders and team members	Develop specific tasks and actions to reach identified short term targets or overcome problems and barriers
Do	Visually communicate action plan	As needed	Team leaders and team members	Use clear and easy to understand charts and graphs to communicate action plan to all relevant teams and team members. (i.e. SCRUM charts, One Page Project Plan, A3 Report)
	Implement action plan	As needed	Team leaders and team members	Implement action plans, completing tasks and action items, using processes such as SCRUM and One Page Project Management
	Track operations plan implementation	As needed	Team leaders and team members	Track and record action plan implementation progress using processes such as SCRUM, One Page Project Management and Playbook
Check	Monitor implementation progress	As needed	Team leaders and team members	Monitor whether tasks and actions are being carried out
	Check status of short term targets and goals	Weekly to quarterly	Team leaders and team members	Evaluate whether short term target and goals are reached and with how much effort
Act	Identify ineffective and/or inefficient processes	Weekly to quarterly	Team leaders and team members	Identify processes that hinder plan implementation
	Identify misaligned targets and goals	Weekly to quarterly	Team leaders and team members	Identify targets and goals that are no longer valid due to new problems or changes in the larger context
	Start the PDCA cycle again	Weekly to quarterly	Team leaders and team members	Go to the Plan stage of the PDCA cycle and start the process again.

Conclusion

In conclusion, CQI is a holistic, sequential, and collaborative process that incorporates best practices and results in actionable information. Although the PDCA cycle described in this chapter originated in industry, it is increasingly used in human service organizations to facilitate organizational changes that enhance both personal outcomes and the organization's effectiveness and efficiency. As we understand CQI and its application in not-for-profit organizations it becomes increasingly apparent that it is a parallel process at the individual, team, and organization levels, and that the PDCA cycle can be applied at each of these three levels. This parallelism and comprehensiveness facilitate both the successful application of quality improvement strategies as a core component of organization transformation and the incorporation of CQI into an organization's mindset and culture.

CHAPTER 10
ORGANIZATIONAL TRANSFORMATION

JOS VAN LOON and PETER VAN WIJK

Introduction and Overview

Today many organizations providing supports to people with ID face fundamental challenges that question their existence in their current form. An important development across countries is to transition from congregated settings to community-based support. For example, in 2013 the European Association for People with Disabilities (EASPD) discussed deinstitutionalization and the promotion of community-based services in Europe: " . . . It is time to put forward concrete planning for deinstitutionalization and community-based settings involving persons with disability and all mainstream and disability stakeholders."

But there are more challenges, such as decreasing resources, a movement from vertical to horizontal organization structure, a shift from general services to individualized supports, the need to align values with service delivery practices, the focus on evidence and evidence-based practices, and the need for capacity building in reference to organization-based self-assessment, strategic planning, and performance evaluation (Schalock & Verdugo, 2012b). Important in this respect is also the influence of the CRPD (United Nations, 2006). The conclusion is that many organizations supporting people with disabilities face the need for organizational transformation.

These developments had and have a prominent place in Arduin, a Dutch organization providing services for people with ID. Arduin was established in 1969 under the name Vijvervreugd as a residential facility serving persons with ID. In 1994, when the organization came under new management, there was clearly insufficient quality of care in several respects and a course of action was drawn up. The new Arduin became an independent, refocused organization. The action plan that was developed to bring about the necessary changes was based on a QOL focus and the supports paradigm. Arduin was transformed from an institution to a new community-based organization, focusing on supporting each individual, who determines what he or she needs (van Loon & Van Hove, 2001).

At present, Arduin serves about 800 persons: 533 for 24 hours per day (living and work/daily activities), 37 who receive support in their homes, 25 short-stay (weekends and holidays), and 205 who come to Arduin for support in work/daily activities. People live in more than 150 houses in communities spread over a wide region, work full time in a variety of businesses or day centers, and are supported according to their needs. The transformation to a community-based organization is not done yet. Recent developments in the field of support to people with ID, and the move toward accountability, require new responses.

In this chapter we focus on two important factors and themes in organizational transformation: the process of deinstitutionalization and the process of continuously adjusting to new developments. In doing so, we use Arduin as an example. However, we emphasize that the factors playing a role in Arduin's transformation can largely be seen as universal factors in any organization's transformation. These factors can be considered as guidelines, presented in the shaded boxes throughout the chapter.

Deinstitutionalization Process of Arduin: Quality of Life as Leading Principle

Before

The essential and consequent attitude in the process of reorganization, leading to deinstitutionalization, was that a person with ID should be empowered to decide how to give meaning and completion to his or her life. This necessitated a completely different way of thinking: namely, the individual person as the smallest organizational unit, including the splitting up of home living and care (van Loon & Van Hove, 2001). This new way of thinking led to closing Vijvervreugd, the institution in the town of Middelburg.

> The separation between the three life spheres—accommodation, work/daily activities, and leisure—was seen as fundamentally important in the process of deinstitutionalization and promotion of QOL.

After

The concept of QOL was operationally defined and implemented through the eight core domains found in the international QOL literature (Schalock & Verdugo, 2002).

From a large action research project we concluded that from these eight domains, inclusion, self-determination and personal development were especially influential in the shift from "total care"—as organized within the traditional institutional care—to "support." These three domains were considered fundamental to the best possible QOL for the clients of Arduin (van Loon, 2005; van Loon & Van Hove, 2001).

> A focus on QOL and on the support paradigm was continuous during the program changes.

Within the new approach, the individual was encouraged to develop from a position of dependence to one of self-determination, with a clear focus on long-term person-referenced outcomes. It was essential in the process of change that the implications of the focus on QOL was carried through consistently in all of the resolutions made.

> Every decision at the organizational level as well as at the level of the individual client had to contribute to the personal outcomes of clients.

Because every decision had to contribute to the personal outcomes of clients, the eight QOL domains were used as guidelines in the transformation of the organization. Thus, whatever organizational policy decision the management team took had to contribute to the QOL of clients and result in increased self-determination, inclusion, and personal development. This "right-to-left thinking" (Schalock, 2001) was accentuated in the decision to dismantle the institution, choosing a coaching style of management directed toward autonomy and self-direction, abolishing a lot of bureaucracy, developing a person-centered support system, and implementing a housing bureau and a vacancy bank for clients. One of the problems we encountered in deinstitutionalization was that staff who trained to work in an institution are not automatically trained to work in supporting people in community-based working and living situations. Therefore a new education for this profession was suggested and implemented (van Loon, 2005).

> In this consequential policy of focusing on QOL and supports, sometimes a lot of creative thinking was necessary.

For example, because of the expanding costs of transport, Arduin once started its own taxi company, to reduce the costs of buying cars (a taxi company has lower taxes when buying a car). There are no problems, only challenges.

> Regarding the focus on QOL: There is no "yes BUT, ..."

Quality Management: Evidence-Based and Focusing on QOL

In Arduin the choice was made to focus quality management on QOL instead of quality of care, and on what is necessary in the organization to enhance personal outcomes. From a quality of care orientation, staff and facility perspectives are usually more influential than the perspectives of the clients. The results that are important in a quality of care system are often conceived in an easy-to-reach and measured way. This means that value-based evaluation is less popular. The quality of care system gives no guarantee that existing knowledge about good predictors for QOL, such as social inclusion, self-determination, and personal development, are implemented (van Loon & Van Hove, 2001). Thus, one frequently finds an emphasis on impairment, categorization, homogenous grouping, health and safety, and control (De Waele & van Hove, 2005; De Waele, van Loon, van Hove, & Schalock, 2005). The main concern for quality of care strategies is typically the process (Hatton, 1998). This focus on the process allows organizations to invest a lot of time and energy in their own management structures and arrangements that sometimes inhibit decisiveness and in some cases lead to the abandonment of principles.

Basic to an organization committed to enhancing QOL are the fundamental beliefs that QOL of people with disabilities is: (a) composed of the same factors that are important to all persons; (b) enhanced by empowering persons to participate in decisions that affect their lives; (c) enhanced by the acceptance and full integration of persons into their local communities; and (d) enhanced through the provision of individualized supports (Brown & Brown, 2003; Schalock & Verdugo, 2008).

Adapting to New Developments

In addition to using the QOL concept and the supports paradigm as the overarching framework for organization transformation, we have had to adjust to new developments that involve the universal rights of persons, integrating the supports paradigm with individual support planning, using evidence-based outcomes, and employing a collaborative approach to organization self-assessment.

Universal Rights

The CRPD (United Nations, 2006) presents a profound and challenging agenda for government institutions, service commissioners and providers, and practitioners. It provides specific direction on how we assess the adequacy of our current systems and structures and identify what must be done to bring them into compliance with the Convention, and more importantly, how our practice and supports measure up to these fundamental obligations to recognize, protect, and promote the rights of people with ID (Stainton & Clare, 2012). As Stainton and Clare noted, issues of concern to the ID community are well represented in the Convention's Articles, including Article 12 (equal recognition before the law), Article 19 (living independently and being included in the community), and Article 17 (the right to respect for physical and mental integrity).

With the CRPD also comes a need for evidence-based instruments that help in the promotion of these rights. Verdugo et al. (2012) found a close relation between the QOL domains and the Convention Articles; these Articles can be evaluated by assessing indicators associated with the eight QOL domains (see Chapter 15). This means that indicators for good quality of an organization that wants to conform to the articles of the CRPD should in the first place be evidence based and use outcome-based indicators that are linked to the QOL of clients.

In this respect the data from the use of the Personal Outcomes Scale (POS; van Loon et al., 2008) can generate important evidence-based outcomes on an individual as well as an organizational level (van Loon, Bonham, Peterson, Schalock, Claes & Decramer, 2013). This process also answers another challenge: the need to focus on evidence and evidence-based practices.

Integrating the Supports Paradigm with Supports Planning

> Important for the embedding of improved QOL in an organisation is consumer involvement (Schalock et al., 2007): an essential organizational strategy involves incorporating consumers in meaningful roles.

An important motto in the UN Convention is "Nothing about us, without us." For a service provider, the essential question here is, to what degree are consumers involved in the development and implementation of their Individual Supports Plan (ISP)? To address this question, Arduin developed an individualized supports system that is person-centered (i.e., based on the person's interests, preferences, needs, and natural support network); responsive (i.e., based on a dialog between the person and those involved in the supports plan); flexible across the life span; proactive (i.e., equalizing opportunities with fellow citizens, empowering the person, generating effective social inclusion, and increasing social/community participation); and data based (i.e., based on the pattern and intensity of support needs) and evaluated in terms of facilitating personal outcomes (van Loon et al., 2010).

> The outcomes of an individual supports plan for a person should be an enhanced QOL. Determining whether this outcome occurs, requires the reliable and valid assessment of QOL-related domains.

The POS (van Loon et al., 2008), which is based on the QOL conceptual model and measurement framework by Schalock and Verdugo (2002), was developed as an instrument to assess personal, QOL-related outcomes. The POS has two optional assessment formats: a self-report and a report by others. Both formats are administered in an interview conducted by a well-trained, certificated interviewer. The interviewer completes the self-report, preferably with the client, or the report of others (if self-report is not possible)—a parent, direct support worker, or professional. The POS has six items for each QOL domain. For comparability purposes, the content of each item is the same for the self-report and report of others formats. The POS results in scores for the three factors and eight domains from both formats.

In the person-centered support system there is an alignment between the wishes and goals of a person, his or her support needs as measured by the *Supports Intensity Scale* (Thompson et al., 2004), the ISP, and his or her QOL as measured with the POS. This alignment among wishes and goals, assessed support needs, ISP components, and QOL outcomes, creates an excellent opportunity to enhance clinical decisions regarding how to support people methodically in improving their QOL. In Arduin this support system is communicated electronically in web-based applications (van Loon, Claes, Vandevelde, van Hove, & Schalock, 2010; van Loon, van Hove, & Schalock, 2009). In developing Individual Support Plans the two most important, and at the same time quite simple, questions are: (1) What does the person want? and (2) Which support does the person need? The third question then is: (3) What is the purpose of support? What should be the outcome of the supports given to the person? And also here the answer is simple: the outcome should obviously be a good QOL.

> A central element in a support methodology is the dialogue with the person.

A dialogue with the person is ongoing during the process of developing and implementing the ISP. Supports can be adjusted at any time as a consequence of this dialogue. Thus, the process of developing an ISP is an ongoing process. Within our program, the personal assistant is the professional responsible for dialogue with the person on the ISP. Each client has a personal assistant whom he or she can call upon for support in the dialogue with the organization, in formulating wishes and support requests directed to the organization. The personal assistant also maintains communication between the various staff members of the organization, the client, his or her family and/or legal representative, and assures the agreed service and care is carried out in conformity with the wishes of the individual client. Figure 10.1 provides an overview of the person-centered support system.

In the development of an ISP, a structured interview focusing on the person's desired life experiences and goals is held first. This interview involves the person and his or her parents. This is Component 1. In this interview the person is asked on each domain of QOL what his or her wishes and goals in life and an ideal situation would be. This is written in a web based program. Then the SIS (Component 2) is (electronically)

```
                    ┌──────────────────────────────┐  ┌──────────────────────────────────────────┐
                    │        COMPONENT 1           │  │              COMPONENT 2                 │
                    │ Wishes, personal aspirations │  │ 2.a. Determining Support Needs: to and   │
                    │ and goals: structured        │  │      for the person                      │
                    │ interview with the client    │  │      e.g. Interview with Supports        │
                    │                              │  │      Intensity Scale                     │
                    │                              │  │ 2.b. if needed: additional               │
                    │                              │  │      diagnostics/assessment              │
                    └──────────────────────────────┘  └──────────────────────────────────────────┘
```

COMPONENT 3: Developing an Individual Supports Plan
a. The client (with his personal assistant) synthesizes the wishes and goals with the support needs and come to an idea for an individual support plan: how do I want to be supported?
b. This idea is discussed with the supportworkers/professionals (and the psychologist).
c. Together they decide on a ISP on which support the person wants so he can fully participate in the community.

COMPONENT 4: Implementation
Those involved in the support of the person: the natural network and the professional supportworkers

COMPONENT 5: Monitoring
To what extent are goals and wishes realised? ←— Dialogue with the client —→ Does the person get the support he/she needs?

COMPONENT 6: Evaluation of the Individual Support Plan
Measuring QOL by measuring Personal Outcomes with the POS

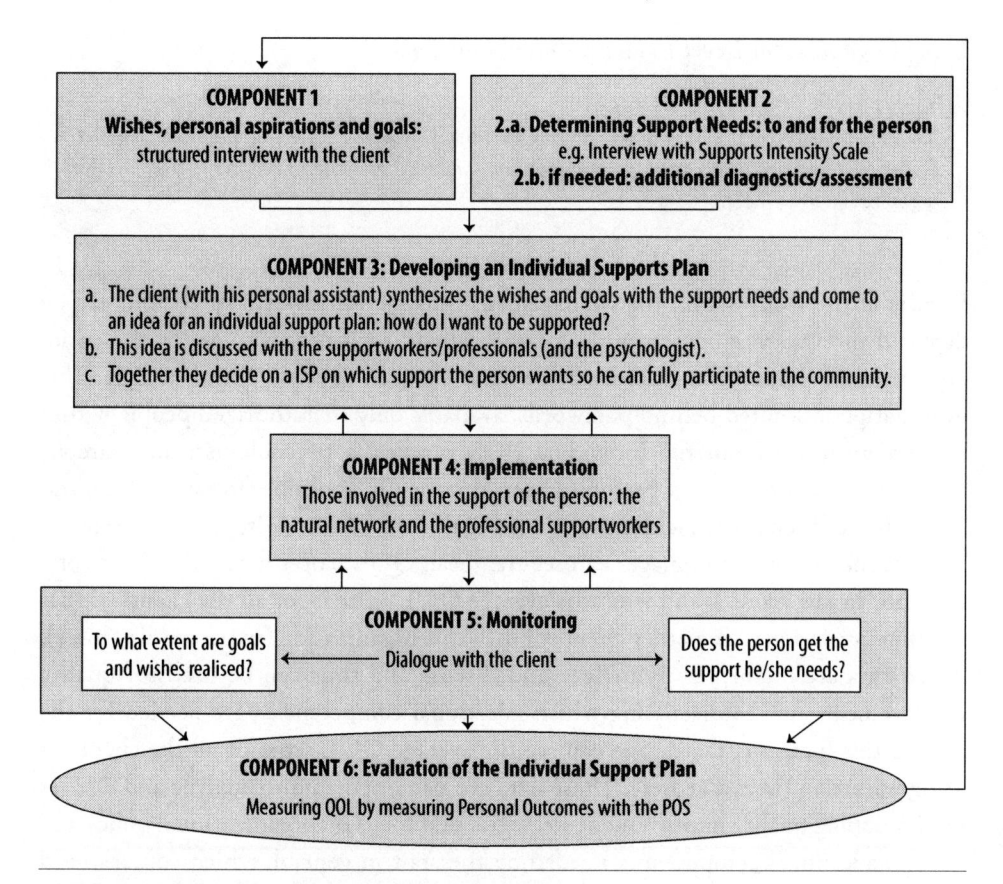

FIGURE 10.1. Design of a person-centered support system

administered, which again involves the person and his or her parents or relatives. The data from Component 1 (the interview on the person's desired life experiences and goals) and Component 2 (the SIS) are then combined into a computer-based application, giving an overview of the person's goals and the supports needed to achieve these goals, within a QOL framework. The ISP is written by the personal assistant, in dialogue with the client and support workers (Component 3), and then implemented by support staff and the person's natural network (Component 4). The outcomes of the supports are monitored on the same elements (Component 5) and evaluated by measuring personal outcomes through interview with the person (or an important other) with the *Personal Outcomes Scale* (Component 6). The results of this evaluation lead to an adjustment of goals, perspectives, and supports. All elements of this supports system are developed electronically in web-based applications. This alignment between SIS, ISP, and QOL creates an excellent opportunity to support people methodically in improving their QOL: measuring QOL gets a place in a support methodology, with the aim of continuous improvement.

Using Organization-Level Evidence-Based Outcomes

> The data collected in the interviews with the Personal Outcomes Scale are aggregated to give evidence-based outcomes information regarding the individual, organization program, or the organization as a whole.

Results of the POS within the Management Information System of Arduin can be depicted in raw score or percentile for each client, each program, or for the entire organization. Comparisons can easily be done between any two points in time. This information is secured behind passwords, available only to authorized people within the organization. From the individual POS profiles, a psychologist, for example, involved in the support of a person can see first the QOL profile (in raw scores), and how this profile compares with other clients of the organization (in percentile scores). As a second example, a manager can see the mean QOL scores for all the clients of a location (in raw scores), and what the average QOL score is for all the clients of that location in relation to the other clients of the same organization (in percentile scores). These data are important to analyze and discuss and thus can be used for quality improvement such as discussing which additional competencies are needed for the staff of this location. Third, one can see the average QOL score of all the clients of an organization (in raw scores). These data are also important to analyze and discuss for developing quality improvement strategies that focus on organizational policy and change, additional competences needed by the staff in general, which courses need to be developed for clients and staff, and determination of significant predictors of personal outcomes. Finally, these POS profiles are important to use as key results in a quality management model. When accountability is the question, what is more important than the personal outcomes that reflect the QOL of the clients who are supported by an organization?

Organization Self-Assessment

> In the process of change, human service organizations can use an evidence-based self-assessment approach to organization evaluation to facilitate continuous quality improvement and organization change.

Despite the implementation in Arduin of the supports paradigm and the QOL concept, and the commitment to outcomes evaluation, there was a perceived need to look at both evidence-based indicators based on best practices and a wider perspective on performance evaluation and management. For that purpose, the Organization Effectiveness and Efficiency Scale (OEES; the scale) was used. The purpose of this scale, developed by the International Research Consortium on Evidence-Based Practices (2013), is to assist not-for-profit organizations to meet the increasing need to be more effective in achieving their intended results, more efficient in their resource utilization, and more sustainable in adapting to change and providing a range of sound service delivery opportunities and practices.

The OEES measures four performance-based perspectives, which reflect a balanced approach to performance evaluation and management: the customer perspective, the growth perspective, the financial perspective and the internal processes perspective. Assessment scores obtained from the OEES result in profiles summarizing scores for each of these four performance-based perspectives, and *three evidence-based indices: (a) an effectiveness index* based on measures related to the customer and organization's growth; (b) an efficiency index based on measures related to the organization's financial analyses and internal processes; and (c) a sustainability index, which is the sum of the effectiveness and efficiency indices. These four perspectives and three indices also reflect a balanced-scorecard approach to evaluating and managing organization performance (Schalock et al., 2014; Schalock & Verdugo, 2012b; Tsai, Chou, & Hsu, 2009; Wu, Lin, & Chang, 2011).

The Arduin management team assesses the organization using the OEES. A trained external interviewer administers the Scale and members of the management team serve as the respondents. The intent of the self-assessment is to better understand the process of collaborative evaluation and to use the resulting information for quality improvement. Based on the results of one recent OEES assessment, a quality improvement plan was developed that included developing a strategy within the management team in which data collected were more structurally combined, analyzed, evaluated, and discussed, and conducting a study into the possibilities of current assistive technology devices and strategies.

Conclusion

In conclusion, changes in the Arduin program reflect what is happening in many human service organizations undergoing change and transformation. In general, these changes have involved making the person central, shifting from general services to individualized supports, aligning person-centered values (e.g. QOL, self-determination, inclusion, empowerment, and equity) with service delivery practices, assessing personal goals and person-referenced support needs, providing an individualized system of supports, and evaluating personal outcomes. Additionally, we have moved beyond focusing on deinstitutionalization that was based on the QOL concept and the supports paradigm to adjusting to new developments and challenges related to universal rights of persons with a disability, integrating the supports paradigm with individualized supports planning, using organization-level evidence-based outcomes, and employing a collaborative approach to organization self-assessment.

The transformation of organizations, such as Arduin, that face the challenges of increasing financial issues and contemporary developments in supports provision requires a conceptual framework that gives guidance for change. The QOL framework continues to give excellent guidelines to organizations for this process as well for measuring outcomes for use on both individual and organizational levels.

SECTION IV
QUALITY OF LIFE AT THE MACROSYSTEM LEVEL

Section Overview

In the preceding two sections, the authors addressed quality of life from the perspective of the individual and family, and the organizations providing services and supports to persons with intellectual disability. Collectively, these chapters provide a mosaic that reflects the interdependency among people, organizations, and the larger society. In this section of the text, contributing authors present a number of societal or macrosystem practices that potentially enhance the QOL of people with ID. These practices center on meta-level outcomes measurement, individualized supports provision, positive psychology, service delivery system changes, universal human rights and their relation to core QOL domains, and the evolution of QOL perspectives in the developing world.

In selecting contributors to this section of the book, we turned to individuals with experience and expertise in these societal-level practices. As in Section III, we begin with the end in mind, and discuss the importance of applying systems-level outcome indicators to service planning, benchmarking, evaluation, and continuous quality improvement. Once the desired outcomes are identified, then right-to-left thinking can be used by policy makers, funding agencies, and organizations to implement systems of supports that enhance desired personal and organization outcomes and bring about systems change. We next provide a chapter that focuses on the commitment of the international community to the rights of individuals with disabilities, and international efforts to align these rights with QOL-referenced domains and enhancement strategies. The section concludes with a chapter discussing social relational world view influences on the evolution of the QOL perspective in low-income countries, and the centrality of social collective supports to living a life of quality.

CHAPTER 11

A FOCUS ON SYSTEM-LEVEL OUTCOME INDICATORS

VALERIE J. BRADLEY, DOROTHY HIERSTEINER, and ALEXANDRA BONARDI

Introduction and Overview

The focus on the QOL of people with IDD and the concomitant outcomes associated with a "life well lived" has intensified as changes in the field have brought more attention to individual well-being. The emergence of personal experience as a legitimate measure of quality has evolved as each wave of reform has uncovered a deepening understanding of the mission of services and supports to people with IDD (Schalock, et al., 2002).

For purposes of this chapter, the modern reform era in this field began in the years following the end of World War II, when the overcrowded conditions in public institutions (and the accompanying neglect and paucity of resources devoted to care and treatment) became increasingly apparent through exposés (e.g., Rivera, 1972; Terry, 1968). The increased attention to the conditions in public institutions led to appeals for redress through class action law suits in states including Alabama, Minnesota, Maine, Michigan, and Massachusetts. (Bradley, 1978). The redress sought was to upgrade physical facilities, improve clinical and professional capacity, and increase staffing ratios—all input measures. These enhancements were aimed primarily at health and safety.

As the community system grew and expanded as an alternative to institutional care, new service models emerged that supported improved functioning, communication, learning, health, and socialization. As community offerings became more sophisticated, performance measurement moved to "model coherency" and compliance with clinical standards and programmatic licensing standards (Waddington, 2001).

The dominance of professional voices as arbiters of quality in the field began to wane in the latter years of the 20th century, as the voices of self-advocates and families became more prominent (Schalock et al., 2002; Schalock et al., 2007). The mantra of self-advocates, "nothing about us without us," infused a growing conversation across the field about whether the services and supports that had been put into place had done more than ensure safety and improved functioning and had in fact improved people's lives—improvements that reflected the desires of those who were system beneficiaries (Bell, 2014). Since then, the commitment to measure outcomes for people—outcomes that are important to *them*—has grown both in the United States and internationally (Bradley, 1996). Long after Wolfensberger (1972) advanced the notion of "normalization" as a benchmark to assess the legitimacy of services, the field finally began to develop measures to assess whether the people receiving the services and supports were in fact achieving the same goals that motivate all of us.

The purpose of this chapter is to provide an overview of how the commitment to measures of outcomes for people at the systems level has played out over the last two decades. We begin with a review of the precursors to meta-level measurement and the international QOL movement. Then we summarize how systems-level outcome measures have emerged in the United States. During the course of measuring systems-level outcomes, we have learned a lot about the importance of sustained measurement and the application of outcome data to quality improvement. We conclude the chapter with a discussion of the key role that common language plays in allowing for international research and cross-cultural comparisons.

Precursors to Meta-Level Measurement

One of the first attempts at the national level to measure outcomes was mandated in the U.S. in the 1987 amendments to the Developmental Disabilities Assistance and Bill of Rights Act of 1987 (P.L. 100–146). The statute required Developmental Disabilities (DD) Councils to complete a review and analysis of consumer satisfaction with state agencies providing developmental disabilities services, using independence, productivity, and integration as the benchmarks. To accomplish this goal, a standardized interview protocol was designed. DD Councils were then charged to use the results of the state-by-state surveys to develop priorities for new projects. The findings of the Congressional mandate were memorialized in *The 1990 Report* (Temple University, 1990).

In 1993, the Accreditation Council on Services for People with Disabilities issued the new *Outcome Based Performance Measures*, which moved the Council from standards based solely on inputs and process to an accreditation template that included information derived directly from individuals. Accreditation—once based almost entirely on paper reviews and site visits—became a more holistic picture of provider performance, including responses from individuals being served. The Council, now the Council on Quality and Leadership, continues to move to a more and more robust focus on outcomes (Gardner & Carran, 2005).

Data on individual outcomes were also collected as part of studies that followed people coming out of institutions such as Pennhurst, Belchertown, and Laconia (Bradley, 1986; Bradley, et. al., 1992; Conroy & Bradley, 1985). However, these studies used different interview protocols and ended when the research project ended. There were a few other forays into outcome measurement, including the Ask Me! Survey, administered by self-advocates under the auspices of the Maryland Arc (Bonham, et al. 2004). That survey, based on the Quality of Life Questionnaire (Schalock & Keith, 1993), collected data over many years. The results, however, could not be compared to results in other states; and the survey was given only to people in structured residential settings.

Interest in outcomes and the QOL of individuals with ID also developed within the international community. The first World Assembly, in Singapore in 1981, held by Disabled Peoples International, encouraged international acknowledgement of the systemic oppression of people with disabilities. International attention brought by the Assembly prompted recognition of a social movement advocating for the rights of people with disabilities. With the encouragement of advocates, disability came to be defined as more than a diagnosis or medical issue, but as a structural and social issue. People with disabilities were therefore seen as disabled by society rather than by their bodies. This transition from an individual, medical perspective of disability to a structural, social perspective created a desire to measure QOL, well-being, and satisfaction beyond access to income and welfare (WHO, 2011).

The conception of what makes up a quality life is highly personal and varies significantly by culture and region (Keith & Schalock, 2000). Recognition of the subjective nature of QOL spawned an international network of researchers interested in measuring culturally-specific QOL, as well as the development of more standardized measures (Skevington, Bradshaw & Saxena, 1999; WHOQOL Group, 1995, 1998). Researchers from countries such as the U. S., Canada, Australia, United Kingdom, and Finland have come together to enhance cross-cultural understanding of the QOL concept, including its conceptualization, measurement, and application (Matikka, 1994; Schalock, et al., 2002).

Emergence of System-Level Outcome Measures in the U.S.

The desire for an expanded understanding of the experiences of people receiving public services was animated by more than just a desire to capture whether the ideology and mission of the field were being realized. The creation of tools to measure outcomes was also necessitated by a variety of other contextual factors. For example, the landscape of services became extremely complex as the number and types of residential and day supports proliferated.

Further, the proliferation of services coincided with rapid expansions of state and federal budgets for services and supports to people with IDD. In Fiscal Year 2012, total

Medicaid spending, including federal and state funds, devoted to Home and Community Based Waiver services for people with IDD was 29.5 billion dollars. The total budget for Intermediate Care Facilities for People with Intellectual and Developmental Disabilities (ICF/IDDs) in the same year was 12.3 billion dollars (Larson, et al, 2014). As the expenditures for services became a more prominent proportion of state budgets, the pressure for accountability to taxpayers also grew. Public managers increasingly found themselves called upon to answer the question, "Is all of this public money having the desired impact?"

In 1997, a number of state IDD directors came together under the auspices of the National Association of State Directors of Developmental Disabilities Services (NASDDDS) and the Human Services Research Institute (HSRI) to discuss the launch of a standardized data collection effort that would allow public managers and other stakeholders to compare outcomes across states. The conversation that ensued began with identification of those domains or aspirations that characterized the consensus of the field. Domains selected included Employment, Community Inclusion, Relationships, Family Support, and Health and Safety. The group was then challenged to identify concrete outcomes or indicators that would suggest that outcomes in those domains were being met. Table 11.1 provides examples of how statements of concern and indicators line up within the overarching domains.

Table 11.1. *Domain, Subdomain, Concern, Indicator, and Data Source Crosswalk*

DOMAIN: SYSTEM PERFORMANCE	**Overview:** The system performance indicators address the following topics: (a) service coordination; (b) family and individual participation in provider-level decisions; (c) the utilization of and outlays for various types of services and supports; (d) cultural competency; and (e) access to services.		
Subdomain	Concern	Indicator	Data Source
Service Coordination	Service coordinators are accessible, responsive, and support the person's participation in service planning.	The proportion of people reporting that service coordinators help them get what they need.	Consumer Survey
		The proportion of people who were involved in creating their service plan	Consumer Survey
		The proportion of people reporting that service coordinators ask them what they want.	Consumer Survey
		The proportion of people who have met their service coordinators.	Consumer Survey
		The proportion of people who report that their service coordinators call them back right away.	Consumer Survey
Access	Publicly-funded services are readily available to individuals who need and qualify for them.	The proportion of people who report having adequate transportation when they want to go somewhere.	Consumer Survey
		The proportion of people who feel their support staff has been appropriately trained to meet their needs.	Consumer Survey
		The rate at which people report that they do not get the services they need.	Consumer Survey

With funding primarily from the states and more recently from the federal government, those early efforts spawned a burgeoning movement—National Core Indicators (NCI)—that as of 2014 had been implemented in 42 states (including the District of Columbia) and 22 sub-state entities. Data collection tools include: (a) an adult consumer survey that is administered in-person to a valid and reliable sample of at least 400 individuals; (b) three family surveys that are mailed to families with children, families with an adult living at home, and families with an adult living outside the home; and (c) system-level protocols, including a tool to measure provider staff stability and retention, and a canvass of mortality data.

The availability of a national database encompassing outcomes has made it possible to explore multiple programmatic and demographic issues affecting people with ID and their families. Over the past decade and a half, NCI staff have produced data briefs focusing attention on such issues as overuse of psychotropic medications, access to primary health care, challenges facing individuals with autism, and the importance of outcomes and choice as predicators of other outcomes. The data have also formed the basis for articles in peer-reviewed journals on such topics as race and ethnicity, health surveillance, and human rights (National Core Indicators, n.d.).

Because of the success of NCI, there has recently been a move to introduce this approach to outcomes measurement in another field—aging and disability. During the last two years, the National Association of States United for Aging and Disability and HSRI have been in the pilot phase of development of an adult consumer survey for people who are aging and who have physical disabilities. Termed NCI-AD, the new survey was implemented initially in twelve American states in 2015. Because there is some overlap between the original NCI and the new NCI-AD, some cross-population comparisons will be possible.

Lessons Learned

Importance of Sustained Measurement

During the almost two decades since NCI began, professionals in the field have learned important lessons about the variables or preconditions that predict whether aggregate data on outcomes are applied to the improvement of state systems and ultimately individual lives. One important lesson was that the presence of these data did not automatically translate into policy or system change. Most states had—and many continue to have—limited analysis and evaluation capacity. Over time, as more states discovered the utility of the data, peers learned from peers about the importance of the resource they had at their disposal. NASDDDS and HSRI helped to accelerate this process by disseminating these experiences and making sure that emerging leaders received a platform to inform others (Bradley & Pell, 2012).

Another important contributor to the success of NCI is that data are collected on a regular basis. This allows managers to track progress over time, using protocols that change only minimally from year to year. Thus, states have been able to track outcomes such as increases in access to health services, declines in the use of psychotropic medication, changes in the percentages of individuals participating in their individual plans, and numbers of individuals employed.

As state agencies began to expand the collection of outcome measures, pressure mounted on states from the federal level to generate evidence regarding Medicaid compliance. In the early 2000s, the Centers for Medicaid and Medicare Services began to standardize state reporting requirements associated with management of Home and Community Based Waiver services (HCBS; Medicaid.gov, n.d.). The new requirements directed states to collect systematic evidence that assurances such as health and safety, plans of care, and provider capabilities were being met. Data from NCI were integrated by many states into evidence submissions. More recently, the promulgation of new HCBS regulations concerning the character of residential and other settings supported by Medicaid funding has also led many states to include results of their consumer and family surveys as indications that requirements are being met. That these states were able to incorporate NCI findings into evidence reports and transition plans is testimony to the continuing relevance of the domains and indicators (Pell, 2014).

Another important lesson—one that contributes to the sustainability of national data collection—is that the survey protocols are designed to minimize respondent burden. Although there are many things that would be interesting to know about consumer and family perceptions, it was and is important to be parsimonious in the number of questions included in a survey. Further, the tool continues to benefit from the fact that it is valid and reliable and that the samples in each state are drawn using correct parameters. Without these assurances, the information generated would be subject to question.

From the beginning, a very important assumption about NCI data was that they would be shared publicly and that state-by-state comparisons would be available as well. This commitment to transparency was a bold step by members of NCI and has enhanced the use and utility of the information. However, simply making the information available does not mean that people will seek it out, nor, if they do, that they will find it interesting and/or understandable. To ensure that the information is accessible, NCI staff members have designed user-friendly report templates that can be used by a wide variety of audiences. The reports include graphic as well as written depictions of key outcome indicators (for more information, see www.nationalcoreindicators.org/resources/reports).

Application of Data to Quality Improvement

Participating NCI states provide several examples of how system-wide outcome data can be used as a basis for quality improvement. For example, Arizona uses NCI data to identify areas of low performance. These data are then presented to the Statewide Management Team, which works to develop priorities and strategies to improve performance in the low performing areas. NCI data have contributed to the Division's decision to increase provider rates to incentivize Community and Supported Employment initiatives. In addition, NCI data have contributed to the creation and allocation of District Employment Specialist positions.

Georgia also uses NCI data to identify areas for improvement. Specifically, public managers in the state noted a troubling yearly increase in the rate of use of psychotropic medications. Using NCI data, state quality management staff found there was an increase in psychotropic medication use over time for all clients with IDD receiving services through the Medicaid Home and Community Based Services program, and that the rate of psychotropic drug use was increasing even faster for individuals who were transitioning out of institutional settings. They also noticed that the use of psychotropic medications varied by certain demographic characteristics. Based on these findings, the state agency implemented a series of trainings for providers and support coordinators on what informed consent means, the importance of obtaining informed consent for prescription of psychotropic medications, and who can provide informed consent if an individual is unable to do so. In addition, the Georgia Human Rights Council reviews the case records of all individuals who are prescribed five or more psychotropic medications. Based on these reviews, the Council makes recommendations concerning the ongoing medication regimen. Subsequent evaluation has shown a decrease in psychotropic medication use.

In 2010, the Kentucky National Core Indicators Quality Improvement Committee presented a series of recommendations to the Kentucky Division of Developmental and Intellectual Disabilities (DDID). These recommendations were based on NCI data, and included goals regarding employment, health and exercise, medications, and loneliness. As a result of these recommendations, the DDID initiated several changes to their service delivery systems; however, as of 2013, several of these changes were yet to be implemented. The changes included:

- Changes to the Supports for Community Living (SCL) Waiver to increase rates of individuals receiving supported employment and to decrease the use of non-work day activity/day habilitation services
- Amendment to the SCL Waiver menu of services to include a service called "community access" to support people with disabilities in engaging in community life
- Initiation of partnerships with the Human Development Institute at the University of Kentucky and the University of Illinois-Chicago. This collaboration has led to pilot projects such as an evidence-based wellness and health curriculum.
- Development of various health risk screening tools and scales, as well as new services to increase health and wellness

Yearly, Washington State convenes a group of volunteers recruited by the Developmental Disabilities Council. This committee reviews and makes systems change recommendations to the Division on Developmental Disabilities (DDD) based on the NCI data reports. Some examples of policy and programmatic changes resulting from these recommendations include:

- Development of a website and a podcast from which information for families and caregivers is easily accessible
- Development of a project to help schools prepare people leaving school for a more inclusive life
- Development of an information template that goes annually to each person/family receiving services, informing them of the costs of the services they received in the past fiscal year
- Revised case manager training that emphasizes the need to encourage service recipients to ask for what they want
- Development of training for individuals with disabilities on general safety
- Collaboration between DDD and staff from the University of Washington working on finding ways to impart information to primary care doctors on the unique care needs of individuals with developmental disabilities

Many states, including Tennessee and Michigan, convene committees and quality improvement councils to annually assess data and generate priorities for presentation to stakeholders and lawmakers. In addition, some states use the NCI data for regulatory reporting to the national Centers for Medicare and Medicaid Services.

Common Language that Allows for International Research and Comparisons

The momentum toward comprehensive, system-level, QOL outcome measurement is not limited to the United States. In the 1960s, the burgeoning women's rights, gay rights, and anti-racist movements across the globe encouraged a movement advocating for the dignity and human rights of people with disabilities. Previously, concern for the rights of individuals with disabilities had been focused on welfare and right to adequate rehabilitation and medical care. Since the 1960s, disability issues have begun to be considered issues of civil rights and justice (Waddington, 2001). Throughout the next few decades, the expanding emphasis on the rights of individuals with disabilities encouraged international entities to coalesce behind various treaties, conventions, and declarations aiming to enhance the opportunities to experience high QOL.

The CRPD was adopted in December, 2006, and is a legally binding document reflecting an international consensus on the preservation of human and civil rights of individuals with disabilities (see also Chapter 15, this volume). Many nations use CRPD articles as a model for legislation on disability issues and CRPD has been defined as a "moral compass" of disability policy reform (Quinn, 2007), specifying the steps to take to ensure the rights of individuals with disabilities (Ticha, et al., in press). Participation in the CRPD signifies a commitment to a process of systems change toward a more inclusive society. Although the CRPD delineates broad steps that must be taken to achieve that vision, there are no international standards by which participating nations can benchmark, assess, or compare their progress. Furthermore, individual nations that sign and ratify the Convention are required to execute the Convention and monitor the process of implementation (Articles 31 and 33); however, the design of specific strategies for monitoring is left to the discretion of each participating nation. Therefore, how can a participating nation measure the progress of its systems on guidelines outlined in the Convention? And how can nations measure how implementation of the CRPD affects the lives and well-being of individuals with disabilities?

As demonstrated earlier in this chapter, the data that result from NCI surveys are often used to inform strategic planning, produce legislative reports, prioritize quality improvement initiatives, and benchmark performance. The indicators addressed in the National Core Indicators surveys are measurable data points that can be used to assess a system's performance in various domains of interest, such as (but not limited to) relationships, satisfaction, choice and decision-making, health, wellness, access, and service coordination. In aggregate, a system's performance on the domains of interest can be used to monitor progress toward a greater goal of enhanced QOL for individuals with IDD.

Ticha et al. (in press) found overlap between the measurement of rights in the NCI adult consumer survey and the CRPD. Beyond the measurement of rights, NCI can be used as an internationally comparable disability dataset to monitor a nation's progress as it works toward the progressive goals outlined in the CRPD. Although cultural and political differences may require a modification of some of the content of NCI, the major outcome areas coincide with much of the CRPD. Table 11.2 demonstrates how specific NCI indicators align with selected CRPD articles. The work summarized in Table 11.2 and that presented later in Table 15.1 represent initial attempts to operationalize the UN Convention articles into measurable NCI indicators (as in Table 11.2) or QOL-related domains and indicators (as in Table 15.1).

The International Classification of Functioning (ICF) and Outcome Measurement

Looking to the future of outcome measurement at the system level, with particular reference to monitoring the progress toward the rights outlined in the CRPD, it is possible to imagine a framework that will enable policy-makers, stakeholders, and advocates to review a more holistic and multidimensional picture of a system's performance. Using the functional paradigm envisioned by the authors of the International Classification of Functioning (ICF) in combination with a tool like the National Core Indicators Adult Consumer Survey, it may be possible to link capacity with functioning and outcomes.

In 2001, the WHO proposed the ICF as a standardized system to describe and synthesize health and disability elements into one framework, and member states agreed to

Table 11.2. *Crosswalk of Selected CRPD Articles and NCI Indicators*

CRPD Article	NCI Indicator
Article 9 - Accessibility	Proportion of people who report having adequate transportation when they want to go somewhere.
	Proportion of individuals who report being able to use the phone/internet without restrictions
	Proportion of people who feel their support staff have been appropriately trained to meet their needs.
	Rate at which people report that they do not get the services they need.
Article 14 - Liberty and security of person	Proportion of people indicating that most staff treat them with respect.
	Proportion of people whose basic rights are respected by others.
	Proportion of people who make choices about their everyday lives, including: housing, roommates, daily routines, jobs, support staff or providers, what to spend money on, and social activities.
	Proportion of people who report that they feel safe in their home, neighborhood, workplace, and day program/ at other daily activity.
	Proportion of people who report having someone to go to for help when they feel afraid.
Article 19 - Living independently and being included in the community	Proportion of people who regularly participate in everyday integrated activities in their communities.
	Proportion of people who make choices about their everyday lives, including: housing, roommates, daily routines, jobs, support staff or providers, what to spend money on, and social activities.
	Rate at which people report that they do not get the services they need: If Does Not Get Needed Services Needs If Does Not Get Needed Services Needs Social/Relationships
	Proportion of people who can go out on a date if they want to.
	Proportion of people who are able to see their families and friends when they want.
	Proportion of people who have a close friend, someone they can talk to about personal things.
	Proportion of people who have friends and caring relationships with people other than support staff and family members.
	Proportion of people who feel lonely.
Article 25 - Health	Proportion of people in poor health
	Proportion of people who receive Medicare
	Proportion of people age 50 and older who have had a screening for colorectal cancer within the past year.
	Proportion of people described as having poor health.
	Proportion of people reported as having a primary care doctor.
	Proportion of people who have ever had a vaccination for pneumonia.
	Proportion of people who have had a complete annual physical exam in the past year.
	Proportion of people who have had a flu vaccination within the past 12 months.
	Proportion of people who have had a hearing test within the past 5 years.
	Proportion of people who have had a routine dental exam in the past year.
	Proportion of people who have had a vision screening within the past year.
	Proportion of women 18 and over who have had a Pap test in the past year.
	Proportion of women over 40 who have had a mammogram within the past 2 years.
	Proportion of people taking medications for mood, anxiety, behavior problems, or psychotic disorders.
	Proportion of people who maintain healthy habits in such areas as smoking, weight, and exercise.
	Rate at which people report that they do not get the services they need
	Rate at which people report that they do not get the services they need.

Table 11.2. *Crosswalk of Selected CRPD Articles and NCI Indicators (continued)*

CRPD Article	NCI Indicator
Article 27 - Work and employment	Proportion of people who have a job in the community.
	Of people who have a job in the community, the average length of time they have been working at their current job.
	Of people who have a job in the community, the percent who receive vacation and/or sick time benefits.
	Of people who have a job in the community, the percent who were continuously employed during the previous year.
	Average bi-weekly earnings of people who have jobs in the community.
	Average number of hours worked bi-weekly by people with jobs in the community.
	Percent of people earning at or above the State minimum wage
	Proportion of people who do not have a job in the community but would like to have one.
	Proportion of people who do volunteer work.
	Proportion of people who go to a day program or have some other daily activity.
	Proportion of people who have a goal of integrated employment in their individualized service plan.
	Rate at which people report that they do not get the services they need.

adopt the ICF as the basis for uniform health and disability data worldwide. The new scheme was developed in recognition of the fact that diagnosis and traditional measures of population health—such as mortality and morbidity—are not accurate predictors of functional status, level of disability, or service costs.

The ICF framework builds on the social-ecological model of disability. The environment in which a person lives, including the supports and services received, interacts with and influences the level of the person's community activity and participation. The notion that functioning is a dynamic process tempered by the extent to which functional deficits are accommodated by formal and informal supports was also a foundational concept in the 11th edition of the AAIDD definition manual, *Intellectual Disability: Definition, Classification, and Systems of Support* (Schalock et al., 2010).

In addition to measuring functioning and supports, the ICF has been promoted as a tool that can be used for management and outcome evaluation, including a means of answering questions such as "how useful are the services we are providing?" Although the ICF does provide a relevant and useful way to think about the interrelationship of individual and social factors that affect the experience of disability, it may be a stretch to suggest that it provides adequate guidance in the evaluation of the relation between personal factors, the environment in which the person lives, and the outcomes or "usefulness" of services provided.

As noted earlier in this chapter, the NCI adult consumer survey is used to collect information at the individual level and that yields an aggregate view for interpretation of system performance. Given the importance of measuring outcomes to gauge the

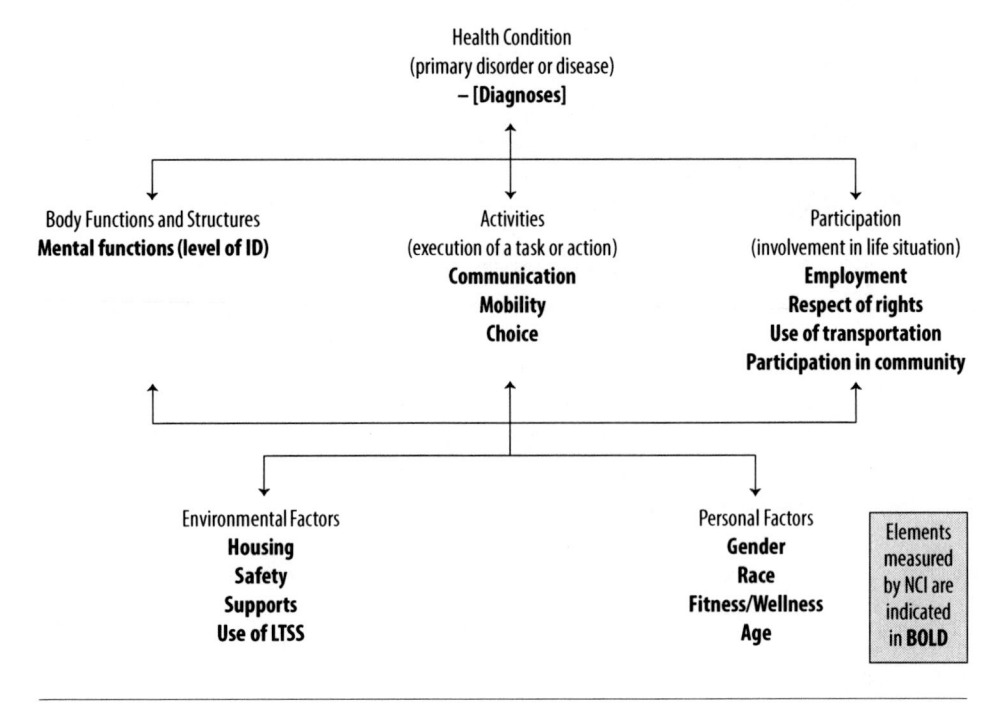

```
                          Health Condition
                      (primary disorder or disease)
                            – [Diagnoses]
                                 ↑
            ↓                    ↓                    ↓
Body Functions and Structures  Activities          Participation
Mental functions (level of ID) (execution of a task or action)  (involvement in life situation)
                            Communication          Employment
                              Mobility            Respect of rights
                               Choice           Use of transportation
                                              Participation in community
            ↑                    ↑                    ↑
            ↓                                         ↓
      Environmental Factors               Personal Factors      ┌─────────────┐
           Housing                            Gender            │  Elements   │
           Safety                              Race             │  measured   │
          Supports                      Fitness/Wellness        │  by NCI are │
         Use of LTSS                            Age             │  indicated  │
                                                                │  in BOLD    │
                                                                └─────────────┘
```

FIGURE 11.1. ICF model and elements measured by NCI

implementation of the CRPD, as well as to advance international metrics to assess outcomes generally, the possibility of interpreting some of the domains of NCI using ICF coding as a framework should be explored. An initial framework showing the extent to which elements measured by NCI align with the ICF model is presented in Figure 11.1.

Conclusion

Over the past several decades, progress has been made in measuring the outcomes of public services and supports for people with IDD. In the U.S., the NCI have made it possible for states to not only compare their performance but also to use outcome measures as a basis for systems reform. The adoption of the CRPD provides an opportunity to measure progress at the individual level and at the state, provincial, regional, and national levels. CRPD also provides an opportunity to adopt methods that make it possible to adopt a common language and framework for international research and comparisons. The combination of standardized outcome measures make it possible to understand at both the individual and systems level the connections among capacity, functioning, supports, and outcomes. The next chapter discusses the critical role that individualized supports play in this process.

CHAPTER 12

THE SUPPORTS PARADIGM

ROGER J. STANCLIFFE, SAMUEL R. C. ARNOLD, and VIVIENNE C. RICHES

Introduction and Overview

Supports have been defined by the American Association on Intellectual and Developmental Disabilities (AAIDD) as "resources and strategies that aim to promote the development, education, interests, and personal well-being of a person and that enhance individual functioning" (Schalock et al., 2010, p. 105). As such, supports represent a broad concept including, but not limited to, adaptive equipment (e.g., computerized text readers), universal design and/or environmental modifications (e.g., signs in public places using symbols instead of text), and personal support from an individual such as a caregiver. In this chapter we focus on paid and unpaid personal supports provided by other people. We recognize that other forms of support are important and interact with personal supports. For example, the availability of a power wheelchair reduces the need for personal support for mobility (e.g., a caregiver pushing a wheelchair).

The nature of support is values-driven and relates to the outcomes intended to be achieved through provision of support. The AAIDD definition of ID includes the assumption that "with appropriate personalized supports over a sustained period, the life functioning of the person with intellectual disability will improve" (Schalock et al., 2010, p. 1). In discussing support and providing examples of what we consider to be appropriate support, we will deliberately highlight support that is enabling.

For example, students need to travel to school each day. In Australia, for example, many students without disabilities travel to school by public transportation, whereas students with disability are often provided with specialized, segregated, door-to-door travel. Haveman, Tillmann, Stoppler, Kvas, and Monninger (2013) showed that many, but not all, students with ID can learn to travel to school independently by public transportation; yet Australian governments spend large amounts of money transporting students with disabilities, but little or nothing on travel skills training. For many students, such specialized transport is a potentially disabling form of support that creates unnecessary long-term dependence. Travel skills training is enabling, not only for the journey to school, but also as a basis for future independent travel to work or for leisure. In addition, such enabling support has the potential to free current support resources to provide support for other important outcomes to be achieved.

In this chapter we will briefly describe the supports paradigm and examine a variety of examples of how supports have been operationalized. Specifically, we will analyze (a) what is the supports paradigm, (b) conceptualization of support needs, (c) support-needs assessment, (d) resource allocation, (e) active support, (f) support, function, and outcomes, and (g) culture and support. As appropriate, these analyses will focus on the individual level (microsystem), the organization level (mesosystem), and the level of service systems and society (macrosystem).

What is the Supports Paradigm?

In the IDD field, the supports paradigm has been described in detail by a number of authors in recent years (Buntinx, & Schalock, 2010; Luckasson et al., 2002; Schalock, 2004b) and is a central feature of the AAIDD conceptualization of ID (Schalock et al., 2010). Figure 12.1 shows the centrality of supports in human functioning as proposed by AAIDD.

In turn, the supports paradigm is closely related to our understanding of the nature of disability. This understanding has changed in recent decades, as exemplified by the

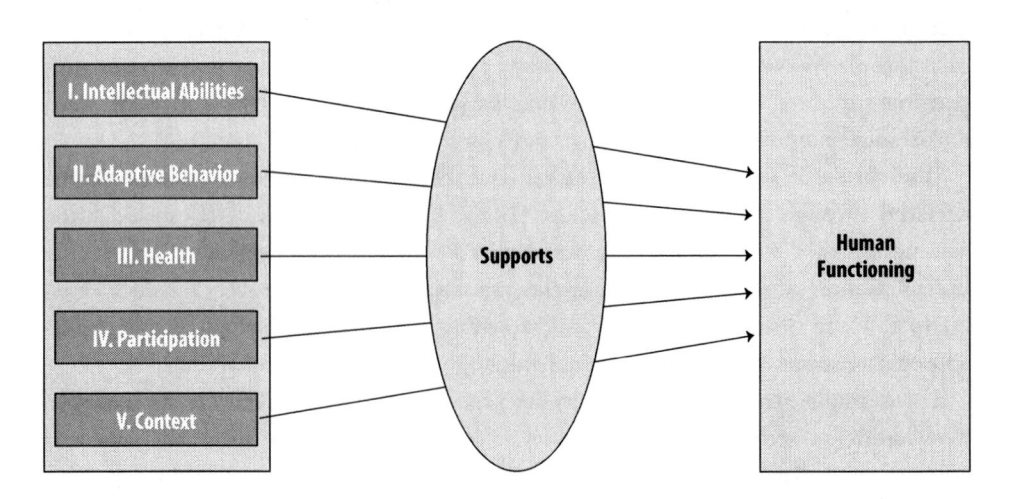

FIGURE 12.1. Conceptual framework for human functioning (from Schalock et al., 2010)

emergence of the ICF model proposed by the WHO (WHO, 2001), with its emphasis on person-environment interaction and a functional understanding of disability. Disability arises not because of impairment per se, but because of functional limitations and participation restrictions in relation to the roles and tasks expected of an individual within a social environment. Disability occurs because of the gap between the person's functioning and participation opportunities without support, and the requirements of the person's social and physical environment. Supports are intended to enhance individual functioning to enable participation.

In addition, the supports paradigm has developed at a time when other significant factors are shaping thinking about disability, disability services, and supports (Schalock, 2004a, b). These factors include: (a) individualization of funding, services and supports; (b) a person-centered approach in which the person's wishes and preferences are central; (c) a focus on outcomes, personal wellbeing and QOL; and (d) widespread recognition of the rights of people with disability (United Nations, 2006). As a result of such factors, disability services and supports have moved away from former care models to the current supports paradigm. To oversimplify somewhat, care involves doing things *to* the person (personal care, health care) based on others' views of the person's best interests, whereas support involves enabling participation in activities and settings, and doing things with the person, based mainly on the person's own goals and preferences.

There is one important caveat concerning these ideas. The supports paradigm has been developed in western countries and is operationalized via person-centered approaches with a presumption of the primacy of the individual. Non-western cultures and developing countries may understand and approach these issues differently, and have access to different types of support resources. These topics are explored in a section on culture and support later in this chapter.

Conceptualization of Support Needs

AAIDD has defined support needs as "a psychological construct referring to the pattern and intensity of supports necessary for a person to participate in activities linked to normative human functioning" (Schalock et al., 2010, p. 105). Our understanding of support needs is still developing (Arnold, Riches, & Stancliffe, in press), as is the capacity to assess support needs and to use this information appropriately with individuals, services, and service systems.

Support needs and adaptive behavior. Brown, Ouellette-Kuntz, Bielska, and Elliott (2009) asked whether support need assessments are simply proxy measures for adaptive behavior. Conceptually, support-need measures deal with the support required to engage in everyday activities, whereas adaptive behavior assessments examine the extent of independence in performing everyday activities. Thus, these measures should be related but could also be seen as different ways of operationalizing the same phenomena. Better developed adaptive behavior should translate into fewer support needs, given that individuals who are independent, by definition, need no extraordinary support in comparison to other community members.

Studies using the Supports Intensity Scale (SIS; Thompson et al., 2004) to assess support needs have consistently reported very strong associations with various measures of adaptive behavior (Brown et al., 2009; Guscia, Harries, Kirby, Nettelbeck, & Taplin, 2005), with correlations as strong as .89 (Brown et al., 2009). That is, there is robust and consistent empirical support for the contention that the SIS support needs and adaptive behavior are very closely related. This strong association may well arise in part because of the standardized approach taken by the SIS and the newer version, the Supports Intensity Scale—Adult Version (SIS—A) to assessing support needs. Like adaptive behavior instruments, the SIS and SIS—A use standard life activity domains and items (activities). They evaluate the frequency and intensity of support needed without specific regard to whether the assessed activities are (a) relevant to the individual (does the person's social and physical environment require this activity?), and (b) important to the person because they relate to preferred activities or goals. Even if the person does not need or want to do the activity assessed in a particular SIS or SIS—A item, this item is scored and contributes to the person's overall support-needs score. We have questioned the legitimacy of including such items in the assessment of an individual's support needs (Arnold, Riches & Stancliffe, 2014). This approach seems out of step with the social-ecological model of disability that conceptualizes functioning in relation to environmental demands.

The support-needs scores that arise from this standardized approach may well be very useful in agency-wide and system-wide planning and resource allocation; however they are less directly applicable to *individual* planning and require additional individual information, as noted by Ivey et al. (2008). An alternative approach to support needs assessment is described below involving the Instrument for the Classification and Assessment of Support Needs (I-CAN; Arnold, & Riches, 2013; Riches, Parmenter, Llewellyn, Hindmarsh, & Chan, 2009). These instruments are analyzed briefly below.

Support Needs Assessment

One of the five assumptions of the AAIDD definition of ID is that "an important purpose of describing limitation is to develop a profile of needed supports" (Schalock et al., 2010, p. 1). Consequently, AAIDD and others have developed tools to assess support needs of people with ID. We will briefly describe two approaches to support-need assessment: the SIS and SIS—A (Thompson et al., 2004, 2015) and the Instrument for the Classification and Assessment of Support Needs (I-CAN; Arnold & Riches, 2013; Arnold et al., 2014; Riches et al., 2009).

SIS and SIS—A. The SIS and the SIS—A assess the pattern and intensity of supports needed for more successful participation in the QOL-related domains of Home Living, Community Living, Life-Long Learning, Employment, Health and Safety,

Social Activities, and Protection and Advocacy. The SIS (and SIS—A) Support Needs Index is the sum of items in each domain, excluding protection and advocacy. The SIS and SIS—A score each item on Frequency, Daily Support Time, and Type of Support scales. Additional domains—Exceptional Medical and Behavioral Support Needs— are scored but do not directly enter into the Support Needs Index. As a standardized assessment, the SIS and SIS—A do not collect person-centered information such as preferred activities and goals (Ivey et al., 2008).

I-CAN. The I-CAN is based on the International Classification of Functioning, Disability and Health (ICF; WHO, 2001). Each item is scored on a 0–5 Frequency of Support and a 0–5 Level of Support scale. The Total I-CAN Score is a sum of the frequency and intensity of support required across all domains. The I-CAN includes optional My Goals, Circle of Support, and Support Services domains, as well as several optional descriptive items, including "About Me" and "I Can Contribute" to contextualize the assessment and work in unison with person-centered planning approaches.

A key difference is in the way these two tools conceptualize and score support needs. As described previously, the SIS—A uses a standardized environmental context, and support needs must be scored for every item even if that item is not relevant to the person. By contrast, the I-CAN is scored in the context of the person's own environment(s), with only relevant items scored. The I-CAN also allows custom questions to be asked to explore additional dimensions of the person's support, such as, is this a met or unmet need, or does this support need require funded or informal supports. In contrast to the AAIDD definition, the I-CAN defines supports as "people, resources, tools, equipment, education, or strategies that enable a person to interact with their environment and pursue a valued life" (Arnold, n.d., p. 12), with key differences being a stronger focus on the person's environmental context and the individual pursuit of a valued life as opposed to increases in functioning. A fuller account of our thinking about the conceptualization and assessment of support needs is set out in Arnold et al. (2014, in press).

Other differences include that the SIS and SIS—A record primarily, although not exclusively, quantitative data, whereas the I-CAN optionally records qualitative data, including person-centered information and goals, allowing for quantitative and qualitative reports, with closer links to person-centered planning. The SIS and SIS—A have been translated into multiple languages and have wide usage, but the I-CAN is currently available only in English and is used in Australia and Singapore.

Resource Allocation

Increasingly, resources (e.g., disability funding) are allocated on an individual basis, and systems are needed to determine such allocations fairly. Therefore, an important question is whether support-needs assessments and adaptive behavior scores are equally effective at predicting resource allocation such as individual funding.

Arnold et al. (in press) found that support-needs assessment using the I-CAN was better at predicting the person's current individual funding allocation than was adaptive behavior (Inventory for Client and Agency Planning [ICAP]; Bruininks, Hill, Weatherman, & Woodcock, 1986). In addition, selecting only those I-CAN items that relate to each individual's need for *funded* support further improved the accuracy of support-needs assessment in predicting individual funding, with I-CAN funded support needs plus age accounting for 87% of variance in individual funding in the Arnold et al. study. These findings suggest that it may be important when assessing support needs to distinguish between support that requires funding (e.g., disability staff) versus support that is freely available to all citizens (e.g., assistance from a bus driver to any traveler needing help) or support provided without cost to someone with a disability by friends, family, or other natural support providers. Just as not all areas of life activity listed in support-needs assessments are necessarily relevant to a specific individual with disability, so too some activities do not require paid support because of the availability of unpaid support.

The SIS and SIS—A have been used in several jurisdictional resource allocation systems, and are typically combined with additional variables in developing a resource allocation algorithm based on regression analysis. One example comes from Louisiana (LeVelle & Meche, 2008), where the LA PLUS was developed. An addition to the SIS—A tool, the LA PLUS covers numerous other support domains. A study of more than 1300 people found that 82.3% of variance in services cost could be explained using the SIS—A, LA PLUS, and personal and other factors, such as residential arrangement and geographical location.

These findings indicate that support-needs assessment scores may well be very useful in individual resource allocation, but the need for additional information in both cases suggests that (a) other factors are at play, and (b) our understanding of the relationship between assessed support needs and individual funding is still developing.

Active Support

Recognizing the central importance of support, key questions arise about the nature of that support and how to deliver it effectively and consistently. In this section, we focus on active support as a well-researched and systematic approach to providing tailored support for participation by people with ID. Active support was originally developed in the UK to promote increased engagement in meaningful everyday activities by people with ID through direct support for active participation from caregivers (Stancliffe et al., 2008). Caregivers are trained to use graded assistance to support participation, using techniques such as requests, step-by-step verbal instructions, gestures, demonstration, and physical assistance. Support is given as needed for activities throughout the day. The primary focus is on supported engagement in real, age-appropriate, everyday activities.

Skill mastery and independence are not required outcomes (but are welcome), as support can be provided indefinitely. Participation in such everyday activities is valued by people with ID (Miller et al., 2008) and contributes directly to QOL.

These support techniques are not new, but active support's comprehensive approach to support and reliable access to meaningful activities has resulted in consistent findings that the person's participation in activities is increased, as is the amount of staff support for client participation. Active support has also been associated with other positive outcomes, such as increases in choice (Beadle-Brown, Hutchinson, & Whelton, 2012), and in adaptive behavior (Mansell, Elliott, Beadle-Brown, Ashman, & Macdonald, 2002), as well as decreases in depression (Riches et al., 2011; Stancliffe, McVilly, Radler, Mountford, & Tomaszewski, 2010).

Support provision has more dimensions than support techniques and making activities available. Stancliffe et al.'s (2008) review noted that active support had been confined to certain types of activity, especially domestic activity, and to group homes with support provided by group-home staff. These authors called for broader implementation of active support. There is scope for expanding *who* provides the support, *where* support is offered, and for *what* type of activities. Since that review, active support initiatives have taken place to address these issues. These include: (a) effective support given by members of the public (i.e., not family or paid disability staff) who received some training (Chng, Stancliffe, Wilson, & Anderson, 2013); (b) support and activities occurring in socially inclusive community settings (e.g., a mainstream community group; Chng et al., 2013; Stancliffe, Bigby, Balandin, Wilson, & Craig, 2014); and (c) support focused on non-domestic tasks such as physical activity and exercise (Lante et al., 2014).

In summary, active support research shows that support is crucial to participation and so to QOL, and that multiple features of support require attention, such as the type and amount of support, together with by whom, where, and for what support is provided.

Support, Functioning, and Outcomes

Active support research provides clear evidence for the importance of support in enabling everyday functioning by people with ID. But what sort of support is best? Are some kinds support less effective or even detrimental? And how much support is appropriate for optimal functioning?

Source of Support

Can some types of support interfere with aspects of functioning? The emphasis on "natural supports" is based in part on findings that the presence of external disability professionals may adversely affect the nature and extent of social interaction the person with ID experiences. For example, Lee, Storey, Anderson, Goetz, and Zivolich (1997) found that restaurant workers with severe disabilities who were trained under a mentoring model interacted more with co-workers without disability than those trained by external disability job coaches.

Opportunities for Participation

While support can facilitate functioning, opportunities for and social expectations of participation are also critical. Providing regular access to meaningful activities with appropriate support is central to the active support model (Stancliffe et al., 2008). Stancliffe and Lakin's (2007) review of independent living found that, across a wide range of activities (e.g., supermarket shopping, independent living, employment, financial decision making, choice making), regular opportunities for independent participation by people with ID with mild to moderate levels of impairment were important for continued independent functioning, as well as for skill acquisition. Environmental demands for independent participation arise more frequently in normative social settings, such as independent living or competitive employment. For example, Stancliffe (2005) found higher levels of participation by people with ID living semi-independently than for matched group-home residents, and argued that frequent periods of staff absence with drop-in staffing in semi-independent settings effectively demanded such participation because there was no alternative for residents but to do things for themselves.

Support Needs and Amount of Support

However, these effects are mediated by level of support need. Individuals with greater support needs do poorly with little support. Gardner and Carran (2005) found that people with ID with mild to moderate levels of impairment who lived independently attained the most positive personal outcomes (80%), whereas those with severe/profound impairments experienced the fewest positive outcomes (52%) in independent living, but did better in settings with more support. Low levels of staff support in independent living may enable better outcomes for people with milder levels of impairment, but independent living provided too little support for individuals with more severe levels of impairment to attain many personal outcomes. The issue appears to be providing enough assistance when needed, without interfering if the person needs no support. Too much and too little support can each be problematic.

Type of Support

To be effective, support should be both acceptable to the individual and matched to his or her capacity to respond to that specific type of support. For example, step-by-step verbal prompts or requests alone may be enough for a person with sound basic understanding of spoken language, but may be insufficient for another individual with more limited comprehension. Smith, Felce, Jones, and Lowe (2002) examined the effectiveness of different types of support (verbal and non-verbal) in enabling adults with ID to participate in activities. They found that, among adults with higher support needs, staff assistance was more effective in eliciting and maintaining participation after active support training because of increased staff provision of, and individuals' responsiveness to, non-verbal support. That is, the non-verbal forms of assistance used by staff more closely matched individual needs and so were more effective.

Culture and Support

In principle, the need for support is universal, but cultural factors may affect the nature of activities and support. Valued activities, appropriate context, understanding of disability, and the type and source of support are all to some extent culturally defined. Contemporary definitions of disability explicitly acknowledge the relevance of social and cultural norms by viewing disability as an individual's limitation in performing roles and tasks expected in a social environment (Schalock, 2004), or by seeing individual functioning as an interaction among biological, psychological, and social and environmental factors (WHO, 2001). Thus, acceptable and preferred support, activities, or roles will differ not only between individuals but also across different sociocultural settings.

Support for transportation, for example, will vary among cultures; in some cultures many people do not have private cars. In such cases, a person with ID living on a farm may wish to learn to ride a four-wheel motorbike, whereas an individual from a large city may opt to be supported to use public transport.

In some cultures, it is acceptable to receive personal support from a member of the opposite sex, but in others it may be inappropriate or even forbidden. Support involving touching the person, such as hand-over-hand guidance, may be unacceptable in some cultures.

Cultural issues also affect understanding of disability and support, and so influence the assessment of support needs. Flaherty et al. (1988) proposed five dimensions of cross-cultural equivalence that are pertinent to assessment and provision of supports to people with disabilities: content, semantics, measurement, criterion, and concepts. How does one plan individual supports, for example, for Anangu Pitjantjatjara Yankunytjatjara (APY) Land Aboriginals in Australia, whose society does not have an overarching term for disability and who are unlikely to attend an interview or engage with paperwork? (Ngaanyatjarra Pitjantjatjara Yankunytjatjara Women's Council, 2014).

Words such as *health*, *disease*, *distress*, and *happiness* can have subtly different meanings, depending on the cultural and linguistic context (Guillemin, Bombardir & Beaton, 1993; Hunt et al., 1991). Cultures may vary in their acceptance of closed-ended interview formats, in their sensitivities about who can be an informant, in what is acceptable to disclose, and in where assessments can be conducted. Criterion or normative data vary across cultures, and concepts such as self-determination and person-centeredness pose challenges in cultures that focus on the society and family before the individual.

Conclusion

Supports are increasingly central to our understanding of disability, whether we focus on ID (Schalock et al., 2010) or disability generally (WHO, 2001). Research on active support has shown the importance of appropriate support as one determinant of a life of quality. However, it is simplistic to assume that more support is always better. Instead, better outcomes are achieved when one matches the type, amount, source, and focus of the support to the needs and preferences of the individual.

The conceptualization and measurement of support needs is still developing, with differing assumptions and practices yielding support-needs assessments that vary in the support domains assessed and the nature of the items that enter into an individual's total support-needs score. Support-needs assessments appear to provide useful data for predicting resource allocation, including individual funding. At the organization/service provider level (mesosystem), and the service-system level (macrosystem), conceptual issues about whether support-needs assessment items are scored based on a standardized environment, or the environment in which the person lives, may not be as crucial as the performance of these assessments in accurately predicting funding. Australia is restructuring its disability service system under the new National Disability Insurance Scheme. Eventually all eligible scheme participants will have individualized funding with the option for self-direction. At present there is no national data-based individual funding allocation methodology. An approach based on a valid assessment of support needs may contribute substantially to ensuring consistent, fair, needs-based funding in Australia and in other countries.

In terms of individuals (microsystem), standardized support-needs assessment does not always fit comfortably with person-centered approaches. Further research and development is needed of the relations among support-needs assessment, person-centered planning, and QOL-related outcomes evaluation. Many important steps have been taken in conceptualizing and operationalizing the supports paradigm, but as we have seen, challenges remain.

CHAPTER 13

POSITIVE PSYCHOLOGY AND A QUALITY-OF-LIFE AGENDA

MICHAEL L. WEHMEYER and KARRIE A. SHOGREN

Introduction and Overview

The emphasis on improving the QOL of people with ID—by now into its fourth decade (Goode, 1988, 1994; Schalock, 1990a, b; Schalock, 1996; Schalock, et al., 2007)—was among the opening salvos in the movement toward strengths-based models of disability that emerged in the early 1990s and have become the standard for understanding ID today (Schalock, et al., 2010; Wehmeyer, 2013).

Strengths-based approaches to disability can be traced to the promulgation of the normalization principle by Neils Erik Bank-Mikkelsen, Bengt Nirje, Wolf Wolfensberger, and others (Hanamura, 1998; Wolfensberger, 1972; Wolfensberger & Kugel, 1969). Schalock and Keith (this volume) define QOL as "a multidimensional phenomenon composed of core domains influenced by personal characteristics and environmental factors." Those domains include concepts and constructs central to positive psychology, including self-determination and various forms of wellbeing. Further, issues of QOL and lifestyle satisfaction are, themselves, key elements in positive psychology and strengths-based approaches.

The normalization principle introduced a number of conceptualizations that became critical to the development of a positive psychology of disability, including the notions of the dignity of risk (Perske, 1972) and self-determination (Nirje, 1972). It took almost two decades, however, before the systems that supported people with ID became aligned with the kinds of systems suggested by the normalization principle. When that occurred, it was the still nascent but growing emphasis on QOL that provided a frame for understanding how such interpersonal characteristics as self-determination, well-being, and lifestyle satisfaction fit into designing and structuring organizations and systems (Wehmeyer & Schalock, 2001). When the field of positive psychology emerged in the early 2000s, the field of ID was situated to move from deficits-based to strengths-based models of disability, in large measure because of the influence of the QOL movement on issues such as self-determination, well-being, and self-advocacy (Wehmeyer, Bersani, & Gagne, 2000; Wehmeyer & Metzler, 1995; Wehmeyer, & Schwartz, 1998).

The purpose of this chapter is to discuss the construct of positive psychology and relate positive psychology principles to strengths-based models of disability and QOL. Throughout the chapter, positive psychology is defined as the pursuit of understanding optimal human functioning and well-being.

Positive Psychology

In 1998, Seligman stated that "psychology has moved too far away from its original roots, which were to make the lives of all people more fulfilling and productive, and too much toward the important, but not all-important, area of curing mental illness" (Seligman, 1999, p. 559). Seligman called for a "reoriented science that emphasizes the understanding and building of the most positive qualities of an individual" (Seligman, 1999, p. 559). As Seligman and Csikszentmihalyi (2000) observed,

> . . . the field of positive psychology at the subjective level is about valued subjective experiences: well-being, contentment, and satisfaction (in the past); hope and optimism (for the future); and flow and happiness (in the present). At the individual level, it is about positive individual traits: the capacity for love and vocation, courage, interpersonal skill, aesthetic sensibility, perseverance, forgiveness, originality, future mindedness, spirituality, high talent, and wisdom. (p. 5)

Ryan and Deci (2000) asserted that in this pursuit for understanding optimal human functioning and well-being, researchers must take into account the agentic nature of human action, noting that the fullest representations of humanity show people to be curious, vital, and self-motivated. At their best, people are agentic and inspired, striving to learn, extend themselves, master new skills, and apply their talents responsibly. That most people show considerable effort, agency, and commitment in their lives indicates the positive and persistent features of human nature.

As in any young field, the focus of positive psychological inquiry remains fluid. Hart and Sasso (2011) conducted a review of the extant literature and identified six major themes: "(a) virtues, character strengths, positive personality traits, abilities, and talents; (b) happiness, positive emotional well-being, fulfillment, and quality of life; (c) development processes associated with growth, fulfillment, actualization of potential, and the authentic self; (d) the good life or the life worth living; (e) thriving and flourishing, and (f) resilience or adaptive functioning/behavior" (Shogren, 2013, p. 21). Among the constructs receiving attention in positive psychology are subjective well-being, optimism, happiness, self-determination, hope, emotional intelligence, resilience, creativity, lifestyle satisfaction, QOL, and positive affect.

Positive Psychology and Intellectual Disability

A primary catalyst for moving toward strengths-based models of disability has been the publication of a series of diagnostic and classification manuals published by AAIDD (Luckasson, et al., 1992, 2002; Schalock et al., 2010) that adopted the social-ecological or person-environment fit model of disability to define and understand the intellectual disability construct. This model views disability in the context of the fit (or lack thereof) between personal capacity and the demands of the environment or context, requiring the design of supports to narrow or close that gap (see also Chapters 8 and 12, this volume). The emphasis in the field on a supports paradigm increased in 2004 with the publication of the *Supports Intensity Scale* (Thompson et al., 2004).

Spurred by the social-ecological model, Shogren, Wehmeyer, Pressgrove, and Lopez (2007) reviewed the application of positive psychology constructs to research in the ID literature between 1975 and 2004. The authors selected five top journals in the ID field and reviewed one randomly selected issue of each journal from 1975–2004, reviewing a total of 144 journal issues and 1,124 research articles or literature reviews/program descriptions. Each article was coded across multiple dimensions relevant to a strengths-based approach to disability and the inclusion of positive psychological constructs. Each article was reviewed to determine whether it focused on human capacities of people with ID; those that did were coded to determine if they adopted a strengths perspective, a deficits perspective, or a mixed or a neutral perspective. Of articles that focused on a human capacity in people with ID, 35% adopted a strengths perspective, although the focus changed significantly over time, from a low of 22% of articles in 1975–1984 to a high of 50% of articles in 1995–2004. Of these articles, 15% included a construct associated with positive psychology as a primary focus and, again, the percentage of articles examining a positive psychological construct increased over time. From 1975 to 1984, only 9% of articles focused on a positive psychology construct; from 1985 to 1995, 15% of articles did so; and from 1995–2004, 24% of articles included such a focus. The most frequently cited positive psychology constructs (across time periods) were personal control (13% of articles), personal relationships (10%), interpersonal skills (5%), satisfaction (3%), and self-determination (3%). Interestingly, happiness, one of the most frequently cited themes in positive psychology research and definitions, appeared in only 1% of studies.

Shogren et al. (2006) also explored the degree to which articles focused on key dimensions of human functioning identified in the AAIDD manuals' conceptual framework of human functioning: intellectual abilities, adaptive behavior, health participation, context interaction and social roles, and health. Older articles focused most commonly on intellectual abilities, due largely to the historical focus on IQ testing and classification by levels of intelligence. However, over time the number of articles focusing on the other human functioning dimensions increased significantly, suggesting more emphasis on the multidimensionality of human experience for people with ID. These findings suggest that there had been a shift in the field, with more focus on a strengths-based perspective that incorporates positive psychology constructs that focus on the multidimensionality of human experiences. This shift is consistent with the shift in the psychology toward a focus on positive constructs and processes.

Shogren (2013) conducted a review of articles published in the field of positive psychology to determine the degree to which disability (in general, not specific to ID) was represented in that literature base. She found only a limited focus on disability issues within *The Journal of Positive Psychology* where, from among 162 articles published between 2006 and 2011, 6 articles (4%) explicitly mentioned people with disabilities or people with health-related issues that could be associated with disability. Of the six articles, the majority focused on specific health-related conditions that may or may not be associated with disability (e.g., asthma, chronic illness, and cancer).

As summarized above, there are clear trends in the ID literature toward a strengths-based/positive psychological focus in research. Three positive psychology constructs have received extensive study. First, there is a robust international literature base concerning factors influencing self-determination (Gomez-Vela, Verdugo, Gonzalez-Gil, Corbella, & Wehmeyer, 2012; Nota, Ferrari, Soresi, & Wehmeyer, 2007; Stancliffe, Abery, & Smith, 2000; Stancliffe & Wehmeyer, 1995; Wehmeyer & Metzler, 1995) and the importance of self-determination to the lives of youth and adults with ID (Lachapelle et al., 2005; Shogren, Palmer, Wehmeyer, Williams-Diehm, & Little, 2012; Shogren, Wehmeyer, Palmer, Rifenbark, & Little, 2015; van Loon, 2005). Second, there is a long-standing literature base showing that people with ID can learn to self-regulate or self-manage actions in ways that reduce their dependence on other people (Agran, King-Sears, Wehmeyer, & Copeland, 2003; Schunk & Bursuck, 2013). Third, there is evidence indicating that people with ID can learn and use problem-solving and decision making skills (Hickson & Khemka, 2013). In addition to these three, hope and character strength, as positive psychological constructs, have begun to receive attention from researchers (Shogren, Lopez, Wehmeyer, Little, & Pressgrove, 2006; Shogren, Wehmeyer, Lang, & Niemiec, 2015).

Finally, some practices predicated on positive approaches have substantial support. Positive Behavior Interventions and Supports (PBIS), for example, which has emerged as an effective approach to problem behavior, is predicated on social-environmental fit models. PBIS examines what environmental or contextual variables are causing problem behavior, and determining what supports (enhanced personal capacity, modification to the context or environment) can make problem behavior unnecessary (Dunlap, Kincaid, & Jackson, 2013). As a second example, supported employment similarly examines person-environment fit issues to enable people with ID to achieve meaningful, integrated employment (Wehman, Brooke, Lau, & Targett, 2013).

Positive Psychology and Quality of Life

The QOL construct serves as a critical framework for understanding personal strengths such as self-determination, well-being, support systems, and lifestyle satisfaction. The construct also provides a framework for thinking about positive psychological constructs more broadly, and how the QOL construct guides the field toward the wider adoption of strengths-based models of disability and the pursuit of an understanding of optimal human functioning and well-being for people with ID.

Schalock and Verdugo (2013a) identified five overarching ways in which a focus on QOL benefits people with ID. Several of these ways speak to the ongoing importance of the QOL concept in moving the field toward strengths-based approaches. QOL, argued Schalock and Verdugo, has provided a framework for a service delivery system "based on the values of dignity, equality, empowerment, self-determination, non-discrimination, and inclusion" (p. 46). If there were no other benefits to a continued role for QOL as a framework for designing systems of supports that focus on optimal human functioning and well-being, this would be sufficient in and of itself. Further, however, Schalock and Verdugo stressed that the QOL concept also provides an outcomes-based evaluation framework associated with specific domains (including self-determination and well-being) that enable both the consideration of personally valued life outcomes and the design of large systems of supports. In that regard, studies show that the positive psychology constructs of hope, optimism, and self-determination are significant predictors of an enhanced QOL for persons with ID (Nota et al.. 2007; Lachapelle et al., 2005; Shogren et al., 2006; Wehmeyer & Schwartz, 1998).

Conclusion

Positive psychology emphasizes optimal human functioning and well-being, and incorporates principles related to virtues and strengths, happiness and positive emotional well-being, positive development, a life worth living, thriving and flourishing, and resilience. These principles not only focus on the multidimensionality of human experiences, but also establish the parameters for best practices regarding services and supports that enhance the well-being and QOL of persons with ID.

The continued emergence of positive psychology within the context of ID (and disability in general) is reliant upon the adoption of the social-ecological model of disability, which provides an understanding of disability that allows for a strengths-based approach. The combination of positive psychology and a QOL framework allows a powerful structure to emerge within which to build systems that operationalize these models and that emphasize personal strengths.

The QOL concept has always asked us to consider how to ensure that people with ID are supported to experience the "good life" (Schalock & Verdugo, 2013a, p. 38). Positive psychology is the pursuit of understanding optimal human functioning and well-being so that people can live rich, fulfilling lives . . . the proverbial good life. Regardless of the society, people with ID deserve the same opportunity as all of the world's citizens to pursue the good life. Positive psychology and a QOL agenda provide a roadmap to achieve this.

CHAPTER 14

CHANGING SERVICE DELIVERY SYSTEMS:

An Example from Community Living–British Columbia

ANDREA BAKER, BRIAN SALISBURY, and DAN COLLINS

Introduction and Overview

Transformations are occurring, both in organizations and systems providing services and in the supports being provided to people with ID. Chapters 7–10 dealt with the movement toward outcomes evaluation, organizational self-assessment, aligning supports planning within a QOL framework, and continuous quality improvement. Chapter 11 dealt with ways in which systems-level outcome indicators can be used for multiple purposes, including demonstrating accountability, establishing benchmarks for quality improvement, and responding more effectively to consumer needs and personal goals.

This chapter describes how a provincial service delivery system (Community Living British Columbia; CLBC) is creating a more aligned, transformed service delivery system based on three change catalysts: values, leadership, and empowerment. The chapter begins by describing the context within which the transformation is occurring. Thereafter, the authors discuss how values, leadership, and empowerment can be used to move from a traditional bureaucratic human service delivery model to one that responds to the unique and evolving needs of individuals and their families. The chapter concludes with a summary of the lessons learned thus far and the challenges that still remain.

The British Columbia Context

Post-World War II human services systems have experienced mixed results in terms of improving the lives of the people they were created to serve. There is a variety of reasons for this situation, including lack of funding, poor system design, political interference, disagreement about program priorities, sectorial and professional in-fighting, poor implementation, and lack of effective evaluation. While operating ostensibly to address a variety of personal needs and to increase social inclusion, many of these systems have simply failed to address people's fundamental citizenship requirements, such as the opportunity to create meaningful relationships, work, and access valued social roles. Advocacy efforts worldwide attest to the fact that those most affected by the services provided to address these needs want a change from the status quo. For those of us who are not labelled and who do not require the support of the state, the things that are being requested are the *sine qua non* of true citizenship.

It can be argued that a major contributor to this situation is a lack of horizontal and vertical system alignment between inputs, throughputs, outputs, and outcomes at the personal, provider, and system level. Most notably, while many state-funded systems use impressive-sounding rhetoric to outline what they hope to achieve, many lack an overarching framework to link desired outcomes with existing structures created to support policy and practice implementation. The results, inevitably, are supports and services that fail to meet people's true needs. The framework developed by Schalock and Verdugo (2012b) holds out great promise that fully aligned systems can in fact be created to focus on the prize of enhanced QOL, while using scarce public funding more effectively and efficiently. This is the path taken by CLBC to create a more aligned system.

CLBC is a crown agency of the government of British Columbia, Canada. It is mandated under the Community Living Authority Act (2004) to fund supports and services through community service agencies for adults with developmental disabilities and their families. CLBC was established following a groundswell of community activism between 2001 and 2005 to create a provincial organization that would support people with developmental disabilities and their families to have more choices (greater self-determination) about how they live, work, and contribute. Very simply, CLBC was created as an arm of government that would, with active citizen involvement, enhance people's QOL.

CLBC's journey since its formal proclamation as a provincial crown agency on July 1, 2005, has been one of attempting to create a system that honors the vision of its proponents and is articulated in the final report of the Community Living Transition Steering Committee (2002). This report, aptly named *A New Vision for Community Living . . . A Vision of Choice and Change*, proposed to government the parameters of a provincial governance structure that would fund and oversee community living services. The change process has involved trying to move from a traditional bureaucratic human service delivery model to one focused on ensuring individuals and families have a real voice in determining their personal goals, while at the same time increasing their opportunities to participate as full and active citizens. In short, moving from a supply-side type of system focused on meeting the needs of people as a group, to using a more demand-driven approach that will enable the system to respond to the unique and evolving needs of individuals and families. It has been the story of one system trying to determine how to enhance QOL for those whom it serves. The adoption of the QOL framework to anchor this system change process is presented on subsequent pages.

Schalock and Verdugo (2012a) identified four basic catalysts for change: values, leadership, empowerment, and technology. In moving from a demonstration project to full implementation, CLBC has attempted to pay attention to three of these factors—values, leadership, and empowerment. This has supported our efforts to initiate the shift. Technology will be our next focus and is something we will rely upon to anchor the changes we have made thus far and to share learning between service providers.

Values and a Clear Vision

Schalock and Verdugo (2012a) stated that "organization change efforts frequently fail because, regardless of the intervention(s) tried, leaders and managers have failed to change the deeply ingrained assumptions, generalizations, and images that help organization personnel understand the world and experience (or visualize) the future" (p. 6). For CLBC, we had to begin with an understanding of our own readiness to adopt the paradigm shift that underscores this initiative—a paradigm that shifts us away from a focus on goal attainment (toward a focus on personal outcomes), away from a reliance on funded services (toward a more holistic view of QOL, one rooted in community), and away from a performance management relationship with our contracted service providers (toward a partnership approach emphasizing continuous quality improvement).

Several key activities helped us understand the values that we were currently holding and those we would need to embrace to support a successful shift to a new way of thinking and being. These included funding a demonstration project, conducting a policy review, developing a logic model, and including expectations related to QOL outcomes in our contracts with service providers.

Demonstration Project

We were searching for a way to accurately assess whether the $850 million of contracted services we were putting in place were truly making a positive difference in the lives of individuals we support. We were immediately attracted to the QOL framework for several reasons. Like other options we had considered, QOL has scientific merit, has the ability to integrate with existing requirements, and is steeped in the philosophy of continuous quality improvement. However, it also has something that was missing in the other models we explored; it has tremendous construct validity and resonates with everyone who hears about it. The fact that the framework is not unique to people with developmental disabilities fits well with CLBC's vision of good lives in welcoming communities.

We began our journey down the path of adopting a QOL framework by funding a demonstration project in one of our operating regions. We confirmed that the QOL survey instrument we had selected (*My Life Personal Outcomes Index*; see Chapter 7, this volume) and the proposed administration process could be used reliably to provide valid information about the QOL of adults surveyed. Additionally, the individuals and service providers who participated in the demonstration project found it to be a positive and informative experience. Based on the success of the demonstration project, we decided to proceed with provincial implementation.

Policy Review

One of the first things we tackled was a review of our organization's foundational policies. The goal was to assess the "lay of the land" and to evaluate our readiness to formally adopt the eight-domain QOL framework. The exercise was conducted by a Master of Social Work practicum student from the University of British Columbia. The review was helpful in that it provided us with an objective assessment of how well the implicit values and explicit language of the selected policies aligned with the QOL framework. Not surprisingly, given the history of CLBC's evolution, we found that many of our core policies (e.g. *Individual and Family Support, Service Provision by Family Members, Role of Formal and Informal Representatives*) were generally aligned and almost foreshadowed our adoption of the framework, while many of our legacy policies (especially those related to resource allocation and quality assurance) did not accurately reflect the direction we were heading. Out of this review came three tangible decisions:

- developing a standard definition of "quality of life" that could be inserted in policies that were being created or revised
- consulting by the policy department with the *include Me!* team (created to oversee implementation of QOL initiatives at CLBC) prior to releasing a new or revised policy to ensure congruence with the QOL paradigm
- prioritizing those policies that were most discordant with the new framework for revision

Logic Model

To ensure that all parties had confidence that this approach to measuring personal outcomes and supporting an environment of continuous quality improvement had been well thought-out, we developed a logic model that could be presented to leadership and other key stakeholders. This is in keeping with the idea of beginning with the end in mind . . . the idea that working backwards from the place you want to arrive will help you begin to anticipate potential challenges and identify central requirements for success. Our logic model was developed with input from numerous sources (academic research, external consultants, internal and external stakeholders). It identified key goals, assumptions, resources, actions, outputs, expected shorter-term outcomes (within 1–3 years of implementation), and expected longer-term outcomes (within 3–5 years of implementation). The logic model was presented to the Provincial Quality of Life Steering Committee that had been established to provide input from key sector stakeholders, and to CLBC's senior leadership team. It was the foundation for budget approval for year one implementation. The logic model is presented in Figure 14.1.

We printed a large poster-sized version of our logic model and hung it in the main reception area of our central provincial office so that it could be seen by all staff as well as external visitors. The model has generated many conversations and continues to be a touchstone for the work we do. We are nearing the end of year three of our implementation and are largely on track to accomplish what we set out to do in June, 2012.

Contractual Obligations

As we were exploring the opportunities associated with measuring and responding to personal outcomes of individuals, CLBC was also reviewing and revising its overall contracting framework. The contract templates we had inherited from our predecessor ministries had not been updated for many years and no longer reflected the needs or values of our sector. Those contracts were developed during an era of case management and lack of standardization. They required service providers to submit reports to CLBC that were time-consuming to produce and served little purpose other than to provide a basic sense that something had been done with the funding provided. The contracts had been amended multiple times in a reactive and *ad hoc* way over time, so they lacked internal consistency and did not align with any particular paradigm or obvious guiding mission.

As the contracts were revised, the manager responsible for *include Me!* worked closely with members of the organization's Corporate Services division to ensure the new templates were consistent with the direction we had set. The result was a schedule addendum to the over-arching terms and conditions that includes expectations for service delivery that clearly signal CLBC's commitment to the QOL framework. The schedule requires all service providers under contract with CLBC to "align their services to further the achievement of the quality of life of individuals served." As we move forward with implementation, providers will be expected to report (in some way) on their experience with delivering services that support continuous quality improvements in the outcomes being achieved by the individuals they serve.

Subsequently, CLBC also revised its overall procurement framework and incorporated expectations related to these outcomes in the submissions we request of providers who are seeking to do business with us. Providers who wish to become part of CLBC's provincial service suppliers list must demonstrate their understanding of and support for a QOL/outcome-driven approach to service delivery. Individuals and families who wish to have input to the selection of the provider they will access for services are given

Measuring and Improving the QOL of Adults With DD Over Time as a Result of Measuring Personal Outcomes and Responding to Results

INPUTS					OUTPUTS	
Goals	**Assumptions**	**Resources**	**Actions**	**Outputs**	**Expected Outcomes (1–3 years)**	**Expected Outcomes (3–5 years)**
provide leadership and strategic direction on provincially implementing the *My Life* survey	the *My Life* survey is a reliable and valid tool that can be used to measure QoL outcomes within this province	the *My Life* survey CLBC infrastructure and funding	develop multi-year implementation/ sampling and communication plans	implementation/ sampling plan communication plan and materials	implementation plans and timelines are met CLBC staff are familiar with and support the initiative as an integral CQI initiative in providing effective services	individuals and families support the survey process as integral to improving the QoL for adults with developmental disabilities QoL domains are central to planning for supports and services
implement a comprehensive plan to measure QoL outcomes of adults with developmental disabilities who access CLBC-funded services	individuals want to participate in the survey process service providers will be interested in supporting the individuals they serve to participate	CLBC staff including the *include Me!* team contractor with expertise in survey administration and data analysis	actively survey in all 5 CLBC regions and conduct a general population survey develop and implement CQI strategies	training material for CLBC staff and service providers survey results for service providers within each CLBC region	service providers are true partners in the process survey results lead to CLBC and service provider CQI initiatives	service provider outcome measurement aligns with QoL domains adults with developmental disabilities experience a QoL that is similar to the general population of BC
report survey results at the agency, regional, and provincial levels	there is political support there are provincial, regional, and service provider resources for this initiative to be successful	service providers under contract with CLBC adults with disabilities and members of their support networks	develop and implement training for CLBC staff and service providers maintain working agreements with a professional survey administration and data analysis firm	aggregated *My Life* survey results for individuals served general population survey results	CLBC and service providers create communities of practice to enhance CQI efforts	CLBC is a recognized leader in measuring personal outcomes and using survey data to inform implementation of CQI strategies at the individual, organizational, and system level
provide strategic advice to CLBC leadership and service providers on survey results and potential CQI implications	a focus on CQI processes will improve the QoL of those served		establish linkages with other jurisdictions establish an evaluation protocol to determine impact of the initiative	CQI plans at all levels contract with data analysis/survey firm evaluation with recommendations about future implementation	survey administration is integrated into core business functions and staff roles/responsibilities QoL framework is supported by provincial policy	

FIGURE 14.1. Include me! logic model

a set of guiding questions that can be used in conversations with potential providers. These questions are framed around the eight QOL domains. This process sets the tone with individuals, families, and new providers about what we view as important. Aligning input (procurement) and throughput (contract) components of our business helps ensure that all parties understand the commitment we are collectively making as a sector to ensure that individuals have access to lives of quality. It also begins to unify the sector in terms of developing a deeper understanding of why we do the work we do and the outcomes we are striving to achieve.

Leadership and Constructive Engagement

Schalock and Verdugo (2012b) reminded us that there is a difference between management and leadership. While management focuses on processes and rules that keep an operation moving, true "leadership is about change. Leadership involves inspiring people and organizations to change, *to want to change*" (p. 7). Effective leaders play a variety of roles—mentoring and directing, coaching and instructing, inspiring and empowering, and collaborating and partnering. Sometimes all of those skills can be found in one place and one person. Sometimes you look to different sources for each of the components. In moving from demonstration project to provincial implementation, CLBC actively sought out champions who would help successfully launch not only the survey project but also the transition from the old paradigm to the new . . . leaders who believed that attending to individual outcomes was what was needed for the community living sector in British Columbia to begin an evolution that would ultimately help bring us to a place of greater efficiency, effectiveness, and sustainability.

External Expertise

We have truly been charting new territory by implementing a survey designed to measure QOL (instead of "consumer satisfaction" with services, sector outputs, goals attained, etc.) and by beginning to focus our entire system on continuous quality improvement efforts that improve outcomes for the individuals we serve. To be successful, we knew we would need outside expertise to ensure we were implementing in a considered and efficient manner. Two parties were especially important as we proceeded with provincial implementation—Dr. Robert L. Schalock and R. A. Malatest and Associates Ltd.

Dr. Robert Schalock. Since the very beginning of this initiative, we have engaged Dr. Schalock to provide us and our service provider partners with guidance and support. His involvement in this initiative has been valuable beyond measure. In addition to providing advice on implementation of the survey, he has offered strategic leadership, unfaltering encouragement, and practical tools to engage the sector and promote partnerships, joint learning, and collective investment in what we are trying to achieve. We have been extremely fortunate to have had the opportunity to work directly with

Dr. Schalock, and his effectiveness is largely due to his depth of knowledge and experience, his extensive connections to like-minded people around the world, his graciousness, his obvious passion for this work, and his genuine approach. However, there is value to simply having an objective expert who can cut through internal politics that naturally exist in a sector where partnerships are struck between a government funder and its contracted service providers.

This kind of external leadership helped us sidestep some of the issues we faced when we have tried to implement other changes within our sector. Through Dr. Schalock, our service providers were introduced to community living leaders around the world. It gave them the opportunity to be involved as knowledge producers (instead of just knowledge recipients) and to be part of a movement with potential to transform community living service provision. This kind of motivation has kept our providers engaged and committed to this approach during a couple of difficult years created by sector budget shortfalls and complex system change.

R. A. Malatest and Associates Ltd. We are entering an era in which we no longer have the time or resources to engage in trial and error, endless consultation, and debate until we stumble upon what may or may not be the solution to a particular problem. We need outside help that is efficient and targeted, and specialized companies such as Malatest are becoming important partners. Involving a professional survey administration and data analysis firm in this initiative has had tremendous benefits. They have provided guidance on successful practice in the area of survey administration, surveyor training/support, data analysis, and reporting. They have been tremendously helpful in sharing information with the many stakeholders involved in this initiative and have identified trends and issues that we would likely have missed without their involvement. Their expertise has made the whole process more streamlined, effective, and impactful. It has added credibility and veracity to the results and has freed us up to focus our own limited time and resources on parts of this initiative where our background, experience, and involvement can have a greater impact.

Internal Champions

Although we expected staff within CLBC to understand and support the initiative, it was not realistic for us to assume that people would simply absorb the work that was required to get this off the ground and to prioritize it, given the multiple day-to-day work demands they must already manage. As CLBC leadership felt strongly about the importance of the initiative and recognized the deep and growing support within the organization and in the broader sector (including individuals, families, and service providers), they committed to fund a small team to focus exclusively on this initiative. The *include Me!* team that has been established includes a provincial project manager, two full-time liaisons who work within the regions in which we are actively surveying, and a part-time self-advocate advisor. The team operates according to principles of high-performing teams, and members work to support service providers, CLBC staff, and other stakeholders to understand the initiative and capitalize on information that is coming out of the survey process. This involves:

- supporting participating providers and their stakeholder groups (individuals, staff, families, etc.) to understand the initiative
- acting as a liaison between the survey administration company and participating providers to respond to emerging issues and facilitate the process of engaging individuals
- keeping CLBC staff up-to-date on activities that are underway within the region
- organizing regional learning tables and communities of practice
- linking providers with mentor agencies
- connecting with provincial stakeholders to ensure that these groups understand and continue to champion the initiative
- educating CLBC staff to interpret survey results and work collaboratively with service providers to support continuous quality improvement efforts
- highlighting and sharing information that will ultimately strengthen the system of support that is available to individuals within this province
- providing advice to the senior management team and Board of Directors on the policy and program implications of data gathered

Members of the *include Me!* team are available as a resource to service providers, CLBC staff, and others. The team supports regional staff to work more efficiently by ensuring that they receive the information that comes out of the survey process, that they understand the results, and that they incorporate it into their day-to-day work. The work of this specialized and dedicated team helps minimize the impact implementation of this initiative has on the day-to-day workload of regional staff.

Sector Leaders

Setting this in motion would have been impossible if we did not have broad support to move in the direction we were heading. Our external experts and internal champions would have taken us only so far. We needed to make sure the momentum was in place outside the boundaries of CLBC. We knew we needed to start small and where we were most likely to have some success that could demonstrate to all stakeholders that this was a valuable and viable direction to pursue. Three sector leadership groups were critical in helping us move from simple demonstration project to actual implementation: our provincial steering committee, self-advocate surveyors, and service provider champions.

Provincial quality of life steering committee. At the conclusion of the demonstration project in the spring of 2011, CLBC established a fifteen-member, multi-stakeholder steering committee that included leaders from the service provider, advocacy, and academic communities as well as CLBC representatives. The role of the steering committee was to support implementation of the QOL framework by providing guidance on issues such as:

- sector-wide change management to enhance efforts to successfully implement the QOL framework and create community living sector understanding and support
- communication with the sector

The work of the steering committee was guided by principles of mutual support, respect, collaboration, solution-focused participation, and proactive problem-solving. Steering committee members represented the diverse interests and perspectives of the community living sector. The steering committee was in place for two years, and disbanded in the spring of 2013 when members agreed that the primary objectives of the committee (supporting initial implementation and communicating with the sector) had been achieved.

Self-advocate surveyors. Following in the footsteps of jurisdictions that were implementing similar processes, CLBC committed to using self-advocates to administer the survey. In the three years since the initiative has been active (post-demonstration project), Malatest has screened, hired, trained, and supported approximately 50 self-advocate surveyors in the parts of the province in which we have been actively surveying. They receive market rate wages for this work and are paid for training they are required to complete.

This group has proven to be one of our best sources for making improvements to the quality of the survey administration process. They are consulted regularly about how to make the process run more smoothly for everyone, and have also become the greatest ambassadors for the initiative, explaining what it is about, telling their own stories, and helping participating service providers and individuals offer the survey in a manner that meets the unique needs of each agency.

Service provider champions. We have invited large accredited service providers (primarily by the Council on Accreditation and Rehabilitation Facilities) to volunteer to support the individuals they serve to participate in the survey. To date we have had more provider interest than we have been able to accommodate with available resources. The first round of surveys was offered in the central urban hub of our province where providers were more familiar with the initiative and where we had access to resources required to support implementation. In years two and three we expanded into areas of the province that were more geographically remote. The leaders of the organizations that have taken part have spoken candidly about the challenges they have faced in having the survey administered within their organizations and in deciding how to make use of the results. We have invited candid feedback and have responded by making procedural adjustments, offering customized support, and connecting providers with one another to share ideas. These agencies have also offered extremely strong support for the initiative and have encouraged their peers to take part. We now have providers who are eager to complete their second round of surveys to see if their efforts in response to the first survey results have had a positive effect, and providers in parts of the province where we are not yet active who are eager for the process to be offered in their communities. Approximately 65 service providers and 3,000 individuals have now taken part in the survey process.

We could not have moved toward full provincial implementation without the support of our service provider partners. In many ways, even with all of our hopes and efforts poured into this, the initiative had to sell itself. If service providers did not see it as providing valuable information and guided by solid values, we would not have been successful in moving this forward. The power of our first two change catalysts—values and leadership—and the valuable use of QOL- related information are clearly evident in the following case study.

CASE STUDY—LANGLEY ASSOCIATION FOR COMMUNITY LIVING

The Langley Association for Community Living (LACL) was eager to participate in the initial phase of include Me! For many years, LACL has participated in a formal accreditation process (CARF), and while this has served the organization well, include Me! provided a novel approach to directly asking the individuals served about their perceptions of their quality of life. Historically, efforts at program or organizational evaluation have resulted in limited feedback related to specific aspects of the lives of the individuals we serve. QOL offered a unifying framework for the many stakeholders connected with LACL. We were interested in and excited by an approach that could support CQI activities that would benefit the individuals served, while at the same time addressing a number of funder accountability requirements.

LACL's initial survey occurred as part of CLBC's demonstration project in the fall of 2011. In preparation, LACL undertook a number of key activities to raise awareness about the survey process. LACL developed a poster that described the eight QOL domains that was widely distributed and posted throughout the organization's various locations. The framework was new to LACL and the management team knew that increasing awareness was very important. A number of gatherings were held with the individuals we served to answer questions they might have about participation in the survey.

The results of our initial survey revealed that individuals served by LACL experienced reasonably high levels of emotional, material, and physical well-being, but efforts to increase self-determination, personal development, interpersonal relations, and social inclusion were warranted. The results served as a catalyst for a number of change initiatives. These included a broad review of the core values that drive the work of the organization, a review of the personal planning system used to help individuals determine their desired outcomes, and training and development activities to increase our understanding of and reliance on social capital.

In order for meaningful change to occur and be sustained across the organization, we decided to address the mental models that stakeholders (particularly direct support staff) have about our efforts to improve quality of life. We undertook a process to renew our organization's core values. Following adoption of these values, we introduced the values to all employees and explored how they are translated into day to day practice. This "values into action" process supports adoption of new ways to improve QOL.

LACL's personal planning process was adapted to align with the eight quality of life domains. In this way, organizational investment in personal supports and resources were aligned with the eight domains. Individuals served were supported to deepen their understanding of the QOL domains and the variety of ways that their QOL can be affected. A focus on ways to improve supported decision making was also essential.

LACL focuses training and development activities on increasing our knowledge of social capital and exploring ways to increase the social connections of the individuals we support. Increased friendships and social connections, as well as increased investments in employment supports, were all implemented.

Recently, the organization participated in its second survey (three years from initial survey). Compared with the first survey, we made improvements in personal development, self-determination, interpersonal relations, and social inclusion (see Figure 14.2). These results affirm our decision to make strategic investments to improve QOL in these areas. Undoubtedly, efforts to increase the number of individuals who are employed have also had a positive impact on the results obtained in the second survey. Fifty-eight percent of the individuals surveyed reported that they were employed. The organization will continue to focus investment in ways that improve QOL outcomes for those it serves.

MyLife Personal Outcome Index™ Quality-of-Life Domain Scores

Domain	2014/15 Scores	Demo Project Scores
Emotional Well-Being	8.6	9.1
Material Well-Being	8.2	7.9
Physical Well-Being	8.1	8.2
Rights	7.4	7.3
Personal Development	7.4	6.9
Self-Determination	7.2	6.2
Interpersonal Relations	7.2	6.5
Social Inclusion	6.5	6.0

Domain Score (0 to 10)

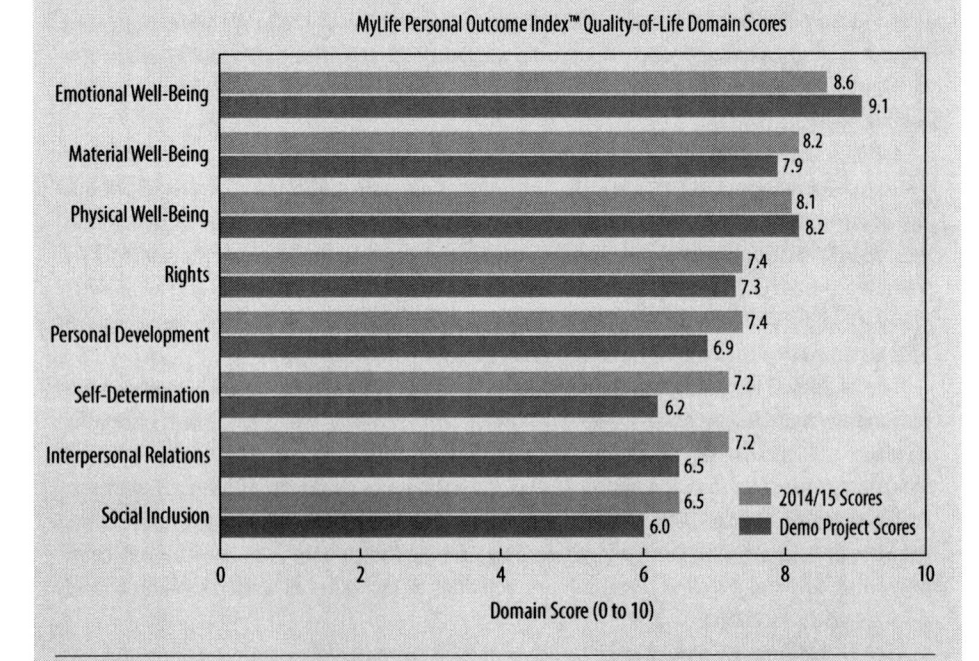

FIGURE 14.2. Representative QOL domain scores

Empowerment and Simple Communication

People want to feel important and involved. They want to feel that their work matters. When this occurs, people become engaged, motivated, team oriented, and change focused. Schalock and Verdugo (2012) stated that human systems function optimally when three basic psychological needs are met: a sense of competence, a sense of relatedness, and a sense of autonomy. They go on to say that "when these three psychological needs are met, people feel empowered [and that] a sense of empowerment greatly influences the degree to which individuals want to be part of any activity" (p. 9). It has been our experience that one of the most effective ways to meet these three needs is to provide people with access to clear, accurate, and timely information that is easy to understand and targeted to the specific needs of the audience. For this reason, attending to communication has been one of the most important aspects of the system's transformation.

Branding and Various Communication Tools

One of the most important aspects of *include Me!* has been ensuring that our many stakeholders are informed about the initiative and are supportive of where we are going. This has meant developing a variety of materials and approaches to meet the diverse communication needs of our audience. Throughout the process, we have consulted with key informants to ensure that our communications are hitting the mark. This began with our initial branding exercise. The name and *include Me!* logo were chosen after a series of focus groups, as well as field testing involving representatives from various stakeholder groups. We worked closely with our communications department and the Quality of Life Provincial Steering Committee to prioritize the development/release of various communication tools and to ensure that all material reflects the core principles of the initiative. The following were critical in communicating with our stakeholders:

- content in every issue of CLBC's bi-monthly newsletter
- high profile presence on the CLBC website with content that is regularly refreshed (http://www.communitylivingbc.ca/projects/quality-of-life/)
- use of CLBC's weekly info flash (for staff)
- social media blitzes at key times during the annual survey life cycle
- technical reports
- series of videos that highlight different aspects of the initiative
- formal briefings for CLBC's senior leadership, Board of Directors, and Minister of Social Development and Social Innovation (the Ministry to which CLBC is accountable through the provincial legislature)
- cornerstone events that included presentations to various stakeholders by external experts
- presentations by various members of the *include Me!* team that were targeted to the specific audience/forum

Wherever possible, we have ensured that communication materials are presented in simple English. We have also offered translation services to those participating in the survey process (including language and American Sign Language interpretation) and have translated our foundational overview document into the ten languages most commonly spoken in the province.

Provincial Conference

A keystone event in our implementation was a major conference held in Vancouver in October 2013. The conference was titled *At the Heart of it All: Practice that Promotes Quality of Life*. It was co-sponsored by CLBC, the Persons with Developmental Disabilities (PDD) division of the Alberta government, and a group of BC service providers who were highly committed to the shift in practice we were promoting (Langley Association for Community Living, Burnaby Association for Community Inclusion, Milieu Family Services, and Community Integration Services Society). The conference featured expert international speakers as well as sector leaders from BC and Alberta.

Aimed at service provider leadership, professionals, and policy makers, the conference featured two days of interactive dialogue that showcased what had been learned from initial implementation in BC and Alberta as well as other jurisdictions around the world that have adopted a similar approach. The conference also featured a one-day leadership summit that was designed to help service provider leaders and their CLBC and PDD colleagues use knowledge gained at the conference to explore how they could begin to align policy, practice, and governance in their organizations to support the achievement of personal outcomes.

The conference encouraged attendees to consider ways to use QOL as a lens to view their work and to guide continuous quality improvement efforts. This conference provided a tremendous opportunity for education, networking, and idea generation. However, it also served another purpose—to signal to internal and external stakeholders that this was an intersection point around which we all could rally, one that we could all get behind in some way, no matter which jurisdiction we work in, what role we play, or how far we were in our respective transformative journey.

Lessons Learned and Remaining Challenges

Lessons Learned

Transforming a service delivery system is hard work that during its continuous process results in some lessons learned. For example, the results of the QOL assessments tell us that the vast majority of individuals who have participated in the survey are experiencing very high scores on the wellbeing domains (physical, material, and emotional). The results are less encouraging for the domains of social inclusion, personal development, and self-determination. However, we are moving in the right direction. The information provided to CLBC and service providers is already being used for its intended purpose of continuous quality improvement and evidence-based decision-making.

The case study provided by LACL is encouraging and clearly demonstrates the power of measuring personal outcomes. In receiving and responding to the results of their first survey, LACL personnel have been able to make significant positive changes in the areas upon which they focused—personal development, self-determination, interpersonal relations, and social inclusion. Other providers are engaged in similar activities and are using their results to shift the manner in which they deliver services and support individuals.

At the systems level, CLBC is beginning to make similar shifts in response to the data, shifts that will create better horizontal and vertical alignment throughout the system. Two pieces of work currently underway illustrate how we are using personal outcome data to improve the overall system. The first is a review of our overall quality assurance framework, using QOL as the lens to evaluate the processes we currently have in place. This will move us away from the dominant focus we have had on health and safety, to a more holistic and person-centered approach to helping to create lives of quality. The second is a major revision of the person-centered planning we currently do so that it moves us away from a goal-attainment paradigm to one that focuses more effectively on individual QOL outcomes. This will help ensure that planning reflects what is important *to* the individual, as well as what is important *for* the individual and that there is an appropriate balance between what are tantamount to personal versus system needs

The results in our province are similar to those of similar jurisdictions in other parts of the world (see, for example Chapters 8–10, this volume). They signify that, while organizations and systems have made great progress in helping people to be *in* the community, supporting them to be *of* the community (a requirement for true active citizenship) remains a key challenge. We are excited to have access to a new and powerful data set that will allow us to respond in ways that will truly make a difference to the individuals we are collectively here to serve.

Remaining Challenges

Although the approach described in this chapter has received sector-wide support from individuals, families, service providers, CLBC staff and leadership, and government, we realize there is work to be done and we face several challenges as we move forward with implementation. Among the most important of these challenges:

- *Leadership change.* A number of key senior staff who were involved in CLBC's creation have recently retired, making the potential for losing the history of how/why this process started very real. We need to pause and give the new leadership the time and information they need to understand the rationale and potential importance of this initiative so we can move forward with confidence and full endorsement of the organization.

- *Funding deficits.* As in virtually every jurisdiction that provides these types of community living services, the demand for funding invariably exceeds supply. *Include Me!* has a price tag that must be defended to those who call for more funding for services.
- *Competing internal priorities.* The reality is that CLBC is a large, modern-day bureaucracy. There is a limited budget for administration, so there are competing demands for funding, staffing, and other resources. The reality is that aligning departments with different functions is a challenge.
- *Political will.* CLBC is a creature of government. As such, it and the various initiatives it supports are susceptible to the vagaries of changing public policy.
- *Time.* CLBC uses a staggered implementation approach to introduce *include Me!* to the 16,000 individuals who are served across the province. This approach is due in part to budget constraints, but also to differing views among senior leadership about the role and place of the imitative. So while the current implementation plan represents a necessary compromise, there remains a real risk that a drift in values/focus will occur.

Although an organizational strategic plan can neatly lay out where an organization wants to head, the reality is that every funding body operates in a dynamic and ever-changing environment. Sometimes, for various political, strategic, or policy-related reasons, priorities change or must go on the back burner. *Include Me!* is one initiative that is at risk in such an environment. However, we remain optimistic about the future. There are a number of next steps that will help to anchor the changes the *include Me!* team wishes to achieve:

- web-based portal to share learning between service providers as a way to develop deeper understanding of how to implement effective continuous quality improvement strategies
- regional learning events (ongoing) to connect CLBC staff, service providers, and others to one another and to support commitment to a common vision
- general population survey (planned for 2015–16) to provide another benchmark of how we are currently doing with our goal of supporting individuals to experience a QOL that is similar to (or better than) others who reside in this province
- documenting efforts and sharing results achieved by providers (ongoing) who have participated thus far so that providers can learn from one another and individuals and families can have a sense of what is truly possible when accessing services of an agency that has made a true commitment to promoting individual QOL in a holistic manner

Conclusion

CLBC has an opportunity to support the development of a service delivery system that works collaboratively to keep its eye on the prize—supporting adults with developmental disabilities to be active and contributing citizens who enjoy a QOL that many citizens take for granted. Describing the efforts to date to reach this goal has been the focus of this chapter. In the material and examples presented, we have suggested that changing a service delivery system requires maximizing three change catalysts: values, leadership, and empowerment. Maximizing values to bring about change and transformation requires demonstrating that change is possible, revising policies and practices so they are aligned with the envisioned change, developing a logic model that communicates clearly the key aspects of the change process, and changing contractual obligations to support the change process. Maximizing leadership to bring about change and transformation requires involving outside experts, internal champions, and sector leaders. Maximizing empowerment involves simple communication and stakeholder involvement.

There have been some early wins and transformational changes. However, adoption of the QOL framework is the easy part. There are challenges ahead and further obstacles to surmount. Creating a more aligned system across various stakeholder groups challenges a very dominant paradigm characterized by a mental model in which professionals know best. Ongoing clear communication about what *include Me!* is, and what it hopes to achieve and how, will be a fundamental requirement, as will ongoing discussions and reflections about how we offer service to others and what this really means in everyday practice. To paraphrase Ghandi, each of us must be the change we wish to see in the world.

CHAPTER 15

HUMAN RIGHTS AND QUALITY-OF-LIFE DOMAINS:
Identifying Cross-Cultural Indicators

CLAUDIA CLAES, HANNE VANDENBUSSCHE, and MARCO LOMBARDI

Introduction and Overview

Societal views on people with disabilities have changed over the last few decades (Schalock & Verdugo, 2002; Abbott & McConkey, 2006; Claes et al. 2009; Verdugo et al., 2012). These changes are reflected in specific international conventions that have been developed to guide policy and practices. After the *Universal Declaration of Human Rights* was promulgated in 1948 (United Nations, 1948) many conventions and agreements evolved, including the *Declaration on the Rights of Mentally Retarded Persons* (United Nations, 1975), and the *Standard Rules on the Equalization of Opportunities for Persons with Disabilities* (United Nations, 1993). In 2006, the Standard Rules were replaced by the CRPD (United Nations, 2006).

The CRPD strives for social-political conditions in the implementation of basic rights related to equality, autonomy, non-discrimination, participation, and inclusion in society. As such, the Convention focuses on macro socio-political conditions, and the need for developing specific regulations and legislation related to people with disabilities. Unfortunately, despite those regulatory efforts, there is a large gap between laws and regulations and the life conditions and rights of people with disabilities (Aznar et al., 2012).

In the field of disability, the construct of QOL evolved from being a sensitizing notion to a measurable construct in which subjective and objective life conditions are assessed. As a person-referenced framework, this multidimensional construct captures essential elements of a life of quality, and strives for empowerment and the improvement of rights and the life situation of individuals and their families (Claes, Van Hove, Vandevelde, van Loon, & Schalock, 2012). In 2012, Verdugo et al. demonstrated that the framework provided by QOL domains could be a vehicle through which the status of the UN Convention Articles is evaluated.

The purpose of this chapter is to summarize current work that focuses on the alignment of CRPD Articles to the eight core QOL domains and measurable QOL domain indicators. We begin the chapter by discussing how the CRPD enforces or protects disability rights and the close relation between Convention articles and the QOL construct. Thereafter, we describe an empirical cross-cultural study identifying measurable indicators associated with each of the article/domain pairings. Based on results obtained in the study, we point out the realistic challenges to policy makers and researchers in identifying and assessing cross-cultural QOL indicators aligned with CRPD Articles. We conclude the chapter with an overview of the next anticipated phase of this work: connecting article/domain indicators to QOL enhancement strategies.

The Need for the CRPD

Human rights provide a global, fertile framework for rethinking how people with disabilities can be included in society and treated as fully human (Stainton & Clare, 2012). In the report *Human Rights and Disabled Persons* (United Nations, 2015), the UN Human Rights Council identified three reasons why it is important to constitute a separate convention for the human rights of people with disabilities.

First, many countries face problems of unwitting discrimination. People with disabilities very often need supports on several domains in daily life; a written right does not ensure that these supports demands are met. People with disabilities may be treated as everybody else, but do not always get all of the opportunities they are entitled to. If we want to respect the human rights of people with disabilities, we need to take into account all of the necessary supports, adjustments in society, and an adapted mentality concerning people with disabilities.

Second, we must also consider the importance of recognizability. People with disabilities have needs that differ from those of the mainstream, and these needs must be met if they are to be able to participate in society. A focus on this minority group in society can help others to highlight and respect necessary policy changes.

Third, recent paradigmatic shifts have moved us from an emphasis on personal defects to a focus on capabilities. Seeing individuals as humans first can facilitate their treatment as full and equal citizens in society (Goodley, 2011; Stainton & Clare, 2012; Van Gennep, 2007).

The CRPD and Quality of Life

In 2012, Verdugo et al. discussed the close relation between the CRPD and the QOL construct, arguing that the QOL construct: (a) reflects the dynamics of personally desired subjective and objective conditions of life, (b) captures the essential domains of an individual's life situation, including his/her human and legal rights, (c) links the general values reflected in social rights and the personal life of the individual, (d) can be the vehicle through which individual-referenced equity, empowerment, life satisfaction, and equal opportunities can be understood and enhanced, and (e) is relevant to both public policy determination and a framework for outcomes evaluation.

The CRPD strives for rehabilitation, independent living, education, health, work and employment, and other endeavors that enhance the rights of people with disabilities. Although regulation is necessary, some authors argue that it is not enough to create social change to improve the QOL of people with disabilities; there is also a need for a framework to understand and evaluate human functioning and personal outcomes related to human rights (Karr, 2011; Verdugo et al., 2012). Such a framework provides a way that political concepts can be translated into evidence-based practices (Schalock, et al., 2011). Thus, the underlying assumption in the study described next is that the QOL domains can be used to provide a best practices framework to analyze the relations among the UN Articles, QOL domains, and measurable indicators.

Relationships Among UN Convention Articles, QOL Domains, and Measurable Indicators

We conducted a three-phase Delphi study to determine the relation among UN Convention Articles, QOL domains, and measurable indicators:

Phase 1: Generating the Initial Items

A focus group composed of 70 self-advocates and service providers in Flanders and The Netherlands was constituted in April, 2013, to generate a pool of potential indicators for each of the CRPD articles. The 40 participants (experts as self-advocates, important relatives, professionals working in the field, and academics) were asked to think about indicators related to the QOL domains and the UN Articles. An indicator was defined operationally as an outcome that can be used to measure the quantity or quality of the results achieved when the respective UN Convention Article is implemented. The following criteria were used to define an indicator: measurable, relevant to the article, and useful for developing supports strategies. This group generated 116 indicators that met both the operational definition and the three criteria.

Phase 2: Finding Consensus on the Initial Items

A Delphi study was conducted to find consensus on the initial pool of 116 items. A Delphi study uses a structured research process where several research rounds are utilized to achieve consensus about a complex problem (Brown, 1968; Keeney, Hasson, & Mckenna, 2001). The Delphi study conducted in Phase 2 resulted in consensus on the initial (i.e., Phase 1) indicators. The purposes of Phase 2 were to: (a) align the CRPD articles to the eight core QOL domains; (b) operationalize the articles in reference to measurable QOL domains and indicators, and (c) reach consensus on those indicators that could become the basis for policies and practices that enhance human rights and QOL. An indicator was defined in Phase 2 as an outcome that can be used to measure the quantity or quality of the results achieved when the respective UN Convention article is implemented.

An online survey provided the opportunity for 50 experts in Belgium and the Netherlands to indicate their agreement with the 116 indicators generated in Phase 1. Based on the data provided by this group of experts (self-advocates, important relatives, professionals working in the field, and academics) 85 items reached the established criterion of 80% agreement that the respective indicator fit the specific article.

Phase 3: Establishing International Consensus

The 85 items upon which consensus was reached in Phase 2 were administered online to a group of 153 individuals from twelve countries. These respondents were members of the AAIDD International Special Interest Group and others recommended by them. The twelve countries were Belgium, Holland, Spain, Catalonia, Portugal, Germany, Czech Republic, Italy, Israel, United States, Canada, and Taiwan. Respondents reached 75% or better agreement on each of the 70 indicators. These 70 indicators, which appear in Table 15.1, summarize our current understanding of the alignment among the UN Articles, the QOL domains, and the specific indicators. As with Phases 1 and 2, an indicator was defined as an outcome that can be used to measure the quantity or quality of the results achieved when the respective UN Convention article is implemented.

Challenges in Determining Cross-Cultural Indicators

Although the three phases of the Delphi study described above resulted in an initial understanding of the alignment among UN Convention Articles, QOL domains, and measurable indicators, the procedures and results described above illustrate six realistic challenges to both policy makers and researchers. These six are: (a) the indicators are not always measurable or objective; (b) indicators with ethical connotations are difficult to reach consensus on; (c) an indicator doesn't always represent a full article; (d) the definition of an indicator impacts the score; (e) indicators identified are not exhaustive; and (f) indicators might fit more than one article.

More specifically, when we analyzed the representation of the eight QOL domains used as an analytic framework, two domains were under-represented in the number of indicators identified: Personal Development and Interpersonal Relations. In reference to Personal Development, the difficulty relates to how to incorporate supports into standards of living and full community or societal participation. In reference to Interpersonal Relations, challenges relate to distinguishing between quantity and quality. For example, one of the indicators of the quality of interpersonal relations is the social network of the person. The network can be understood (and measured) from two perspectives (Forrester-Jones et al., 2006; Lunsky, 2006): a structural one (e.g., in terms of size and frequency) and functional one (e.g., in terms of perceived emotional and practical support).

When we analyzed the representativeness of the UN Articles, we found difficulties with Articles 8, 19, 23, 25, 29, 30. Consensus was lower on these articles. Possible explanations for this lower consensus come from qualitative information provided by the respondents. For example:

- *Article 8* (awareness raising). Confusion arose as to whether participants should try to reach a broader public so that the positions and perspectives of people with disabilities are clear for everyone.
- *Article 19* (living independently and being included in the community). Indicators were viewed as incomplete, too narrow, and too dependent on the person and hence generalized measurement could give a distorted image (e.g., presence in cultural events).
- *Article 23* (respect for home and family). The indicators are specific as to parenting and having a family, but there were concerns expressed about the cultural sensitivity regarding the right of persons with disabilities to establish their own family.
- *Article 25* (health). Concern was expressed by some that the indicators were too general.
- *Article 29* (participation in political and public life). Some participants considered the indicators too vague. If multiple interpretations are possible, indicators can be misused. Other remarks pointed out that it's not easy to measure political consciousness, which is a condition that ensures the article is being implemented.
- *Article 30* (participation in cultural life). There was concern about the quantity and quality of certain concepts. For example, if we consider friendship, the number of friends is less important than the quality of friendship. But the latter isn't easy to measure, whereas the former is. Another remark concerned individual choice: to participate in cultural events implies a certain fascination or interest.

In summary, some of the indicators listed in Table 15.1 were viewed by some respondents as incommensurate, not concrete, or not appropriate for the respective article. On

Table 15.1. *UN Convention Articles, QOL Domains, and Indicators*

Article	QOL domain	Indicators
24 - Education	Personal Development	• Personal skills • Educational setting • Lifelong learning
14 - Liberty and security of the person	Self-Determination	• Freedom of movement • Freedom of choice • Personal autonomy • Safe environment
21 - Freedom of expression and opinion and access to information	Self-Determination	• The level of understanding the information • The use of information • Opportunities to express opinion • Access to information
23 - Respect for home and family	Interpersonal Relations	• Person has the right to set up his own family • Person has the right to be a parent
30 - Participation in culture life, recreation and sport	Interpersonal Relations	• Person participates in cultural events (e.g. concerts, theatre, museums) • Person participates in recreational or leisure events (e.g. hobbies, community activity clubs)
8 - Awareness – raising	Social Inclusion	• Acts of awareness (e.g. projects, campaigns, . . .) to increase social inclusion
9 - Accessibility	Social Inclusion	• Presence in cultural events • Presence in recreation or leisure events
18 - Liberty of movement	Social Inclusion	• Physical access on community streets • Physical access to public transportation
19 - Living independently and being included in the community	Social Inclusion	• Living in a home with minimum intrusion from others
20 - Personal mobility	Social Inclusion	• A way to be personally mobile (e.g. by walking, using a wheelchair, or using crutches) • A way to transport across environments (e.g. a car, a bike, public transportation)
29 - Participation in political and public life	Social Inclusion	• Membership on boards • Running for public office
30 - Participation in cultural life	Social Inclusion	• Presence at concerts • Presence in movie theatres • Presence in museum visits
5 - Equality and non-discrimination	Rights	• Presence in the community • Engages in open employment
6 - Women with disabilities	Rights	• Participation in community life • Receives personalized supports

Table 15.1. *UN Convention Articles, QOL Domains, and Indicators (continued)*

Article	QOL domain	Indicators
7 - Children with disabilities	Rights	• Receives post-natal care • Receives supports to enhance personal growth and development • Involved in educational program • Provided adequate medical care • Included in their family • Included in the community
10 - Right to life	Rights	• Make choices about contraception
11 - Situations of risk and humanitarian emergencies	Rights	• Supplying immigrants with a disability with sufficient legal, financial, and social supports • Access to health care
12 - Equal recognition before the law	Rights	• Accesses legal services • Receives due process • Is considered to be legally competent
13 - Access to justice	Rights	• Has a defense attorney • Participates in one's defense • Are adjudicated by a magistrate, a judge, or a jury • If guilty, receives a fair sentence
15 - Freedom from cruel or unusual punishment	Rights	• Personal injuries caused by others (e.g. torture, maiming) • If guilty, the punishment received is commensurate to that received by others
22 - Respect for privacy	Rights	• Control over personal areas (e.g. bedroom, bathroom, home or dwelling) • Personal access to communication (e.g. letters, e-mails, phone)
16 - Freedom from exploitation, violence and abuse	Emotional Well-Being	• Lives in a safe environment • Is not exploited by others (e.g. sexually, financially, socially) • Is not abused by others (e.g. physical, emotional)
17 - Protecting the integrity of the person	Emotional Well-Being	• Experiences respect • Experiences dignity • Experiences equality
25 - Health	Physical Well-Being	• Physical status • Nutritional status • Chronic conditions
26 - Habilitation and Rehabilitation	Physical Well-Being	• Medical intervention if needed • Emotional intervention if needed • Receives therapy (e.g. physical, occupational, speech) appropriate to the person's condition
27 - Work and employment	Material Well-Being	• Full-time paid employment • Part-time paid employment
28 - Adequate standard of living and social protection	Material Well-Being	• Annual income covers basic living expanses • Annual income allows for discretionary spending • Adequate housing • Unemployment insurance • Public assistance if necessary

the other hand, respondents reported that the indicators identified through the Delphi process can validly measure some of the UN Articles, but some indicators need further elaboration or clarification.

Conclusion

This chapter represents an initial attempt to obtain measureable indicators of the UN Convention Articles within a QOL framework. By using a three-phase Delphi methodology, multiple indicators for each Article/QOL domain pairing were identified by a group of international experts who were familiar with the CRPD Articles and the eight core QOL domains. Although there was consensus on the indicators, further work is required in moving beyond indicators to measurable items because some of the indicators identified are not measureable or objective in their current form, and many have ethical connotations that complicate their measurement.

Despite these challenges, efforts should continue to determine not only the relations among UN Convention Articles, QOL domains, and measureable indicators, but also associated strategies for realizing the UN Convention in local policies and practices. When this is done, then the human rights framework reflected in the CRPD and the principles embedded in the concept of QOL will be translated into both policies and practices.

CHAPTER 16

THE EVOLUTION OF QUALITY-OF-LIFE PERSPECTIVES IN THE DEVELOPING COUNTRIES OF SUB-SAHARAN AFRICA

ELIAS MPOFU

Introduction and Overview

The vast majority of the world's people are citizens of developing countries (also known as low-income, or low- and middle-income countries), and their QOL perspectives are significant to national and federal governments as they adopt support policies. The evolution of QOL perspectives in developing countries has roots in both the local and global cultures. Local influences are culturally sensitive, and explain the QOL indicators that are held to be important and relevant. The local cultural influences on QOL perspectives are aligned to the country's collective worldview about a life worthy of humans (Hofstede, 1984).

The global cultural influences are those acquired from learning from the international community. For instance, most sub-Saharan countries share a historic collectivist worldview grounded in their valuing of the social interconnectedness of people. Cultures with a collectivist worldview emphasize a sense of belonging to a social collective (family, community) and participation in the roles or obligations thereof (Heine, 2012). In collectivist settings, one's humanity is defined in relation to that of others, making for mutual reciprocity in social relations. Such social connectedness and relational support facilitates physical and material well-being within the collectivist culture. Global cultural influences define the generic factors and domains that define QOL regardless of importance or relevance in the local culture. However, the nuances of specific QOL indicators are influenced by local culture (Felce, 1997).

In this chapter I briefly consider social relational worldview influences and the prioritization of collectivist well-being on the evolution of QOL perspectives in the developing countries of sub-Saharan Africa—including Kenya, South Africa, Uganda, Zambia, and Zimbabwe. I discuss relational well-being as a priority for QOL in developing country settings, and especially the centrality of social collective supports to living a life of quality. Next, I describe the role of community-based rehabilitation (CBR) programs in supporting the QOL of people with ID. Finally, I address the importance of living conditions and the disability support infrastructure to the well-being of people with ID in these developing countries.

Relational QOL Perspectives

A worldview rooted in relational support and collectivist culture is one in which QOL is explained and understood in the context of the connectedness of the well-being of oneself and others. A large majority of the world's people live in such collectivist societies, where the role of the group is paramount; this stands in contrast to Western individualistic cultures in which individual interests prevail over those of the group (Hofstede & Hofstede, 2005). Social abilities matter to QOL (Nota et al., 2007). Thus, in many developing world cultures, the primary units in which QOL is realized are the family and community. In this relationship-based worldview, one "is" because others "are" (Mbiti, 1995), and a satisfying life is one in which the individual is a means of life satisfaction for others.

As an example of the translation of collective well-being by families in developing countries, people with disability may be more closely monitored by family and the collective community than are individuals without disability (Ingstad, & Grut, 2007). The social interest of community others in the well-being of a member with disability enhances their chances for social inclusion more than would be the case otherwise (Devlieger, 1998; Mpofu, 2004). For instance, the Neighbourhood Day Centre facility in Uganda brings together people with different disabilities, and sometimes caregivers, to work, counsel each other, share, and rejoice with one another (CBR African Network, 2004). In developing-world contexts, the immediate family of people with ID, especially mothers and extended family members, facilitates daily living activities to enhance their family member's QOL.

Four types of relational supports have been identified in the literature: emotional, affiliational, instrumental, and informational (Langford, Bowsher, Maloney, & Lillis, 1997). In developing countries, these types of support are linked to the collectivist worldview that fosters the mutually supportive roles of self and others. Emotional support refers to perceiving oneself as loved, cared for, and esteemed by others. In developing country settings, emotional support is provided by families and their social networks in the community, which may include relatives and friends. Affiliational support fosters the feeling of belonging to a group with shared interests and participation in social activities, including sports, leisure, arts, and cultural events (Wanderi, Mwisukha, & Bukhala, 2009). Instrumental support involves providing assistance with tasks of living, including housing, food, and respite services. People with ID may need instrumental modifications of the living environment in order to improve safety and accessibility important for one's QOL (Ostensjo, Brogren, & Vollestad, 2003). Such modifications supports are scarce in developing world contexts.

Informational support provides for advice, suggestions, directives, and education about advocacy, supports, and services as well as disability policies (Wehmeyer et al., 2008). However, in developing world contexts, family caregivers of people with ID may lack the knowledge of supports and services they could access for quality care (Kromberg et al., 2008). Information about the ID condition could help family caregivers to acquire the knowledge necessary to development of coping skills (Matousova-Done & Gates, 2006; Meadan, Halle, & Ebata, 2010).

The resource allocation priorities of sub-Saharan countries may under-prioritize the need for systems and services that accord full citizenship rights to people who are vulnerable (e.g., children, women, people with disabilities). Thus, when basic resources have been allocated, people with disabilities have been among the lowest priorities of the governments of developing countries (Mba, 1995; McConkey & O'Toole, 2000), which is a detriment to the QOL of those citizens with disability.

Providing care to a family member with ID, for instance, has a significant impact on the well-being, stress levels, and QOL of the primary caregiver and other family members (Emerson; 2007, 2013; Shearn & Todd 2000). This in turn lowers the QOL of family members with ID (Hatton, & Emerson, 2003). At the same time, caring for a family member with disability can be socially rewarding, although families with more material resources likely provide greater community access and participation to their members than would significantly less advantaged others (see, for example, WHO, 2011).

Global Cultural Influences

Developed countries are members of the global or international community, so that global or world culture is a major influence on their QOL perspectives. The vast majority of developing countries are signatory to international conventions of the rights of people with disabilities, and aspire to the implementation of these conventions (Umeasiegbu, Bishop, & Mpofu, 2013). The realization and practice of citizen rights is a primary QOL quality indicator, including the right to basic human dignity, social inclusion, safety, health, and well-being (United Nations, 2006; WHO, 2011). The progressive implementation of universal citizenship rights policies by developing countries is likely the single most significant influence on the evolution of the QOL-oriented policies and practices of these countries.

As countries develop, they realize opportunities for enhancing citizenship rights for all, including those historically marginalized, such as people with disabilities. For example, Article 9 of the UN Convention underscores the importance of accessibility. By this convention, national governments are encouraged to enable persons with disabilities to live independently and participate fully in a way of life that ensures equal access to amenities for physical and social well-being. These measures include the identification and elimination of obstacles and barriers to access financial, educational, and other service facilities, including workplaces, to enhance the self-determination of individuals with disabilities. In the past decade, the increased pressure to include disability in the national development policy agenda is adding a sense of urgency to national development goals (Albert, Dube, & Hansen, 2005; Kett, Lang, & Trani 2009).

Community-Based Rehabilitation Influences

CBR is a major vehicle for realization of QOL with disability in the developing world context. CBR is a strategy that stresses rehabilitation, poverty reduction, equalization of opportunities, rehabilitation, and social inclusion of all people with a disability (Coleridge, 2007; Mitra et al., 2011; WHO, 2010). Specifically, CBR has two goals directly aligned to the QOL of persons with a disability: (a) maximizing the physical and mental abilities of people with disability, according them access to resources for well-being and full social inclusion; and (b) engaging and supporting communities to promote full community participation.

Families and organizations of and for people with disabilities are partners in seeking the attainment of these two goals (Heinicke-Motsch, 2013). By removing the barriers to developing social services access and utilization, CBR helps reduce poverty and improve the QOL of everyone in the community (Heinicke-Motsch, 2013). Thus, CBR for social inclusion seeks to address major human development barriers, such as poverty, the lack of universal primary education, major public health problems, gender inequity, and a lack of environmental sustainability (WHO, 2010). As an example, the Community Integrated Programme implemented in rural Uganda is a disability and development CBR, whereby people with disabilities and other community members partner on joint projects, such as communal gardens, to increase their food security (Udoh, Gona, & Maholo, 2013). An important quality of CBR is that participants are people with disabilities and other community members who work in partnership, translating aspirations into mutually satisfying lived experiences

CBR is firmly based within a community development framework (Dutch Coalition on Disability and Development, 2005; Udoh et al., 2013). Participants with disabilities engage others on the same terms as would typically be done by other community members, and they are not stigmatized by their disability and perceived difference. Itinerant community health care providers, as part of CBR, address health needs important for physical or mental health and well-being. Effective CBR empowers people with disabilities, their allies, and communities to enhance social inclusion (Harley, Mpofu, Scanlan, Umeasiegbu, & Mpofu, 2015; Udoh et al., 2013).

Furthermore, CBR can be implemented to meet the needs of specific disability groupings (e.g., people with intellectual, physical, sensory impairments) and by age groups (e.g. children, elderly people) or other pertinent demographics (e.g., gender). This type of customization makes for responsiveness to specific disability QOL-related needs. However, segmentation of CBRs by disability type might also take away from social inclusiveness, which often is the ultimate QOL goal (Makuwira, 2013). Additionally, others outside the community (e.g., government department or civic community organization) with a mission to work with a specific disability group, rather than all people with disability, may set the agenda for QOL-related outcomes, perhaps taking away from the QOL principles of self-determination, equity, empowerment, and inclusion. Having people with disabilities on the external CBR agency teams or in an advisory capacity to external partners helps to enhance the ownership by people with disability of the QOL-related outcomes enhanced by an externally initiated CBR.

Poverty or material scarcity at the community level necessitates the participation of agencies from outside the community in CBR development. Such external support of CBR might be necessary to achieve valued outcomes that presume a certain level of manpower and material resources. For example, superior manpower resourcing made for more successful CBR programs in South Africa and Zimbabwe, compared to similar programs in Cameroon and Zambia (Mpofu et al., 2007). Regardless of the packaging of a CBR, qualities for its success include: (a) national level support through policies, co-ordination, and resource allocation; (b) recognition of the need for CBR programs to be based on a human rights approach; (c) willingness of the community to respond to the needs of its members with disabilities; and (d) presence of motivated community workers (Hartley et al., 2009). Conditions associated with the poverty that is characteristic of most developing world settings can be mitigated by full community inclusion of people with disabilities, through the vehicle of CBR.

CBR and organizations for and of people with disabilities, where they exist, allow a platform for advocacy for resources to enhance the QOL of people with ID. Advocacy support enables people with ID and/or their allies to network with others to assist and support efforts to facilitate a life of quality. Family caregivers of people with ID may be reluctant to access supports and services due to unpleasant past experiences with service providers. The advocacy support networking could involve knowledge about disability support laws and policies and practices that affect peoples' lives.

Conditions of Living and Disability Support Infrastructure

Conditions of living are important to the QOL of people with ID (Felce, 1997). In developing country contexts, material poverty is a significant barrier to living with disability. The cyclic link between disability and poverty is well documented (Emerson, 2007; Mitra, 2004, 2005), and the majority of people with disability live in poverty (Coleridge, 2007; Harley et al., 2015). Poverty typically leads to increased disability, and disability in turn leads to increased risk for poverty across the lifespan (Emerson, 2007). People with disability experience disproportional social exclusion from education and employment, placing them at a four- to five-fold risk for poverty, which in turn increases the severity of their disability (Emerson, 2007; Hartley et al., 2009). In resource-limited settings such as developing countries, conditions of living may be marginal, adding to the challenges to those committed to enhancing the QOL of persons with disability. There are also significant challenges to provision of resources to improve conditions of living in developing world countries due to their under-developed physical and disability support policy infrastructure.

Conclusion

QOL views in the developing world, including the sub-Saharan nations, are evolving under the impetus of both local and global cultures and international covenants. Local cultural influences in developing countries are grounded in a collectivist and relational worldview that gives local meaning to QOL. People with ID with social connectedness to family and community likely enjoy superior QOL in developing contexts than others with fewer social supports. Global cultures in which disability rights are increasingly promoted prioritize human worth and dignity and allow for new learning and alternative ways to achieve valued personal and family outcomes. Community-based rehabilitation programs, where they exist in developing countries, are a primary vehicle for this effort. Regardless of the specific quality indicator employed, emphasis on one's context and the availability and accessibility of resources for well-being will likely define in the future the evolution of QOL perspectives in developing countries.

SECTION V
THE CROSS-CULTURAL QUALITY-OF-LIFE AGENDA

Section Overview

A cross-cultural QOL agenda needs to incorporate the concepts, policies, and practices discussed in the preceding 16 chapters. More specifically, the agenda needs to be based on a clear understanding of the concept of QOL and how societal attitudes and behaviors toward people with ID have changed, commensurate with their evolving roles. The agenda needs to:

- *Be person-centered and facilitate self-advocacy, self-determination, personal involvement, and the empowerment of individuals and families to speak for themselves and be actively involved in enhancing both individual and family QOL.*
- *Encourage and support not-for-profit organizations, public service delivery systems, and social enterprises to: align services and supports to personal goals and assessed support needs, evaluate personal and organization outcomes as a part of continuous quality improvement, and be receptive to changes in policies and practices that enhance organizational effectiveness and efficiency.*
- *Be sensitive to cultural, geographic, and social-economic factors in implementing policies and practices that respect and enhance human rights. Services and supports should align with systems-level outcome indicators, and should transform*

service delivery systems to create social value by improving lives, building community, and improving society.

- *Provide an application framework that incorporates the etic or universal properties of core QOL domains and the desire for all people for a life of quality, and reflects quality indicators, improvement strategies, and enhancement opportunities that are culturally based and vary across economic, social, and geographical boundaries.*

The purpose of this section of the book is to propose a cross-cultural QOL agenda whose parameters are framed by the global perspective of QOL and the critical role that a QOL theory plays in such an agenda. To that end, Chapter 17 summarizes the history of QOL research from the global perspective. This summary provides the empirical foundation for the agenda and is consistent with four international disability-related trends: a changed vision of persons with ID, an emphasis on universal human rights, the provision of individualized supports, and the emphasis on personal and subjective well-being. In Chapter 18, we describe an empirically-based QOL theory that incorporates the domains of a life of quality and the components of quality thinking, explores the impacts of various factors impacting one's QOL, focuses on quality improvement strategies, provides the basis for prediction and hypothesis testing, and establishes the parameters for policy development and outcomes evaluation. In Chapter 19, we synthesize material presented in previous chapters to set the parameters for a cross-cultural agenda to enhance the lives of persons with ID. This agenda, which requires working within cultural contexts, targets policy development, the transformation of organizations and systems, professional education and support provider development, and research.

These four agenda components reflect how far we have come since publishing, in 2000, the first edition of this book. In the first edition, we brought together a geographically diverse group of contributors who shared their vision of the QOL concept and its meaning to people with ID. The 31 chapters of the first edition provided a snapshot of how people within the field conceptualized the QOL concept and its application at that point in time. Now, 16 years later, an updated snapshot is available, based on a better understanding of the conceptualization, measurement, and application of the QOL concept. This growth in knowledge and understanding allows us now to set a cross-cultural agenda to enhance the QOL of persons with ID that is sound both empirically and theoretically.

CHAPTER 17

THE GLOBAL PERSPECTIVE ON THE CONCEPT OF QUALITY OF LIFE

KENNETH D. KEITH and ROBERT L. SCHALOCK

Introduction and Overview

QOL and related notions such as well-being and happiness have long been subject of interest to writers across cultures. Aristotle (325 BCE/1962), for example, writing more than two millennia ago, discussed *eudaimonia*—human flourishing and well-being—the perfect or complete goal of life (Tiberius & Mason, 2009). Even earlier, in India, Siddhartha Gautama, the Buddha, began teaching others to seek the path to happiness (Levine, 2009), and the Chinese philosopher Confucius, born 551 BCE, taught about the dimensions of happiness in the work that became known as *The Analects* (Confucius, trans. 2003).

In more recent times, researchers have recognized the importance of culture to QOL (Bonn & Tafarodi, 2013; Hofstede, 1984), and the QOL concept assumed a central role internationally in the work of researchers interested in the lives of people with ID. In this chapter, we discuss the global perspective on the QOL concept by summarizing research efforts that provide an empirical basis for the phenomenon and tracing some of the significant developments in its cross-cultural application. Major sections involve a discussion of the growth of an international movement, the emergence of a new millennium, and the future in a global community.

Growth of an International Movement

The 1990s brought a world-wide proliferation of definitions of QOL (Cummins, 1995), of articles in the psychological literature (Antaki & Rapley, 1996), and of efforts to measure a variety of aspects of the QOL construct (Hughes et al., 1995). At about the same time, Goode (1994) edited a volume that presented international perspectives on QOL of people with disabilities, reflecting researchers' recognition that QOL is a notion existing in a cross-cultural context (e.g., Heal, Schalock, & Keith, 1992; Keith, 1996).

In 1997, Luckasson acknowledged that QOL might well be a guide to good, and "maybe even a right" (p. ix). Despite some reservations about the usefulness of the QOL construct (e.g., Hatton, 1998; Wolfensberger, 1994), extensive work was underway in a number of countries in the mid-1990s, including several efforts to develop approaches to conceptualization and measurement of QOL. In Australia, Cummins (1997) produced five editions of the Comprehensive Quality of Life Scale—Intellectual Disability. Working in the U.S., Heal and his colleagues developed and revised the *Lifestyle Satisfaction Scale* (Harner & Heal, 1993; Heal, Rubin, & Park, 1995), and Schalock and Keith (1993) published the revised Quality of Life Questionnaire and the Quality of Student Life Questionnaire (Keith & Schalock, 1995). In Canada, Oullette-Kuntz & McCreary (1996) developed the Quality of Life Interview Schedule (QUOLIS).

These instruments reflected the multi-dimensional nature of QOL, and were intended for use with people with ID. International researchers (e.g., Perry & Felce, 1995; Raphael, 1996) engaged in discussion of various aspects of measurement, and one instrument, the Quality of Life Questionnaire, was soon the subject of ongoing cross-cultural evaluation (e.g., Caballo & Peláez, 2005; Caballo et al., 2005; Rapley, 2003; Kober & Eggleton, 2002; Verdugo, Prieto, Caballo, & Peláez, 2005), eventually being translated for use in numerous languages, including Chinese, French, Greek, Japanese, Polish, Portuguese, and Spanish.

Furthering the search for universal core dimensions of QOL, and using a semantic differential technique (Osgood, May, & Miron, 1975), Keith et al. (1996) asked people in seven cultures (Australia, England, Finland, Germany, Japan, Taiwan, and the United States) to evaluate critical QOL concepts. Respondents in the seven countries showed surprising agreement in their ratings of ten concepts (rights, relationships, satisfaction, environment, economic security, social inclusion, individual control, privacy, health, and growth and development). In a review of Goode's (1994) book on international perspectives, Heal (1996) found that writers from a variety of cultural backgrounds addressed a similar array of concepts.

Felce (1997), noting the overlap of his ideas with those of others, as well as the broad agreement among researchers, suggested six potential QOL domains (physical well-being, material well-being, social well-being, productive well-being, emotional well-being, and rights or civic well-being). However, Felce and others (e.g., Carbonell, 1999; Hatton, 1998) recognized an international consensus around Schalock's (1996) conceptualization of QOL in terms of eight core dimensions: emotional well-being, interpersonal relations, material well-being, personal development, physical well-being, self-determination, social inclusion, and rights. By the end of the 1990s, QOL had become a compelling international issue.

Late in the 1990s, Keith and Schalock (2000) invited colleagues from 25 nations to assist in developing a compendium of research and practice in the area of QOL of people with ID. The ultimate result of this effort was an edited volume of 31 chapters reflecting work in 21 countries and including personal, community, and cultural perspectives. The contributors addressing the individual or personal (microsystem) perspective included self-advocates from five countries; community and organizational (mesosystem) contributors described programs in seven countries; and those writing about broader (macrosystem) views represented 15 different cultures. As Matsumoto (2000) noted, the contributors to the 2000 volume made clear the powerful influence of culture on people's lives and the fact that the search for a better QOL is shared by all people.

Emergence of a New Millennium

By the end of the 20th century, international recognition of the importance of QOL and its measurement was exemplified by the work of the WHO to develop effective means for assessing the construct (WHOQOL Group, 1998). The new millennium brought an effort to gather and synthesize the international work on conceptualization, measurement, and implementation of QOL in the field of ID (Keith, 2001), as well as a major cross-cultural compilation of conceptual and measurement tools intended for implementation by human service practitioners (Schalock & Verdugo, 2002).

Conceptualization

Writers in the 1990s sometimes suggested that an actual definition of QOL would not be particularly useful. Parmenter (1992), for example, expressed concern that the search for an operational definition of QOL might result in a loss of true meaning. And Schalock (1996b) advocated thinking of QOL as an organizing and sensitizing concept that could provide guidance to service programs and to development and evaluation of core dimensions. Soon after the turn of the century, Rapley (2003) discussed the difficulty in arriving at a universal definition of QOL, and stressed the importance of the role of culture as a determinant of individual QOL. Perhaps the most compelling conceptual movement in the early 21st century, however, was continued progress toward international agreement on core domains or dimensions.

Although some investigators continued to explore varying numbers of dimensions, an international panel (Schalock et al., 2002) reported a strengthening consensus centered on the eight domains (dimensions) previously described by Schalock (1996b), and cross-cultural analysis supported the universality of these domains (Schalock et al., 2005; Wang et al., 2010). However, the international panel concluded that the actual number of domains is less important than recognition of a multi-element conceptual framework that represents the totality of the QOL construct and takes account of the ability of individuals to know what is important for themselves. This latter point was reinforced by cross-cultural research showing a positive relation between self-determination and QOL (Lachapelle et al., 2005).

These domains (or very similar lists) continued to guide conceptual discussion and research well into the first decade of the century (Verdugo et al., 2005; Otrębski, 2005), and at the end of the decade, Schalock, Keith, Verdugo, and Gómez (2010) characterized QOL as a multidimensional construct with core domains and culturally-sensitive indicators. Researchers thus gave explicit recognition to the fact that, as a psychological construct, QOL cannot be directly seen, and therefore must be inferred and measured by reference to observable indicators (Brown et al., 2013; Schalock & Verdugo, 2002). Identification of QOL indicators, whether in the form of direct behavioral observations (e.g., Felce & Emerson, 2000) or as queries about subjective and objective aspects of individuals' QOL, was central to measurement of the construct.

Measurement

Discussion of the relative roles of subjective and objective aspects of measurement of QOL, long an issue for researchers (e.g., Campbell et al., 1976), continued to be a theme in the international research (e.g., Costanza et al., 2008; Keith, 2001), with key researchers (e.g., Cummins, 2002b) arguing in support of the importance and the utility of subjective measures that take account of the views of individuals. Cross-culturally, investigators agreed on the importance of taking account of both subjective and objective aspects of QOL (Schalock et al., 2002; Verdugo et al., 2005).

Researchers also engaged a cross-cultural discussion of the merits of proxy- and self-reports for individuals whose communicative skills might vary greatly (e.g., Stancliffe, 2000), arriving at a consensus that the validity of self-reports is generally greater than that of proxy reports (Cummins, 2002a). For those individuals whose language skills make self-reports difficult or impossible, thoughtful writers (e.g., Emerson, Felce, & Stancliffe, 2013) have proposed alternative means of data collection and meaningful ways to integrate self- and proxy-reports, and researchers in several cultures have explored creative use of peer interviewers to assist in measuring QOL (e.g., Bonham et al., 2004; Perry & Felce, 2004; Verdugo et al., 2005).

Implementation

If the end of the 20th century and the beginning of the 21st century saw global efforts to conceptualize and define the construct of QOL, the ensuing years might be viewed as a period of implementation—a time during which the field has moved more fully toward use of knowledge of QOL to enhance the lives of people with ID and their families.

United Nations. At the international level, one significant development was enactment, on December 13, 2006, of the UN's CRPD, with the avowed intention to "promote, protect and ensure the full and equal enjoyment of all human rights and fundamental freedoms by all persons with disabilities and to promote respect for their inherent dignity" (p. 4). The Convention is much more specific and detailed than earlier UN actions, and is based on a set of general principles addressing a range of concerns, including independence, decision-making, social inclusion, respect, equal opportunity, gender equality, and preservation of identity and autonomy. As of this writing, 159 nations have signed the Convention (i.e., they have indicated intent to sign the Convention), and 152 have ratified the Convention (indicating their intent to assume the legal rights and obligations stated in the Convention; United Nations enable, 2015). Notably absent from the list of ratifying nations is the United States.

Although recognition of rights is no doubt an important contributor to QOL, it remains a fact across cultures that too often the gap between policy and practice is large, and that implementation of the rights of people with disability may be limited by bias, ultimately diminishing QOL (McFadden, 2013). Nevertheless, the articles of the 2006 UN Convention are closely related to the eight consensus core domains of QOL. Although the Convention does not articulate means for implementation that would ensure enhanced QOL, Verdugo et al. (2012) suggested that the Convention articles could be operationalized through: (a) person-centered planning with a focus on QOL-related personal outcomes; (b) publication of provider profiles detailing quality-related outcomes and aggregate QOL measures of service/support agencies; and (c) a program of individualized supports designed to enhance personal outcomes and individual rights.

Supports paradigm. The provision of an array of personal supports is a step toward making the environment exceptional, as Throne (1972) advocated, rather than simply viewing the individual as exceptional. Pursuing this notion, Arnold et al. (2011) argued that assessment of intellectual and physical support needs could replace traditional intellectual and physical diagnoses of disability, and Arnold, Riches, Parmenter, and Stancliffe (2009) suggested that supports are a kind of interface between the person and the environment. As we saw in Chapter 12 of this volume, the aim of individualized supports should be to *enable* the individual's well-being/QOL, personal preferences, and rights. The supports paradigm represents a divergence from a care model, and is person-centered, with potential to improve personal functioning and community inclusion (Rapley, 2004).

An individualized support system provides a significant bridge between a person's current status and a desired functional status, thus making a connection between what is and what could be" (Arnold et al., 2009; Buntinx & Schalock, 2010). The aim, in other words, is for supports to lead in the direction of improved life quality. The supports model is consistent with the ICF (WHO, 2001), which held that disability derives from the interplay between person and environment, and it is that interaction that determines the need for support (Arnold et al., 2011).

Family quality of life. The understanding of the importance of family QOL for people with ID has grown in this century (Cummins, 2001). This increased interest in family QOL has been cross-cultural (Burton-Smith et al., 2009; Svraka et al., 2011), with its foundations in the extensive body of previous work on individual QOL (Wang & Kober, 2011). The developing focus on family QOL is accompanied by a growing understanding of the need for supports and with renewed recognition of the critical role of families as the primary environment for children and for many adults with ID (Samuel et al., 2012).

Like researchers studying individual QOL, those investigating family QOL have described the construct as multidimensional, and have concluded that measures should be both subjective and objective. Although a number of instruments have appeared (Hu et al., 2011), two have received cross-cultural recognition as psychometrically sound measures: the *Beach Center Family Quality of Life Scale* (Beach Center on Disability, 2005) and the *Family Quality of Life Survey* (*FQOLS-2006*; Brown et al., 2006). The *FQOLS-2006* had a clear international focus from its beginning, and is used across the lifespan for families. The Beach Center instrument, although originally developed for use by families of American children, has also given rise to international versions (e.g., Cordoba-Andrade et al., 2008; Davis & Gavidia-Payne, 2009; Wang et al., 2007). Clearly, family well-being is an important area of global implementation of the QOL construct in the new millennium.

The Future in a Global Community

Bogdan (1988) argued that "How we view people with disabilities has less to do with what they are physiologically than with who we are culturally" (p. 146)—a notion consistent with a social constructionist perspective on disability (e.g., Keith & Keith, 2013; Rapley, 2004). In Chapter 1, we suggested the importance of ecological variables, a capacities approach to disability, a supports paradigm, and person-centered planning as key contributors to QOL. Each of these notions is tied not to immutable characteristics of the person, but rather to the context—including culture—in which the individual lives and interacts. Thus, although there are no doubt etic characteristics of the QOL concept, there are also emic features (Schalock et al., 2005) and potential for cultural bias in QOL measurement (Collinge, Rüdell, & Bhui, 2002). This suggests a critical role for continuing sensitivity to cultural variations.

QOL may be viewed differently across cultures (Hofstede, 1984), and as Mpofu makes clear in Chapter 16 of this volume, the extent to which cultures are relational or individualistic may determine the manner and extent to which supports, as one example, are used to enhance QOL. Yet the broad ideas remain the same: We must attempt to identify the cultural variables capable of enhancing QOL. All people, without regard to individual capacity, should be allowed opportunity to participate in their cultures, and all people should receive the supports necessary to allow such participation. Planning should focus on the individual needs and desires that will enable the person to move toward a satisfying life. These assertions are consistent with the application principles we identified in Chapter 1, and with the United Nations intention to promote international freedom and dignity for people with disability. However, there remain wide discrepancies in the extent to which cultures achieve these aims.

Matsumoto and Juang (2013) observed that the cultural changes occurring over the past century were little short of astounding. Similarly, international work on the QOL of people with ID has expanded dramatically in the past quarter century. As the global community continues to become smaller, we can hope for an ongoing expansion of the role of QOL as a sensitizing concept capable of influencing public policy and cultural practices aimed toward inclusion of all citizens in meaningful participation in the life of their communities.

CHAPTER 18

THE ROLE OF A QUALITY-OF-LIFE THEORY IN A QUALITY-OF-LIFE AGENDA

ROBERT L. SCHALOCK and KENNETH D. KEITH

Introduction and Overview

A QOL theory is based on a conceptual model that explains the QOL concept, organizes knowledge, specifies core QOL domains and indicators, and suggests the relation between QOL domains and personal and environmental variables. In addition, a QOL theory explores how various factors influence the concept, and provides a framework for its application. Thus, a QOL theory is an integrative construct whose definitional, explanatory, and predictive components are used to explain relations, generate hypotheses, and guide application (Schalock et al., 2016).

This chapter discusses a sequential process that integrates the QOL conceptual model presented throughout the text with a theoretically based application framework for QOL that establishes the parameters of a cross-cultural agenda. The chapter has four sections that: (a) describe the components of the QOL conceptual model referenced throughout the text, (b) analyze contextual factors that impact the model's application, (c) discuss the components of a QOL theory, and (d) present an application framework based on the theory. We define a theory as an integrative construct in which investigators arrive at a level of explanation and prediction on the basis of their specific observations and/or systematic inquiries. Furthermore, we stress that a theory is used to generate hypotheses, explain relations, and guide application.

Quality-of-Life Conceptual Model

Our conceptual model of individual QOL, as shown in Figure 18.1, has three components: QOL domains, moderator and mediator variables, and enhancement strategies. The graphics in the figure shaped like cogs denote and depict the connectivity and interactional nature of these three components.

Quality-of-Life Domains

As discussed throughout the text, QOL is a multidimensional phenomenon composed of core domains that constitute personal well-being. The eight core domains depicted in Figure 18.1 were initially synthesized and validated through an extensive review of the international QOL literature in the areas of IDD, special education, behavioral and mental health, and aging (Schalock & Verdugo, 2002). Common to this QOL conceptual model, as well as those promulgated by others, has been the inclusion of QOL domains

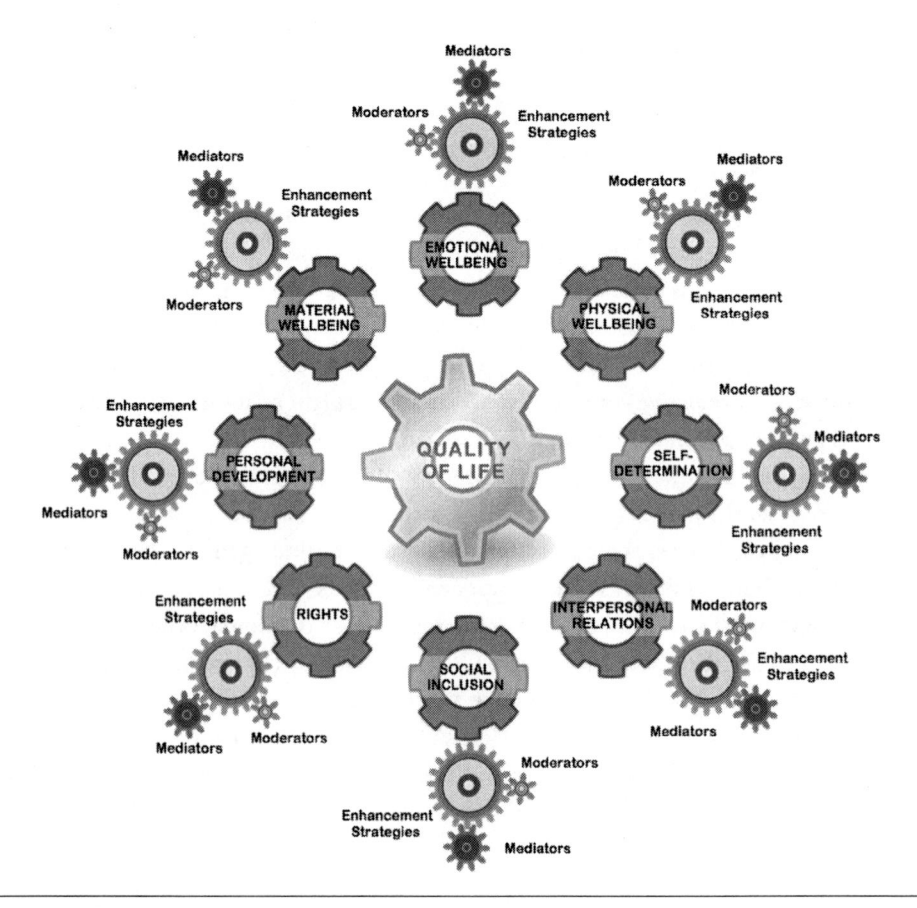

FIGURE 18.1. QOL conceptual model

that are the factors composing personal or family well-being, and quality indicators that are QOL-related perceptions, behaviors, and conditions that give an indication of a person's or family's well-being. The measurement of QOL involves assessing items related to these indicators. The assessment is based on self-report or the report of others.

Moderator and Mediator Variables

The conceptual model that is at the heart of the QOL theory presupposes a contextual understanding of disability as a condition resulting from the interaction of individual and environmental factors. This ecological model of disability also focuses on the congruence between personal competence and environmental demands and opportunities resulting from moderating and mediating variables. A *moderating variable* alters the relation between two variables and thus modifies the form or strength of the relation. A *mediating variable* influences the relation between the independent variable and outcome and exhibits indirect causation, connection, or relation. Moderator and mediator variables will be discussed in more detail later in conjunction with the explanatory component of the QOL theory.

Enhancement Strategies

The third component of our conceptual model involves enhancement strategies that encompass developing personal talents, maximizing personal involvement, providing individualized supports, and facilitating personal growth opportunities.

Contextual Factors

In Chapter 1 we discussed four contextual factors that interface with the QOL concept and affect its evolution and application. As summarized in Figure 18.2, these four contextual factors involve the approach to disability, organization transformation and systems change, professional education and support provider development, and research.

There is currently a concerted effort to understand both the concept of context, and its influence on QOL-related personal outcomes (Shogren et al., 2015). As discussed by Shogren et al. (2014, p. 110), context can be defined as "the totality of circumstances comprising the milieu of human life and human functioning." In understanding the influence of contextual factors on one's QOL, context can be viewed as an independent variable, an intervening variable, or an integrative approach to unifying supports across the micro-, meso-, and macrosystems.

- As an independent variable, context includes personal and environmental characteristics that are not usually manipulated, such as age, language, culture and ethnicity, gender, and family.
- As an intervening variable, context includes personal strengths and assets that can be maximized through personal growth and development opportunities, and

Approach to Disability
- Ecological Model of Disability
- Capacities Approach
- Supports Paradigm
- Person-Centered Planning

Organization Transformation and Systems Change
- High Performance Teams
- Continuous Quality Improvement
- Outcomes Evaluation
- Social Entrepreneurship

Quality-of-Life Concept

Research
- Participatory Action Research
- Evidence-Based Practices
- Methodological Pluralism
- Multivariate Research Designs

Professional Education and Support Provider Development
- Professional Standards
- Professional Ethics
- Critical Thinking Skills
- Best Practices

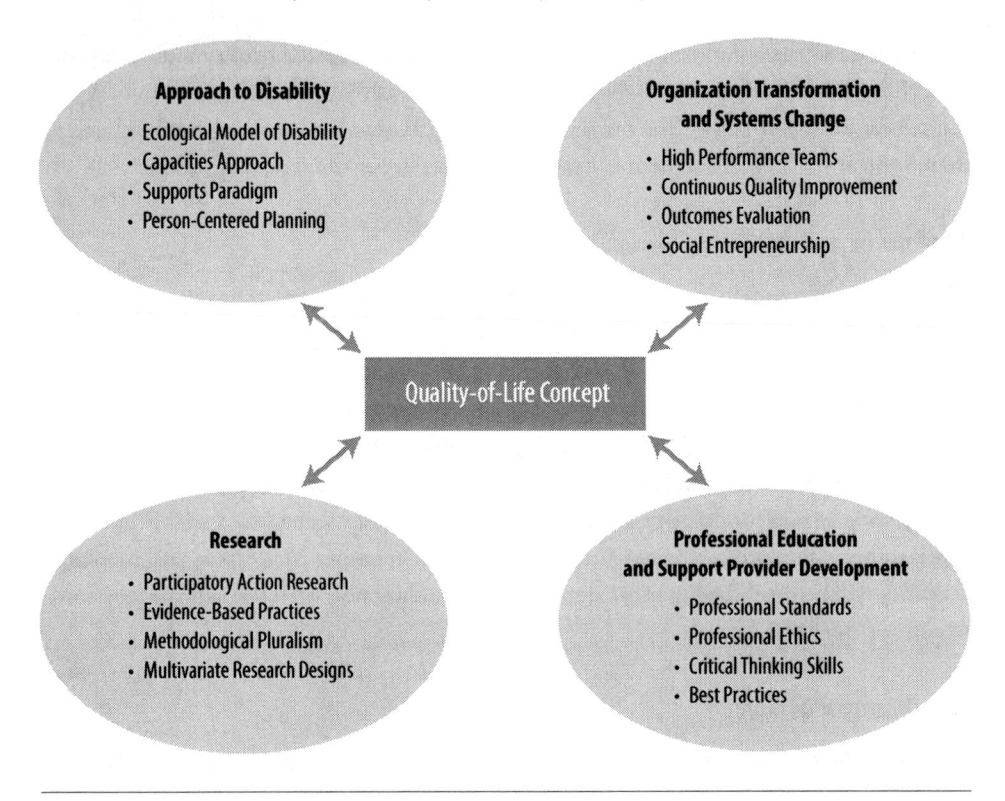

FIGURE 18.2. The context of QOL application

policies and practices at the community, organization, system, and societal level that can be manipulated to enhance personal outcomes.
- As an integrative approach, context provides a framework for describing and analyzing factors that influence personal outcomes such as personal and environmental factors, supports planning, policy development, and integrating systems of supports across ecological systems to enhance the lives of persons with ID. The importance of viewing context from an integrative perspective is that it augments a theoretically-based QOL application framework.

Quality-of-Life Theory Components

As an integrative construct, a QOL theory has various components, at the heart of which is the conceptual model presented in Figure 18.1. The *definitional component* involves "cogs" representing the eight core QOL domains; the *explanatory component* involves moderator and mediator variable "cogs" representing personal characteristics and environmental factors that influence QOL-related personal outcomes; and the *predictive component* involves hypothesis testing and focuses on quality enhancement strategies.

Definitional Component

We define individual QOL as a multidimensional phenomenon composed of core domains that constitute personal well-being. These domains are influenced by personal characteristics and environmental factors. One's QOL is the product of these factors and can be affected positively through public policy, quality enhancement strategies, quality thinking, and outcomes evaluation.

Explanatory Component

The explanatory component involves moderator and mediator variables that presuppose a contextual understanding of disability. A moderator variable alters the relation between two variables, modifying the form or strength of the relation between the two variables. In reference to theory, a *moderator effect* is an interaction in which the effect of one variable is dependent on the level of the other. A moderator variable can be continuous or categorical.

A mediating variable influences the relation between the independent variable and outcome and exhibits indirect causation, connection, or relation. In reference to theory, a *mediating effect* is created when a third factor intervenes between the independent and outcome variable. A mediating variable is generally continuous. The role that these two variables play in the explanatory component of a theory is discussed in Baron & Kenny (1986), Farmer (2012), and McKinnon (2008). A listing of the QOL-related moderator and mediator variables studied to date appears in Table 18.1.

Prediction Component

The prediction component of a QOL theory involves hypothesis testing and focuses on quality enhancement strategies. In focusing on quality enhancement strategies, the emphasis should be on: (a) personal growth opportunities that facilitate the actualization of individual possibilities (Reinders & Schalock, 2014); (b) personal involvement that enhances one's level of motivation through increased self-regulation, autonomy, and self-determination (Schalock, 2004a; Shogren et al., 2014); (c) strategies that reflect

Table 18.1. *QOL-Related Moderator and Mediator Variables Studied To Date*

QOL Moderator/Mediator Class	Specific Variables Studied to Date
QOL Moderators: • Personal demographics • Organization culture • Family-unit factors	• Gender, race, intellectual functioning, adaptive behavior, social-economic status • Level of personal involvement of the client, level of personal growth opportunities • Family income, size of family, family geographical location, religious preference, family structure
QOL Mediators: • Personal status • Provider system • Community factors	• Residential, employment, health, level of self-determination, subjective well-being • Services, individualized supports • Normative expectations, attitudes, media influence

the interplay among individual potential, family and organization policies and practices, and societal-level circumstances (Chiu et al., 2013; Schalock et al., 2007; Schalock & Verdugo, 2008); (d) opportunities that reflect both a capacities approach to people with ID and the notion that development does not only pertain to realized outcomes, but also to the processes involved (Brown et al., 2013; Nussbaum, 2009, 2011); and (e) a system of supports that includes natural supports, technology, prosthetics, education (new skills), environmental accommodation, incentives, personal strengths/assets, and professional services (Schalock & Luckasson, 2014).

Hypotheses can be generated (and subsequently tested) on the basis of the potential impact of moderator and mediator variables and/or quality enhancement strategies. Two examples:

Hypothesis #1: Individualized support strategies related to choices and decision making will increase the QOL domain scores of personal development and self-determination.

Hypothesis #2: An organization that aligns resources with individualized support strategies focusing on the eight QOL domains will achieve enhanced personal outcomes of service recipients.

Testing each hypothesis requires clear operational definitions of both the independent variable (e.g., individualized support strategies and alignment) and the dependent variable (e.g., assessed QOL domains and personal outcomes). The reader is referred to Claes et al. (2012), Gómez et al. (in press), Reinders and Schalock (2014), and Schalock et al. (2016) for additional examples of QOL theory-based hypotheses.

Theoretically Based Application Framework

To summarize what was presented above, a QOL theory is based on a conceptual model that explains the QOL concept and incorporates relevant contextual factors that include moderator and mediator variables and quality enhancement strategies. The conceptual model, which provides the basis for a QOL theory, integrates the three components just discussed: definitional, explanatory, and predictive. As depicted in Figure 18.3, these three components lead to a theoretically based application framework involving policy development, quality enhancement strategies, quality thinking, and research. As we will see in the following chapter, this framework can be used to establish the parameters of a cross-cultural QOL agenda.

Policy Development

Public policy influences practice through its effects at the micro-, meso-, and macrosystem levels. Public policy changes over time and is based on social factors, core concepts of disability, and the changing conception of disability. As Turnbull and Stowe (2014) and Shogren and Turnbull (2010) suggested, *disability core concepts* fall into three overarching principles: constitutional (e.g. life, liberty, equality), ethical (e.g. dignity, family as foundation, community), and administrative (e.g. capacity, individualization, accountability).

Following publication of the CRPD (United Nations, 2006), efforts have been made to relate the 34 articles contained in the Convention to either core disability concepts or QOL domains. In addition to those efforts described in Chapters 11 and 15 of this volume, Shogren and Turnbull (2014) analyzed the congruence between the core disability concepts listed above and the Articles of the CRPD and found a significant overlap, suggesting the international applicability of these core concepts and overarching principles. Similarly, Verdugo et al. (2012) showed the close alignment between the eight core QOL domains listed in Figure 18.1 and the 34 Convention Articles. These findings were the basis for the statement by Buntinx (2013, p. 12) that "It is important to realize that the fundamental values expressed in the QOL concept and the Convention are identical."

Within the context of a QOL theory, policy development needs to integrate values, practices, and outcomes with disability core concepts and the values and principles inherent in the QOL concept. A proposed framework to guide policy development from this perspective appears in Table 18.2.

Quality Enhancement Strategies

Factors that influence the enhancement of QOL are not limited to personal characteristics and circumstances; they include organizational and societal conditions as well. The extent to which programs and services actually contribute to one's QOL depends on the design and performance of formal or informal systems, and the degree to which they involve the individual and the person's social network, provide individualized supports that are based on the individual's personal goals and assessed support needs, and focus on relevant QOL domains.

The direct relation between policy development and quality enhancement strategies is depicted in Figure 18.3 by the unidirectional arrow between the two framework components. The quality enhancement strategies provided need to be aligned with the

Table 18.2. *A Proposed Framework to Guide Policy Development*

Component	Exemplary Indicators
Values	• Life, liberty, equality, dignity, safety, autonomy, self-determination, empowerment, inclusion, equity, family integration
Practices	• Organization services and supports
	• Managerial strategies (e.g. individualization, systems perspective, decision making, supports collaboration and coordination, best practices)
Outcomes	
• Personal and family	• QOL domain scores
• Societal level indicators	• Socio-economic status, health status, subjective well-being
• Organization and systems change indicators	• Funding patterns, program options, service access, systems of supports

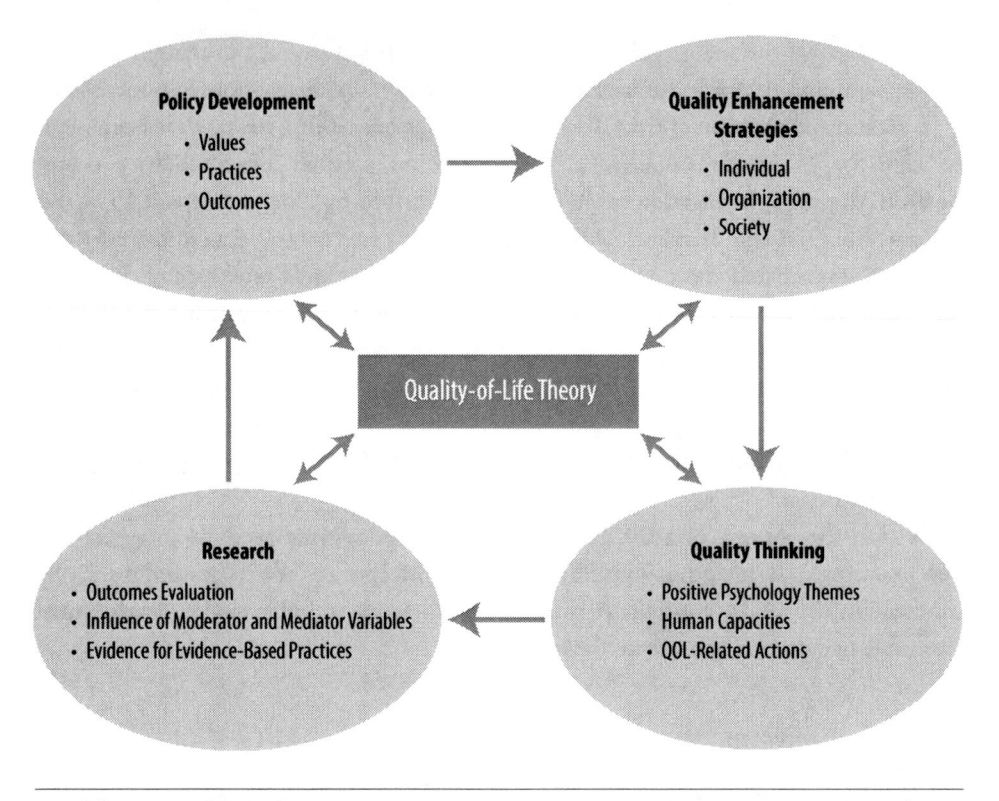

FIGURE 18.3. Application framework

Policy Development
- Values
- Practices
- Outcomes

Quality Enhancement Strategies
- Individual
- Organization
- Society

Quality-of-Life Theory

Research
- Outcomes Evaluation
- Influence of Moderator and Mediator Variables
- Evidence for Evidence-Based Practices

Quality Thinking
- Positive Psychology Themes
- Human Capacities
- QOL-Related Actions

---

policy-related values and practices promulgated by the respective jurisdiction. Table 18.3 provides a listing of exemplary quality enhancement strategies based on the QOL-related principles that play out at the micro-, meso-, and macro-system levels.

Thinking About Quality of Life

The successful application of the QOL concept requires that people engage in a language of QOL thought and action. This engagement is critical in professional education and support provider education. As summarized in Table 18.4, this concept can be organized around the common components of a language of thought (Pinker, 2005), and operationalized through integrating themes from positive psychology (Hart & Sasso, 2011; Lopez & Snyder, 2009), human capacities (Burchardt, 2004, 2008; Nussbaum, 2009, 2011), and QOL-related actions (Schalock & Verdugo, 2014; Schalock et al., 2016; Wehmeyer, 2013).

Research

Research has played a significant role in validating the QOL conceptual model depicted in Figure 18.1, and in explaining the role that moderator and mediator variables play

Table 18.3. *Quality Enhancement Strategies*

Systems Level	QOL-Related Principles	Exemplary QOL Enhancement Strategies
Individual (Microsystem)	Empowerment Skill development Personal involvement	• Decision making, goal setting, self-advocacy • Functional training, use of technology • Participation, inclusion, knowledge sharing
Organization (Mesosystem)	Personal growth opportunities Safe and secure environments Individualized supports	• Integrated environments, social networks • Safety, security, predictability, personal control • Aligning individualized supports to personal goals and assessed support needs
Society (Macrosystem)	Accessibility Attitudes Environmental enrichment	• Human and legal rights • Knowledge and positive interactions • Nutrition, cleaner environments, safer environments, adequate housing and income

Table 18.4. *Quality of Life as a Language of Thought and Action*

Components of a Language of Thought	Positive Psychology Themes	Human Capacities	QOL-Related Actions
A cast of basic concepts	Virtues, character strengths, personality traits, abilities, talents	Life, health, bodily integrity	Equity, inclusion, empowerment, self-determination, human and legal rights
A set of relationships	The good life or the life worth living	Individual, family, social life	Interactions, social networks, community participation, valued roles, positive experiences
A system of spatial concepts	Thriving, flourishing, resilience, adaptive functioning	Participation, influence, voice	Inclusion, active participation, being in and of the community
A family of causal relationships	Developmental processes, actualization of potential	Adequate standard of living, education and learning	Autonomy/personal control/choices, self-advocacy, individualized supports
The concept of a goal	Happiness, positive emotional well-being, fulfillment, quality of life	Legal security, identity, self-expression, self-concept, production, valued activities	Personal outcomes, inclusive education, integrated employment, community living, possessions

in the QOL-related predictors and outcomes summarized in Table 18.1. In a general sense, research efforts related to the QOL concept have explained the complexities of QOL and the complex relations among its properties; generated and tested hypotheses regarding the effect of specific moderator and mediator variables and quality enhancement strategies; and contributed to the growth of information by integrating considerable knowledge regarding personal and environmental factors influencing a life of quality (Schalock et al., 2016).

In pursuing a cross-cultural QOL agenda based in part on a QOL theory, it is important to consider how research can further theoretical and practical developments and provide a guide for the cross-cultural application of the principles embedded in the core QOL domains. In our judgment, QOL-related research can further these goals by focusing on outcomes evaluation and determining the role of moderator and mediator variables in explaining the complexities of QOL.

Outcomes evaluation. Outcomes evaluation involves the assessment of personal, family, or societal changes or benefits that follow as a result or consequence of some activity, intervention, support, or service. Specifically, outcomes evaluation can be used to assess the status of public policy outcomes such as personal and family-related QOL, organization and systems change indicators, and societal-level indicators (Schalock & Verdugo, 2012b; Shogren et al., 2014). In addition, outcomes evaluation can provide: (a) formative feedback that can be used for reporting, benchmarking, monitoring, evaluation, and continuous quality improvement (Schalock et al., 2008; van Loon et al., 2013); and (b) the evidence that is used as the criterion for evidence-based practices (Claes et al., 2015; Schalock et al., 2011).

Influence of moderator and mediator variables. One's QOL is influenced by multiple contextual factors that can be approached empirically from the perspective of moderator or mediator variables. We previously defined a moderator variable as a variable that alters the relation between two variables, and a mediating variable as one that exhibits indirect causation, connection, or relation. Although studying the influence of these two classes of variables can be complex methodologically and statistically, they play a significant role in influencing one's QOL because they encompass personal characteristics, such as capabilities and limitations, and environmental factors, such as social-economic status, societal attitudes, and organization and systems-related policies and practices. The moderator and mediator variables listed in Table 18.1 are a beginning for determining the influence of these variables, but a cross-cultural focus requires that research efforts focus not only on determining the general influence of moderator and mediator variables, but also understanding their cultural relevance and impact.

Conclusion

Four events have significantly influenced the disability field over the last three decades. The first is the ecological model of disability, with its focus on person-environmental interaction and the congruence between personal competence and environmental demands (Schalock & Luckasson, 2014; Shogren et al., 2014). The second is the supports paradigm, based on the assessment of support needs across major life activity areas and the provision of individualized supports that reduce the discrepancy between personal competence and environmental demands (Brown et al., 2013; Nussbaum,

2009, 2011; Thompson et al., 2014). The third is the infusion into the disability field of the principles of positive psychology, including valued subjective experience, positive individual traits, civic values, and QOL (Hart & Sasso, 2011; Wehmeyer, 2013). The fourth is the international recognition of the rights of persons with disabilities and the potential of a conceptual QOL model to operationalize the major articles contained in the CRPD.

A QOL theory should reflect these four events and integrate them into a values-based, person-centered, and systematic approach to services, supports, and outcomes evaluation. How well it does this depends on how well its advocates address the contextual factors depicted in Figure 18.2, and the fidelity of the theory's application. Application fidelity consists of three related factors: adherence, competence, and differentiation (Bigby et al., 2014; Hogue & Dauber, 2013). Adherence refers to the quantity or extent to which the components of a QOL theory are expressed in societal attitudes and public policies, and are delivered within an organization's culture, policies, and practices. Competence, which refers to the quality or skill of delivery, relates directly to developing skills across caregivers, professionals, and organization staff that result in the operationalization and implementation of QOL-related enhancement strategies (Reinders & Schalock, 2014). Differentiation refers to the degree to which application focuses on quality of life and not merely quality of care (DeWaele et al., 2005).

Regardless of its role and effectiveness, a QOL theory should be testable (Bortolotti, 2008; Kuhn, 1970; Newton-Smith, 2001). To that end, it should make accurate predictions; explain factors affecting the lives of persons; guide changes in ID-related practices and outcomes; and allow for theoretical and practical development. The QOL theory described in this chapter meets these criteria, and thereby can serve as a basis for focusing change and implementing quality improvement strategies that lead to an enhanced QOL of persons with ID. In the following chapter we describe how various components of the theory provide a catalyst and guide for the cross-cultural QOL agenda.

CHAPTER 19

SETTING THE CROSS-CULTURAL QUALITY-OF-LIFE AGENDA TO ENHANCE THE LIVES OF PEOPLE WITH INTELLECTUAL DISABILITY

ROBERT L. SCHALOCK and KENNETH D. KEITH

Introduction and Overview

A successful cross-cultural QOL agenda needs to have a clearly stated goal, a rationale reflecting the current zeitgeist, an empirical basis, and a specific plan of action. The goal is reflected in the book's title: "to enhance the lives of people with disabilities." This goal is increasingly possible due to world-wide awareness of the human rights of people with disabilities, and research indicating the close relationship between those rights and QOL-related personal and family outcome categories. The empirical basis for the proposed cross-cultural QOL agenda was summarized in Chapter 17, in the discussion of the global nature of the QOL concept and research indicating its etic and emic properties, and in Chapter 18, in the description of the components of an empirically based QOL theory that provides the definitional, explanatory, and predictive basis for the agenda. The purpose of this chapter is to discuss a proposed plan of action—an agenda—that builds on the material presented in the previous eighteen chapters. The agenda encompasses four components and specific actions regarding policy development, organization and systems transformation, professional education and support provider development, and research.

The proposed cross-cultural QOL agenda will play out within the context of a world in which the global situation for humanity continues to improve in. However, that is not the case for everyone. On the one hand, despite cross-cultural disparities, people around the world are becoming healthier, wealthier, better educated, more peaceful, increasingly more connected, and living longer (Glenn, 2014; Millennium Project, 2013). For people with disabilities—and especially those in low-and middle-income countries (LAMIC)—this scenario is less positive. Here one finds a threat to legal and human rights, poorer health and less access to appropriate health care, and lower rates of education, employment, and adequate housing (Cohen, Brown, & McVilly, 2015; Emerson, 2013; Pelka, 2012; Saxena et al., 2007; WHO and World Bank, 2011). Thus, before discussing the proposed cross-cultural QOL agenda, we need to consider three cross-cultural factors that can act as positive catalysts to enhance the agenda's positive influence on the lives of people with ID and their families. These three factors are global opportunities, the rise of interdependency, and the changing social construction of disability.

Cross-Cultural Catalysts

Global Opportunities

In a recent article titled "The UN Convention on the Rights of Persons with Disabilities: Implementing a Paradigm Shift," Mittler (2015, p. 79) suggested that the CRPD, with the new UN commitment to ensure the inclusion of people with disabilities in the post-2015 Sustainable Development Goals, provide an important catalyst for a radical reappraisal of policies and practices among governments, advocacy groups, organizations and services providing services and supports to people with disabilities, professional organizations, and researchers. Mittler proposed further that such a reappraisal, with accompanying actions, is an overarching priority for organizations and individuals committed to improving the QOL of people with disabilities.

As discussed throughout the preceding chapters, the CRPD is based on a number of principles that provide a framework for focusing global opportunities and thereby enhancing a cross-cultural QOL agenda. These principles include:

- Respect for inherent dignity and individual autonomy
- Equality and nondiscrimination
- Full and active participation and inclusion in society
- Accessibility
- Respect for the evolving capacities of children with disabilities and the right to preserve their identities

CRPD-related global opportunities are further enhanced through a number of UN-related actions associated with implementation of the Convention. Chief among these are: (a) reporting progressive realization of a National Plan for action over a given period of time to the UN Office of the High Commission for Human Rights; (b) establishing guidelines to ensure that people with a disability are explicitly included in the whole range of UN-sponsored aid and development programs; and (c) including in the Sustainable Development Goals the assurance that the needs and benefits of all persons with disabilities will be taken into account in considering poverty eradication, social inclusion, full and productive employment and decent work, and basic social services (Mittler, 2015, pp. 80–82).

Interdependency

The world is becoming more interdependent. As Friedman (2015) noted, an interdependent world comes down to behaviors guided by sustainable values, such as humility, integrity, and respect, that build healthy interdependencies. As a cross-cultural QOL enhancement catalyst, interdependency also:

(a) underlies our concern for the health, welfare, and safety of those around us,
(b) involves the reality that "what is good for all is also good for me," and
(c) results in a vested interest in the lives of our fellow human beings (Matsumoto, 2000).

Interdependency occurs at many levels. For example, a beginning has been made showing the relation between the Articles promulgated in the CRPD and both the core QOL domains and systems-level outcome indicators. Other interdependencies occur when one partners with self-advocates and self-advocacy groups, involving people in decisions that affect their lives and actions, and placing them at the fulcrum of QOL enhancement activities. One also sees interdependency in the person-centered changes occurring in organizations, systems, and professional education and support provider training. Furthermore, interdependency is fostered when research includes consumers and emphasizes evaluation of quality enhancement strategies and determination of personal outcome predictors.

Interdependency is at the heart of the relational world view that encompasses the belief that one "is" because others "are," and that a satisfying life is one in which one is a means of life satisfaction for others (Mpofu, this volume). As Mead (1964a, p. 103) argued, "There must be other selves if one's own is to exist." Accordingly, personal well-being is explained and realized with and for the well-being of self and others, and when relational supports are interlinked to the mutual advantage of self and others. This relational worldview is consistent with the notion of an interdependent construct of self (Markus & Kitayama, 1991), by which the individual is defined in terms of relationships with others. This perspective provides the rationale and basis for community-based rehabilitation (CBR), which is widely used in low- and middle- income countries. The strategy focuses on community development, poverty reduction, equality of opportunities, rehabilitation, promoting and protecting human rights, and the social inclusion of people with disabilities (Mpofu, this volume; WHO, UNESCO, ILO, and International Disability and Development Consortium, 2010).

Social Construction of Disability

The social construction of disability is based on the belief that disability is what a culture says it is (Rapley, 2004). Thus, if a cultural group decides to change its conception of ID, as the American Association on Mental Deficiency (now American Association on Intellectual and Developmental Disabilities) did in 1973, thousands of people may be removed from (or added to) the ranks of those with a disability. In this case, changing the basis of the construct from one to two standard deviations below the average IQ score resulted in a changed label for a large number of people, although the people, of course, did not change at all (Grossman, 1973; Trent, 1994). Thus, as Blatt (1985) asserted, the categories into which we group people are our own inventions, and people are considered to have a disability at least in part because someone said so.

There are still major differences across geographical areas in terms of how cultures conceptualize disability and how they view and treat people with a disability. Some authors in fact have construed disability as a culture in itself (e.g., Conyers, 2003). The social construction of disability is changing to encompass the social-ecological model of disability, human capacities and their enhancement, and the human rights of people with ID (see, for example, Memari & Hofizi, 2015; WHO, 2011), as well as the need for cultural competence in dealing with people with disability (Eddey & Robey, 2005). These changes reflect the influence of international covenants on human rights, positive psychology, the effectiveness of self-advocacy, the supports paradigm, and the QOL movement (Mittler, 2015; Oliver, 1996; Wehmeyer, 2013).

The social construction of disability has the advantage of offering a more optimistic future in which people with ID can have a better life. A social model recognizes that problems do not lie exclusively within the individual; rather, the individual may be disabled or disadvantaged by the environment (e.g., Boxall, 2002). Thus, cross-cultural QOL requires a sensitivity to context—to the local culture—and to working within that cultural context. As Bogdan (1988, p. 146) observed, "How we view people with disabilities has less to do with what they are physiologically than with who we are culturally." And who we are individually is inseparable from our culture (Rapley, 2004).

Cross-Cultural QOL Agenda Components

In the remaining sections of this chapter, we discuss the four components of the plan of action: policy development, organization and systems transformation, professional education and support provider development, and research. These components are depicted in Figure 19.1.

We recognize that these four components must be contextualized to reflect potential differences across countries and cultures. In reference to policy development, for example, the personal outcome domains related to outcomes-driven policy disability goals may need to focus initially on those outcome domains most needed or significantly lacking in

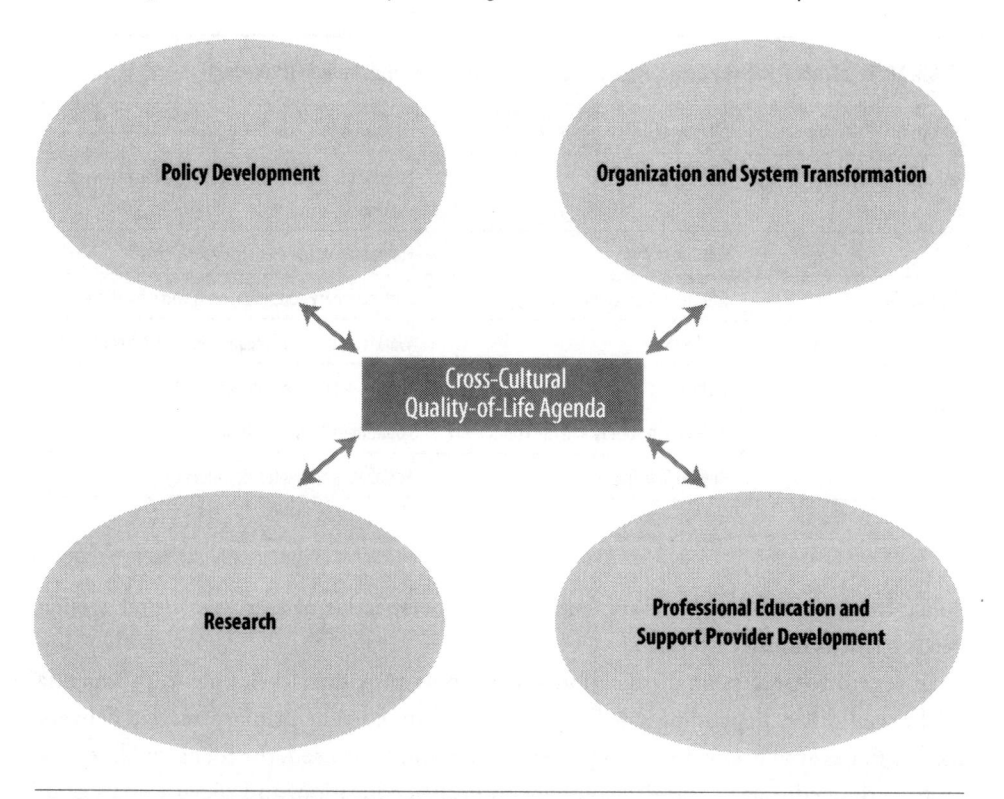

FIGURE 19.1. Cross-cultural QOL agenda components

a particular society. Specifically, human dignity and autonomy as a disability goal might emphasize full citizenship, whereas human endeavor emphasizes well-being, and human engagement focuses on inclusion in society and the community (see Table 19.1).

In reference to organization and systems transformation, social welfare agencies, in partnership with professionals and other NGOs, may work jointly to support health, education, and social welfare staff in providing assistance, services, and supports to people with disabilities and their families (Mannan, MacLachlan, & McAuliffe, 2012; WHO, UNESCO, ILO, & International Disability and Development Consortium, 2010). In addition, organization and systems transformation will be reflected through social entrepreneurship activities and entities that result in creating social value by improving people's lives, building community, and improving society.

Turnbull and Stowe (2014) proposed that disability-related public policy should focus on and promote progressive, *outcomes-driven policy*. As these and other researchers (e.g., Schalock & Verdugo, 2012) have discussed, most public policies related to people with disabilities have historically been based on humane societal concepts and values, and how best to implement value-based policies in terms of resources, statutory changes, service delivery framework, and managerial strategies. Thus, to date there has been more emphasis on process-driven policy formation than on outcomes-driven

Table 19.1. *Disability Policy Goals, Personal Outcome Domains, and Domain Indicators*

Disability Policy Goals	Personal Outcome Domain	Exemplary Outcome Domain Indicators
Human Dignity & Autonomy	Self-Determination	Freedom to make choices, participation in decision making
	Full Citizenship	Fundamental freedoms, privacy, rights
Human Endeavor	Education/Life-Long Learning	Postsecondary education, on-going education
	Productivity	Work/employment, meaningful engagement
	Well-Being	Health and wellness, integrity of the person
Human Engagement	Inclusion in Society and the Community	Community living and inclusion
	Human Relationships	Social networks, inter-dependency

policy formation. Policy development from the perspective of a cross-cultural agenda needs to focus on the latter.

In regard to professional education and support provider development, the agenda might well differ, depending on the country and its current primary service delivery model. For example, in countries where the CBR model is used, the focus will likely be on providing education and development to health, education, and social welfare staff who already work in the community but often lack confidence or motivation to extend their skills to people with disabilities and their families (Mannan et al., 2012; Mittler, 2015). In developed countries where direct support staff provide care, supervision, and supports, the focus will more likely be on team development (Buntinx, 2008) and competency-based training (Bogenschutz, Nord, & Hewitt, 2015).

In developing countries, the focus of research may be on establishing common terminology and data collection, analysis, and reporting (Lysaght, Siska, & Koening, 2015). Elsewhere (and eventually everywhere), research will probably focus on: (a) demonstrating effective approaches to intervention (Tomlinson et al., 2014), (b) determining the moderator and mediator variables that significantly influence QOL outcomes (Schalock et al., 2016), and (c) evaluating the effectiveness and efficiency of the supports paradigm (Thompson et al., 2014).

Policy Development

Policies drive practices, and practices influence people's lives. Currently, the time is right for jurisdictions throughout the world to critically analyze policies toward people with disabilities, and align current and future policies not only with the UN Convention Articles concerning the rights of people with disabilities, but also with the principles underlying the QOL concept—principles that embrace inclusion, equity, self-determination, and empowerment. How jurisdictions do that is critical and requires them to distinguish between process and outcomes. Historically, most public policies related to people with disabilities have entailed process-driven policy formation. This formulation is based on societal concepts and values, and how best to implement these value-based policies in terms to resources, statutory changes, rules and regulations, a service delivery framework, and managerial strategies. Conversely, , outcomes-driven policy formation should delineate the desired outcomes first, and then use right-to-left thinking to develop strategies and rules and regulations to maximize those outcomes (Turnbull & Stowe, 2014). The advantages of a cross-cultural QOL agenda based in part on outcomes-driven policy formation is that policy development as an agenda item reflects the changed vision of persons with ID; incorporates and operationalizes the QOL-related 2006 UN Convention Articles; focuses on personal and family outcomes related to human dignity and autonomy, human endeavors, and human engagement; and establishes clear and unambiguous personal outcome categories for individuals and their families.

The parameters of a QOL outcomes-driven policy framework are provided by three lines of investigation. The first, that of Shogren et al. (2015), is based on an analysis of national (US) and international disability policy statutes and documents. This analysis identified explicitly stated policy goals and related outcomes. As summarized in Table 19.1, these goals and related outcomes are aligned with personal outcome domains and associated indicators that parallel the eight core QOL domains discussed throughout this text. The respective indicator can be used to assess personal outcomes that can be aggregated at the organization, system, and/or national level to evaluate the effects of the respective disability policy goal.

The second line of investigation is based on the work of Verdugo et al. (2012), Bradley et al. (this volume), and Claes et al. (this volume). As envisioned by these authors, the articles of the 2006 UN Convention provide a framework to develop disability-related policy, because they are closely related to the eight consensus core domains of QOL. Although the Convention does not articulate means for implementation that would ensure an enhanced QOL, the Convention Articles can be operationalized through policies related to: (a) person-centered planning with a focus on QOL-related personal outcomes; (b) publication of provider profiles detailing quality-related outcomes; and (c) a program of individualized supports designed to enhance QOL-related personal outcomes and individual rights.

A third line of investigation involves developing policies to build environments that facilitate community integration. For example, Christensen and Byrne (2014) described the "built environment" as one that: provides the setting for human activity; mediates access to community resources, physically and socially; facilitates participation in community life and everyday activities and relationships; provides opportunities for self-determination; and allows individuals to build social capital, engage in competitive employment, and be more independent. This approach echoes the early advice of Throne (1972) that we should make environments exceptional, rather than treat individuals as exceptional.

Organization and System Transformation

The cross-cultural research summarized in Chapters 17 and 18 identified many of the factors that operate at the level of the individual, organization/system, and larger society to influence human functioning and personal and family QOL-related outcomes. Thus, a systems perspective must be used to understand the factors that influence QOL-related outcomes and help set the cross-cultural QOL agenda. Examples at the microsystem level include choices/opportunities, supported decision making, self-advocacy, social networks, social support, and information and assistive technology devices. Examples at the mesosystem level include education; residential and employment opportunities; a person-centered and holistic planning focus; safe, stable and predictable environments; and inclusive community involvement. Examples at the macrosystem level include legal and human rights and protections, community-based alternatives, and systems of support.

Organizations and systems internationally are beginning to transform their policies and practices to successfully address these influencing factors (e.g., Brown & Farber, 2014; Evans, Howlett, Kremer, Simpson, Kayess, & Troller, 2012). At the microsystem level, for example, there is an increasing emphasis on inclusion, equity, self-determination, personal involvement, self-advocacy, personal well-being, and personal outcomes. At the mesosystem level, disability organizations are transforming their service delivery systems along the following lines (Schalock & Verdugo, 2013b): (a) the person as central (e.g. person-centered planning, individualized supports, and personal outcomes); (b) streamlined organizations and the use of horizontally-structured support teams composed of the individual, the person's family/advocate, direct support staff, a supports coordinator, and relevant professionals; and (c) continuous quality improvement that incorporates a learning culture, knowledge generation and sharing, and quality improvement strategies. At the macrosystem level, national policies are increasingly reflecting both a focus on personal and family outcomes and the general principles embedded in the CRPD articles (Mittler, 2015; Shogren & Turnbull, 2010; Turnbull & Stowe, 2013).

Two concepts facilitate organization and systems transformation: contextual analysis and social entrepreneurship. Contextual analysis involves two processes: identifying factors that can be "unfrozen" to overcome resistance to change and enhance the adoption of new practices (Manchester et al., 2014), and using a systematic approach to discrepancy analysis and action planning (Schalock & Verdugo, 2012a). Unfreezing activities involve identifying four factors: change inhibitors, forces that drive change, change promotion strategies, and ways to increase stakeholder participation. The systematic approach involves two steps: (a) use of a logic model (with its input, throughput, and output components) to identify the major discrepancies or disconnects between where one is and where one wants to go in reference to application of the QOL concept and agenda, and (b) development of an action plan that uses a simple planning matrix organized around the four "unfreezing" factors.

Social entrepreneurship represents an innovative approach for dealing cross-culturally with major challenges faced by individuals and their families, organizations, and societies. Social entrepreneurship is a systematic process that builds on values, opportunities, innovation, and maximized resources; involves social entrepreneurial strategies; and results in creating social value by improving peoples' lives, building community, and improving society. Social entrepreneurial strategies involve combining resources in new ways, using resources primarily to explore and exploit opportunities to create social value by stimulating social change or meeting social needs, offering valued services and supports, and transforming current service delivery organizations and systems or creating new ones. Three activities are essential to social entrepreneurship: (a) creating social enterprises that combine the effectiveness and efficiency of a business mindset and the values and mission of not-for-profit organizations; (b) increasing networking that involves partnering to achieve a common goal and offering services and supports through networks composed of for-profit, not-for-profit, and public entities; and (c) building capacity that involves designing and implementing activities related to enhancing the organization's effectiveness and efficiency in terms of supports delivery, resource development, and research and evaluation.

Professional Education and Support Provider Development

Our premise as we address this component of the cross-cultural QOL agenda is that the term "professional" refers to individuals with professional degrees, direct support staff, and CBR personnel who have tacit knowledge and insight based on extensive experience and who are essential in the planning, implementation, monitoring, and evaluation of individual support strategies. Professional education and support provider development involve developing an understanding of what one's professional responsibility is, QOL indicators that can be used to guide observation and judgment, and mental models that can either facilitate or inhibit change.

Professional Responsibility

Professional responsibility starts with respect for the individual and is characterized by giving focused attention to the person, showing concern for the person, emphasizing the person's human and legal rights, and engaging in person-centered practices that facilitate personal well-being. Respect involves supporting personal autonomy, informing people about important matters in their lives, involving people in individual supports planning and provision, providing opportunities for personal development and involvement, and assuring individual emotional, physical, and material well-being. As summarized in Table 19.2, professional responsibility is based on awareness, competence, ethics, and critical thinking skills (Schalock & Luckasson, 2014).

Table 19.2. *Critical Components of Professional Responsibility*

Competency Area	Content Area
Being aware of current international trends impacting the field	• UN Convention on the Rights of Persons with Disabilities • Quality of life concept and its application • Supports paradigm • Consumer empowerment
Being well trained in current best practices	• Best practices are based on current best evidence that is obtained from: (a) credible sources that used reliable and valid methods; and/or (b) information based on a clearly articulated and empirically supported theory or rationale • Best practices encompass: (a) the principles underlying the quality of life concept; and (b) individual support strategies composing a system of support
Acting in accordance with a code of ethics	• Justice (treating all people equitably) • Beneficence (doing good) • Autonomy (respecting the authority of every person to control actions that primarily affect him- or herself
Exercising critical thinking skills	• Analysis: to examine and evaluate component parts of a phenomenon and weigh any contradictory explanation of findings • Alignment: to place or bring processes into a logical sequence of input, throughput, and output • Synthesis: to integrate different types of information and information from multiple sources • Systems thinking: to focus on the multiple factors that affect human functioning at the micro, meso, and macrosystem levels

QOL Indicators

One of the challenges to the success of a cross-cultural QOL agenda is to overcome the belief held by many that the QOL of persons with ID cannot change and improve because their condition precludes development and inclusion. To overcome this misperception, it is essential to educate individuals regarding behaviorally based indicators reflecting growth, development, and change (Bigby et al., 2014; Reinders & Schalock, 2014). These indicators can be used by multiple stakeholders and support providers to guide observations and judgments about the results of personal growth opportunities and the effects of services and supports. An overview of these indicators appears in Table 19.3.

Mental Models

Mental models are deeply ingrained assumptions, generalizations, and images used to understand the world. Mental models form the lens through which one sees the world

Table 19.3. *Quality Indicators of QOL-Related Outcomes*

QOL Domain	Exemplary Outcome-Related Indicators
Personal Development	• People engage in a range of meaningful activities • People try new things and have new experiences
Self-Determination	• People express preferences and make choices • People take part in person-centered planning and other decision-making processes
Interpersonal Relations	• People experience positive and respectful interactions • People are positively regarded by staff
Social Inclusion	• People have a presence in the local community • People have a valued role and are known in the community
Rights	• People are treated with dignity and respect in all their interactions and have privacy • People can physically access transport and community facilities that they would like to or need to access
Emotional Well-Being	• People appear content with and comfortable in their environment • People appear at ease with staff presence and support
Physical Well-Being	• People live healthy lifestyles • People access healthcare promptly when ill
Material Well-Being	• People have their own possessions • People have enough money to afford the essentials and at least some nonessentials

and forms the vision and culture of individuals, organizations, systems, and societies. Mental models can either facilitate or inhibit change. Facilitators include the social-ecological model of disability, the emphasis on social/community inclusion, and the incorporation of values such as equity, self-determination, inclusion, and empowerment into one's thinking and practices. Five mental models that can inhibit change are that professionals know best, individuals with ID have limited capacity, line staff and/or family members lack skills, being around individuals with ID produces a sense of discomfort, and individuals with ID cannot be fully included in the community (Schalock & Verdugo, 2012b).

Because they are deeply ingrained, overcoming these inhibitory mental models presents a challenge. Although not a panacea, incorporating the QOL language of thought and action, described in Table 18.4, into a professional education/support provider development program is promising. Incorporating a QOL-related language of thought and action allows one to integrate positive psychology and the concept of human capacities with QOL-related actions. This integration also facilitates the involvement of people with ID and their families in decisions that affect their lives; in the development, implementation, and monitoring of individualized plans; and in participating in research endeavors.

Research

Research plays a major role in how we conceptualize, measure, and apply the QOL concept. Specifically, research has validated the eight first-order QOL domains; established a measurement framework based on best practices; identified some of the factors (i.e., moderator and mediator variables) influencing QOL-related outcomes; suggested application guidelines related to personal involvement, individualized supports, and personal growth opportunities; and provided an empirical basis for the following definition of individual QOL that can be used as a basis for cross-cultural QOL research.

> QOL is a multidimensional phenomenon composed of core domains that constitute personal well-being. These domains are influenced by personal characteristics and environmental factors that act as moderators or mediators. One's QOL can be enhanced through quality enhancement strategies that encompass personal involvement, individualized supports, and personal growth opportunities.

QOL-related research needs to focus on research priorities at the global level and on gaining a better understanding of the factors influencing QOL outcomes. In reference to the first priority, Tomlinson et al. (2014) described the results of a study involving an international expert group who systematically listed and scored research questions regarding persons with developmental disabilities according to five criteria: answerability, feasibility, applicability and impact, support within the context, and equity. Results indicated clearly "that the important priorities for future research relate to the need for effective and efficient approaches to early intervention, empowering families supporting a person with a developmental disability, and addressing preventable causes of poor health in people with ID and autism" (p. 1121).

As part of a cross-cultural QOL agenda, research should encompass (a) guidelines for QOL-related research, (b) a framework to guide research concerning the factors influencing QOL outcomes, and (c) the components of a supports model that can be used as a framework to determine the influence of individualized supports on personal outcomes.

Research Guidelines

QOL-related research has a rich history, as reflected in the extensive list of references found at the end of this book. Based on this research, we suggest the following six guidelines regarding QOL-related research endeavors:

1. Approach the conceptualization and measurement of QOL from a multidimensional perspective that reflects the etic (i.e., universal) properties of the core QOL domains and the emic (i.e., culture-bound) properties of QOL indicators.

2. Use personal, QOL-related outcomes as dependent variables in multivariate research designs.
3. Evaluate the generalizability of the QOL concept and its application across geographical regions and across cultural and language groups.
4. Determine the factors (i.e., moderator and mediator variables) that affect QOL outcomes.
5. Base QOL theory construction on the etic properties of QOL domains, the emic properties of QOL indicators, and the moderator and mediator variables affecting QOL outcomes.
6. Involve individuals with ID and their families and support providers in research endeavors.

Factors Influencing QOL Outcomes

A basic aspect of the QOL theory discussed in Chapter 18 is that the eight core QOL domains appearing throughout the text are influenced by personal characteristics and environmental factors that act as moderator or mediator variables. As discussed by Schalock, Keith et al. (2010) and Schalock et al. (2016):

- A *moderator variable* alters the relation between two variables and thus modifies the form or strength of the relation between the independent and dependent variable. A moderator effect is an interaction in which the effect of one variable is dependent on the level of the other. A moderator variable can be continuous or categorical.
- A *mediator variable* influences the relation between the independent variable and outcome and exhibits indirect causation, connection, or relation. A mediating effect is created when a third factor intervenes between the independent and outcome variables. A mediating variable is generally continuous.

As summarized in Table 18.1, research efforts to date have identified a number of moderator and mediator variables that effect QOL-related outcomes. Moderator variables include personal demographics, organization culture, and family-unit factors; mediator variables include personal status, [characteristics of the] provider system, and community factors. We suggest that these moderator and mediator variable classes/categories can provide a framework and benchmark to guide subsequent cross-cultural research endeavors to identify the factors influencing QOL outcomes.

Supports Model

The supports paradigm and the provision of individualized supports have become the primary service delivery mechanism throughout much of the world. The use of individual supports to enhance the QOL of individuals with ID as well as to develop an outcomes-driven policy necessitates that researchers have a clear understanding of the

Table 19.4. *A System of Supports Components, Exemplary Strategies, and Potential Outcomes*

System Component	Exemplary Strategy	Potential Outcomes
Natural supports	Support networks (e.g. family, friends, colleagues, generic agencies)	Increased social inclusion, interpersonal relations, social-emotional well-being
Technology based	Assistive and information technology	Increased cognitive functioning, self-determination, and life-long learning
Education and training	Universal design for learning	Enhanced adaptive behavior and personal functioning
Environmental accommodation	Smart homes, modified transportation, job accommodation	Enhanced personal development, community living, and integrated employment
Incentives	Involvement, recognition, personal goal setting	Increased motivation and achievement
Personal strengths	Incorporating interests, skills and knowledge, and positive attitudes into support plans	Increased self-regulation, autonomy, and self-determination
Professional Services	Access to allied health services	Increased personal development, physical and behavioral health, interpersonal relations, and emotional well-being

components of a system of supports, specific support strategies associated with each component, and the intended outcome of the specific support strategy. Table 19.4 provides an overview/summary of these factors.

Conclusion

Our purpose in this concluding chapter is to assist readers in seeing that the opportunity is here to enhance the quality of life of people with disabilities. Perhaps for the first time, there are strong cross-cultural factors that will facilitate the process. These are the three cross-cultural catalysts we discussed earlier in the chapter: global opportunities, the rise of interdependency, and the changing social construction of disability. In addition, the agenda framework provided allows policy makers, service delivery system administrators, support providers, and researchers to see how these catalysts can apply to policy development, organization and systems transformation, professional education and support provider development, and research. And finally, we have suggested a number of strategies that assist readers to align agenda components with outcomes-driven policy formation (Table 19.1), professional responsibility (Table 19.2), and systems of supports (Table 19.4).

The world is complex, and the needs and situations facing individuals with ID and their families, service providers, service delivery systems, and the larger society are not only complex, they are also extremely challenging. Our goal in developing this book, and drawing on the experiences, knowledge, and wisdom of its contributors, is that its content and vison will provide insight into where we have been, where we are, and where we need to go to enhance cross-culturally the QOL of persons with intellectual and closely related developmental disabilities. It's a big challenge, but a worthy goal. A strong foundation has been laid through the significant work of those who have contributed to this book and to so many others who are referenced throughout the text.

It is now up to each of us to continue those journeys described throughout the text. Just as the first edition of this book was a snapshot of how we viewed and approached the concept of QOL in 2000, the current text is a snapshot of how we view the concept today.

QOL is not static; nor should a cross-cultural QOL agenda be inflexible and never changing. We all know that over the next fifteen years progress will continue in how we conceptualize, measure, and apply the QOL concept. As our thinking and actions evolve, it is important that we not get locked into today's model. We need to be creative, stand outside the box, build on the knowledge that local and global opportunities provide us, and be open to new ideas and strategies to enhance the quality of life of everyone.

REFERENCES

Abbott, S., & McConkey, R. (2006). The barriers to social inclusion as perceived by people with intellectual disabilities. *Journal of Intellectual Disabilities, 10*(3), 275–287.

Abery, B., Stancliffe, R., Smith, Dunlap, G., Kincaid, D., & Jackson, D. (2013). Positive behavior supports: Foundations, systems, and quality of life. In M. Wehmeyer (Ed.), *The Oxford handbook of positive psychology and disability* (pp. 303–316). Oxford, UK: Oxford University Press.

Agran, M., King-Sears, M, Wehmeyer, M. L., & Copeland, S. R. (2003). *Teachers' guides to inclusive practices: Student-directed learning strategies*. Baltimore, MD: Paul H. Brookes.

AIRIM (2010). Guidelines: Definition of standards for quality to project live outcomes for people with intellectual and developmental disabilities. Brescia, Italy: Vannini.

Albert, B. A., Dube, S. K., & Hansen, T. C. (2005). Has disability been mainstreamed into development cooperation? Disability Knowledge and Research Programme. Retrieved 11 December 2015 from: http://www.disabilitykar.net/research/red-poverty.html

Albuquerque, C. P. (2012). Psychometric properties of the Portuguese version of the Quality of Life Questionnaire (QOL-Q). *Journal of Applied Research in Intellectual Disabilities, 25*, 445–454.

Allard M. A., Howard, A. M., Vorderer, L. E., & Wells, A. I. (Eds.). (1999). *Ahead of his time: Selected speeches of Gunnar Dybwad*. Washington, DC: American Association on Mental Retardation.

Antaki, C., & Rapley, M. (1996). "Quality of life" talk: The liberal paradox of psychological testing. *Discourse & Society, 7*, 293–316.

Aristotle (1962). *Nichomachean ethics* (M. Ostwald, Trans.). Indianapolis, IN: Bobbs-Merrill (original work c. 325 BCE).

Aristotle (1988). *Politics* (S. Everson, Trans.). Cambridge, UK: Cambridge University Press (original work c. 350 BCE).

Arnold, S. R. C. (2016). *The conceptualisation and measurement of support needs.* Unpublished doctoral dissertation, University of Sydney, Sydney, NSW, Australia.

Arnold, S. R. C., & Riches, V. C. (2013). *I-CAN: Instrument for the Classification and Assessment of Support Needs, instruction manual V5.075.* Sydney, Australia: Centre for Disability Studies, University of Sydney.

Arnold, S. R. C., Riches, V. C., & Stancliffe, R. J. (2011). Intelligence is as intelligence does: Can additional support needs replace disability? *Journal of Intellectual & Developmental Disability, 36,* 254–258.

Arnold, S. R. C., Riches, V. C., Parmenter, T. R., & Stancliffe, R. J. (2009). The I-CAN: Using e-health to get people the support they need. *Electronic Journal of Health Informatics, 4*(1), e4.

Arnold, S. R. C., Riches, V. C., & Stancliffe, R. J. (2014). I-CAN: The classification and prediction of support needs. *Journal of Applied Research in Intellectual Disabilities, 27*(2), 97–111.

Arnold, S. R. C., Riches, V. C., & Stancliffe, R. J. (in press, accepted 7/9/14). Does a measure of support needs predict funding need better than a measure of adaptive and maladaptive behavior? *American Journal on Intellectual and Developmental Disabilities.*

Aznar, A. S., & González Castañón, D. (2005). Quality of life from the point of view of Latin American families: a participative research study. *Journal of Intellectual Disability Research, 49*(10):784–788.

Aznar, A. S., González Castañón, D., & Olate, G. (2012). *The ITINERIS Scale on the Rights of Persons with Intellectual Disabilities:* Development, pilot studies and application at a country level in South America. *Journal of Intellectual Disability Research, 56*(11), 1046–1057.

Azuma, H., & Kashiwagi, K. (1987). Descriptions for an intelligent person: A Japanese study. *Japanese Psychological Research, 29,* 17–26.

Bachrach, L. L. (1976). *Deinstitutionalization: An analytical review and sociological perspective.* DHEW Publication No. (ADM) 786-351. Washington, DC: U.S. Government Printing Office, Washington, D.C.

Balboni, G., Coscarelli, A., Giuntia, G., & Schalock, R. L. (2013). The assessment of the quality of life of adults with intellectual disability: The use of self-report and report of others assessment strategies. *Research in Developmental Disabilities, 34,* 4248–4254.

Baron, R. M., & Kenny, D. A. (1986). The moderator-mediator variable distinction in social psychological research: Conceptual, strategic, and statistical considerations. *Journal of Personality and Social Psychology, 51,* 1173–1182.

Beach Center on Disability (2005). *The Beach Center Family Quality of Life Scale.* Lawrence, KS: The University of Kansas, in partnership with families, service providers, and researchers.

Beadle-Brown, J., Hutchinson, A., & Whelton, B. (2012). Person-centred active support—increasing choice, promoting independence and reducing challenging behaviour. *Journal of Applied Research in Intellectual Disabilities, 25*(4), 291–307.

Bell, B. (2014, August 5). The global disability rights movement: Winning power, participation, and access. *The Huffington Post* (p. 3).

Bentham, J. (1798). *An introduction to the principles of morals and legislation.* London, UK: British Library, Historical Print Editions.

Berkson, G. (2006). Mental disabilities in western civilization from ancient Rome to the Prerogativa Regis. *Mental Retardation, 44,* 28–40.

Bérubé, M. (2010). Equality, freedom, and/or justice for all: A response to Martha Nussbaum. In E. F. Kittay & L. Carlson (Eds.), *Cognitive disability and its challenge to moral philosophy* (pp. 97–109). Chichester, UK: Wiley-Blackwell.

Bigby, C., Knox, M., Beatle-Brown, J., & Bould, E. (2014). Identifying good group homes: Qualitative indicators using a quality of life framework. *Intellectual and Developmental Disabilities, 52*(5), 348–366.

Bigby, C., Knox, M., Beadle-Brown, J., Clement, T., & Mansell, J. (2012). Uncovering dimensions of culture in underperforming group homes for people with severe intellectual disability. *Intellectual and Developmental Disabilities, 50,* 452–467.

Blatt, B. (1981). How to destroy lives by telling stories. *Journal of Psychiatric Treatment and Evaluation, 3,* 183–191.

Blatt, B. (1985). The implications of the language of mental retardation for LD. *Journal of Learning Disabilities, 18,* 625–626.

Blatt, B. (1987). *The conquest of mental retardation.* Austin, TX: Pro-Ed.

Blatt, B., & Kaplan, F. (1966). *Christmas in Purgatory: A Photographic Essay on Mental Retardation.* Boston, MA: Allyn & Bacon.

Bogdan, R. (1988). *Freak show: Presenting human oddities for amusement and profit.* Chicago, IL: The University of Chicago Press.

Bogenschutz, M., Nord, D., & Hewitt, A. (2015). Competency-based training and worker turnover in community supports for people with IDD: Results from a group randomized controlled study. *Intellectual and Developmental Disabilities, 53,* 182–195.

Bonham, G. S., Basehart, S., Schalock, R. L., Marchand, C. B., Kirchner, N., & Rumenap, J. M. (2004). Consumer-based quality of life assessment: The Maryland Ask Me! Project. *Mental Retardation, 42,* 338–355.

Bonn, G., & Tafarodi, R. W. (2013). Visualizing the good life: A cross-cultural analysis. *Journal of Happiness Studies, 14,* 1839–1856.

Bortolotti, L. (2008). *An introduction to the philosophy of science.* Malden, MA: Piloty Press.

Boxall, K. (2002). Individual and social models of disability and the experiences of people with learning difficulties. In D. G. Race (Ed.), *Learning disability—A social approach* (pp. 209–226). London, UK: Routledge.

Bradley, V. (1978). *Deinstitutionalization of developmentally disabled persons: A conceptual analysis and guide.* Baltimore, MD: University Press.

Bradley, V. (1986). *Conduct of a two year longitudinal study of services to developmentally disabled persons in New Hampshire (1984–1986)*. Retrieved on 2/17/15 from http://www.hsri.org/project/conduct-of-a-two-year-longitudinal-study-of-services-to-developmentally-dis/overview/

Bradley, V. (1996). Foreword in J. Mansell and K. Ericsson (Eds). *Deinstitutionalization and community living: Intellectual disability services in Scandinavia, Britain and the USA* (pp. 1–9). London, UK: Chapman and Hall.

Bradley, V., Feinstein, C., Lemanowicz, J., & Allard, M. (1992). *Results of the survey of current and former Belchertown residents and their families*. Retrieved on 2/17/15 from http://www.hsri.org/files/uploads/publications/378_Results_of_the_Survey_of_Current_and_Former_Belchertown_Residents_and_Their_Families.pdf

Bradley, V., & Pell, E. (2012). *Using National Core Indicators (NCI) data for quality improvement initiatives*. Retrieved 2/17/15 from http://www.nationalcoreindicators.org/upload/core-indicators/using_national_core_indicators_data.pdf

Bramston, P., Bruggerman, K., & Petty, G. (2002). Community perspectives and subjective quality of life. *International Journal of Disability, Development and Education*, 49, 385–397.

Brown, B. B. (1968). *Delphi process: A methodology used for the elicitation of opinions of experts*. Rand document nr. P-3925. Santa Monica, CA: The Rand Corporation.

Brown, H. K., Ouellette-Kuntz, H., Bielska, I., & Elliott, D. (2009). Choosing a measure of support need: implications for research and policy. *Journal of Intellectual Disability Research*, 53, 949–954. doi: 10.1111/j.1365-2788.2009.01216.x.

Brown, I. (2009). *The boy in the moon: A father's journey to understand his extraordinary son*. New York, NY: St. Martin's Press.

Brown, I., & Brown, R. (2003). *Quality of life and disability: An approach for community practitioners*. London, UK: Jessica Kingsley Publishers.

Brown, I., Brown R., Baum, N. T., Isaacs, B. J., Myerscough, T., Neikrug, S., et al. (2006). *Family Quality of Life Survey: Main Caregivers of People with Intellectual or Developmental Disabilities*. Toronto, Canada: Surrey Place Centre.

Brown, I., Hatton, C., & Emerson, E. (2013). Quality of life indicators for individuals with intellectual disabilities: Extending current practices. *Intellectual and Developmental Disabilities*, 51, 316–332.

Brown, I., Keith, K. D., & Schalock, R. L. (2004). Quality of life conceptualization, measurement, and application: Validation of the SIRG-QOL consensus principles. *Journal of Intellectual Disability Research*, 48, 451.

Brown, R. I. (Ed.). (1997). *Quality of life for people with disabilities: Models, research, and practice*. Cheltenham, UK: Stanley Thornes.

Brown, R, I., Bayer, M. B., & MacFarlane, C. (1989). *Rehabilitation programmes: Performance and quality of life of adults with developmental handicaps. Vol. I*. Toronto, Canada: Lugus Productions Ltd.

Brown, R. I., Cobigo, V., & Taylor, W. D. (2015). Quality of life and social inclusion across the lifespan: Challenges and recommendations. *International Journal of Developmental Disabilities, 61*, 93–100.

Brown, R. I., & Faragher, R. (2014) (Eds.). *Quality of life and intellectual disability: Knowledge applications to other social and educational challenges.* New York, NY: Nova Science.

Brown, R. I., Hong, K., Shearer, J., Wang, M., & Wang, S. (2010). Family quality of life in several countries: Results and discussion of satisfaction in families where there is a child with a disability. In R. Kober (Ed.), *Enhancing the quality of life of people with intellectual disability: From theory to practice* (pp. 255–264). Dordrecht, Netherlands: Springer.

Bruininks, R. H., Hill, B., Weatherman, R., & Woodcock, R. (1986). *The Inventory for Client and Agency Planning.* Allen, TX: DLM Teaching Resources.

Buntinx, W. (2008). The logic of relations and the logic of management. *Journal of Intellectual Disability Research, 52,* 588–597.

Buntinx, W. H. E. (2013). Disability: A strength-based approach. In M. L. Wehmeyer (ed.), *The Oxford handbook of positive psychology and disability* (pp. 7–18). New York, NY: Oxford University Press.

Buntinx, W. H. E., & Schalock, R. L. (2010). Models of disability, quality of life, and individualized supports: Implications for professional practice in intellectual disability. *Journal of Policy and Practice in Intellectual Disabilities, 7*(4), 283–294.

Burchardt, T. (2004). Capabilities and disability: The capacities framework and the social model of disability. *Disability and Society, 19,* 735–751.

Burchardt, T. (2008). Monitoring inequality: Putting the capacity approach to work. In G. Craig, T. Burchardt, & D. Gordon (Eds.), *Social justice and public policy* (pp. 205–229). Bristol, UK: Policy Press.

Burton-Smith, R., McVilly, K. R., Yazbeck, M., Parmenter, T. R., & Tsutsui, T. (2009). Quality of life of Australian family careers: Implications for research, policy, and practice. *Journal of Policy and Practice in Intellectual Disabilities, 6,* 189–198.

Caballo, C., Crespo, M., Jenaro, C., Verdugo, M. A., & Martinez, J. L. (2005). Factor structure of the *Schalock and Keith Quality of Life Questionnaire (QOL-Q)*: Validation on Mexican and Spanish samples. *Journal of Intellectual Disability Research, 49,* 773–776.

Campbell, A. (1976). Subjective measures of well-being. *American Psychologist, 31,* 117–124.

Campbell, A., Converse, P. E., & Rodgers, W. L. (1976). *The quality of American life: Perceptions, evaluations, and satisfactions.* New York, NY: Russell Sage Foundation.

Carbonell, E. (Ed.). (1999). *El constructe de qualitat de vida.* [The quality of life construct]. Barcelona, Spain: Coordinara de Tallers per a Minusvàlíds Psíquics de Catalunya.

Carlson, L. (2010). *The faces of intellectual disability: Philosophical reflections.* Bloomington, IN: Indiana University Press.

Cavagnola, R., Corti, S., Fioriti, E., Leoni, M., & Lombardi, M. (2015). *Assessment preference for people with profound and multiple disabilities*. Brescia, Italy: Sospiro.

CBR African Network (2004). Community based rehabilitation. Kyambogo, Uganda: Author.

Chiu, C., Kyzar, K., Zuna, N., Turnbull, A., Summers, J. A., & Gomez, V. A. (2013). Family quality of life. In M. Wehmeyer (Ed.), *The Oxford handbook of positive psychology and disability* (pp. 365–392). New York, NY: Oxford University Press.

Chng, J. P. L., Stancliffe, R. J., Wilson, N. J., & Anderson, K. (2013) Engagement in retirement: An evaluation of the effect of Active Mentoring on engagement of older adults with intellectual disability in community activities. *Journal of Intellectual Disability Research. 57*(12), 1130–1142.

Chowdhury M., & Benson, B. A. (2011). Deinstitutionalization and quality of life of individuals with intellectual disability: A review of the international literature. *Journal of Policy and Practice in Intellectual Disabilities, 8*, 256–265.

Christensen, K. M., & Byrne, B. C. (2014). The built environment and community integration: A review of states' Olmstead plans. *Journal of Disability Policy Studies, 25*, 186–195.

Christianson, A. L., Zwane, M. E., Manga, P., Rosen, E., Venter, A., Downs, D., & Kromberg, J. G. R. (2002). Children with intellectual disability in rural South Africa: Prevalence and associated disability. *Journal of Intellectual Disability Research, 46*, 179–186.

Claes, C., Vandevelde, S., Van Hove, G., van Loon, J., Verschelden, G., & Schalock, R. L. (2012). Relationship between self-report and proxy ratings on assessed personal quality of life-related outcomes. *Journal of Policy and Practice in Intellectual Disabilities, 9*, 159–165.

Claes, C., Van Hove, G., Vandevelde, S., van Loon, J., & Schalock, R. L. (2010). Person-centered planning: analysis of research and effectiveness. *Intellectual and Developmental Disabilities, 48*(6), 432–453.

Claes, C., van Hove, G., Vandevelde, S., van Loon, J., & Schalock, R. L. (2012). The influence of support strategies, environmental factors, and client characteristics on quality of life-related outcomes. *Research in Developmental Disabilities, 33*, 96–103.

Claes, C., van Hove, G., van Loon, J., Vandevelde, S., & Schalock, R. L. (2009). Quality of life measurement in the field of intellectual disabilities: Eight principles for assessing quality of life-related personal outcomes. *Social Indicators Research, 98*, 61–72.

Cohen, L. G., Brown, R. I., & McVilly, K. R. (2015). Guest editorial: The World Report on Disability: Challenges to application and translation to individuals with intellectual and developmental disabilities. *Journal of Policy and Practice in Intellectual Disabilities, 12*, 77–78.

Coleridge, P. (2007). Economic empowerment. In: T. Barron and P. Amerena (Eds.), *Disability and inclusive development* (pp. 111–154). London, UK: Leonard Cheshire Disability.

Collinge, A., Rüdell, K., & Bhui, K. (2002). Quality of life assessment in non-Western cultures. *International Review of Psychiatry, 14,* 212–218.

Community Living Authority Act [SBC 2004] CHAPTER 60 – Retrieved from http://www.bclaws.ca/civix/document/id/complete/statreg/04060_01, 2004

Confucius (2003). *The analects* (E. Slingerland, Trans.). Indianapolis, IN: Hackett. (original work c. 500 BCE, probably by students of Confucius).

Conroy, J., & Bradley, V. (1985). *The Pennhurst longitudinal study: A report of five years of research and analysis.* Retrieved 2/17/15 from http://www.nasddds.org/uploads/documents/PennhurstStudy.pdf

Conyers, L. M. (2003). Disability culture: A cultural model of disability. *Rehabilitation Education, 17,* 139–154.

Cordoba-Andrade, L., Gomez-Benito, J., & Verdugo-Alonso, M. A. (2008). Family quality of life of people with a disability: A comparative analysis. *Universitas Psychologica, 7,* 369–383.

Costanza, R., Fisher, B., Ali, S., Beer, C., Bond, L., Boumans, R., . . . & Snapp, R. (2007). Quality of life: An approach integrating opportunities, human needs, and subjective well-being. *Ecological Economics, 61,* 267–276.

Costanza, R., Fisher, B., Ali, S., Beer, C., Bond, L., Boumans, R., . . . & Snapp, R. (2008). An integrative approach to quality of life measurement, research, and policy. *S.A.P.I.E.N.S, 1,* 17–21.

Council on Quality and Leadership. (1997). *Personal outcome measures.* Towson, MD: Author.

Croce, L., Cosimo, F. D., & Lombardi, M. (in press). *A short history of disability aspects from Italy in international history of disability.* Toronto, Canada: University of Toronto Press.

Croce, L., Lombardi, M., Claes, C., & Vandevelde, S. (2014). *Psychometric properties of Personal Outcome Scale Children version.* Paper presented at the 4th IASSID Europe Congress: Pathways to Inclusion, Vienna, Austria.

Cummins, R. A. (1995). Assessing quality of life. In R. I. Brown (Ed.), *Quality of life for handicapped people* (pp. 102–120). London, UK: Chapman & Hall.

Cummins, R. A. (1997). *Comprehensive Quality of Life Scale—Intellectual Disability* (5th ed.). Melbourne, Australia: Deakin University Press.

Cummins, R. A. (2001). The subjective well-being of people caring for a family member with a severe disability at home: A review. *Journal of Intellectual & Developmental Disability, 26,* 83–100.

Cummins, R. A. (2002a). Proxy responding for subjective well-being: A review. *International Review of Research in Mental Retardation, 25,* 183–207.

Cummins, R. A. (2002b). The validity and utility of subjective quality of life: A reply to Hatton & Ager. *Journal of Applied Research in Intellectual Disabilities, 15,* 261–268.

Cummins, R. A. (2004). Instruments for assessing quality of life. In J. H. Hogg and A. Langa (Eds.), *Approaches to the assessment of adults with intellectual disabilities: A service providers guide* (pp. 132–152). London, UK: Blackwell.

Danforth, S. (2008). John Dewey's contributions to an educational philosophy of intellectual disability. *Educational Theory, 58,* 45–62.

Davis, K., & Gavidia-Payne, S. (2009). The impact of child, family, and professional support characteristics on the quality of life in families of young children with disabilities. *Journal of Intellectual & Developmental Disability, 34,* 153–162.

D'Eath, M., Walls, M., Hodgins, M., & Cronin, M. (2003). *Quality of life of young people with intellectual disability in Ireland.* Dublin, Ireland: National Disability Authority.

Descartes, R. (1952). *Meditations* (L. LaFleur, Trans.). Upper Saddle River, NJ: Prentice Hall (original work published 1641).

Developmental Disabilities Assistance and Bill of Rights Act of 1987, Pub. L. 100-146 (1987), U.S.C. 6000, 101 Stat. 840

Devlieger, P. J. (1998). (In) competence in America in comparative perspective. In R. Jenkins (Ed.). *Questions of competence* (pp. 54–75). Cambridge, UK: Cambridge University Press.

De Waele, I., & Van Hove, G. (2005). Modern times: an ethnographic study on the quality of life of people with a high support need in a Flemish residential facility. *Disability and Society, 20*(6), 625–639.

DeWaele, I., van Loon, J., van Hove, G., & Schalock, R. L. (2005). Quality of life vs. quality of care. Implications for people and programs. *Journal of Policy and Practice in Intellectual Disabilities, 2,* 229–239.

Dewey, J. (1922). *Human nature and conduct.* New York, NY: The Modern Library.

Dewey, J. (1957). *Reconstruction in philosophy.* Boston, MA: Beacon Press (original work 1920).

Dudley, M., & Gale, F. (2002). Psychiatrists as moral community? Psychiatry under the Nazis and its contemporary relevance. *Australian and New Zealand Journal of Psychiatry, 36,* 585–594.

Dunlap, G., Kincaid, D., & Jackson, D. (2013). Positive behavior support: Foundations, systems, and quality of life. In M. L. Wehmeyer (Ed.), The Oxford handbook of positive psychology and disability (pp. 303–316). Oxford, UK: Oxford University Press.

Dutch Coalition on Disability and Development (2005). *Human Rights for 139 Persons with Disabilities.* Retrieved October 13, 2013, from, http://aidslex.org/site_documents/DB-0042E.pdf

EASPD (2013). *EASPD renews commitment to de-institutionalisation.* Retrieved December 12, 2014 from http://www.easpd.eu/en/content/easpd-renews-commitment-de-institutionalisation

Eddey, G. E., & Robey, K. L. (2005). Considering the culture of disability in cultural competence education. *Academic Medicine, 80,* 702–712.

Edgerton, R. B. (1996). A longitudinal-ethnographic research perspective on quality of life. In R. L. Schalock (Ed.), *Quality of life, vol. I: Conceptualization and measurement* (pp. 83–90). Washington, DC: American Association on Mental Retardation.

Emerson, E. (2007). Poverty and people with intellectual disabilities. *Mental Retardation and Developmental Disabilities Research, 13*, 1007–1013.

Emerson, E. (2013). Commentary: Childhood exposure to environmental adversity and the well-being of people with intellectual disabilities. *Journal of Intellectual Disability Research, 57*, 589–600.

Emerson, E., Felce, D., & Stancliffe, R. J. (2013). Issues concerning self-report data and population-based data sets involving people with intellectual disabilities. *Intellectual and Developmental Disabilities, 51*, 333–348.

Emerson, E., Hatton, C., Llewellyn, G., Blacher, J., & Graham, H. (2006). Socioeconomic position, household composition, health status and indicators of the well-being of mothers of children with and without intellectual disabilities. *Journal of Intellectual Disability Research, 50*, 862–873.

Emerson, E., & Parish, S. (2010). Intellectual disability and poverty: Introduction to the special section. *Journal of Intellectual & Developmental Disability, 35*, 221–223.

Enea-Drapeau, C., Huguet, P., & Carlier, M. (2014). Misleading face-based judgment of cognitive level in intellectual disability: The case of trisomy 21 (Down syndrome). *Research in Developmental Disabilities, 35*, 3598–3605.

Evans, E. C. (1945). Galen the physician as physiognomist. *Transactions and Proceedings of the American Philological Association, 76*, 374–382.

Evans, E., Howlett, S., Kremser, I., Simpson, J., Kayess, R., & Trollor, J. (2012). Service development for intellectual disability mental health: A human rights approach. *Journal of Intellectual Disability Research, 56*, 1098–1109.

Farmer, C. (2012). Demystifying moderators and mediators in intellectual and developmental disabilities research: A primer and review of the literature. *Journal of Intellectual Disability Research, 56*, 1148–1160.

Felce, D. (1997). Defining and applying the concept of quality of life. *Journal of Intellectual Disability Research, 41*, 126–135.

Felce, D. (2000). Engagement in activity as an indicator of quality of life in British research. In K. D. Keith & R. L. Schalock (Eds.), *Cross-cultural perspectives on quality of life* (pp. 173–190). Washington, DC: American Association on Mental Retardation.

Felce, D., & Emerson, E. (2000). Observational methods in assessment of quality of life. In T. Thompson, D. Felce, & F. J. Symons (Eds.), *Behavioral observation: Technology and applications in developmental disabilities* (pp. 159–174). Baltimore, MD: Paul H. Brookes.

Felce, D. (1997). Defining and applying the concept of quality of life. *Journal of Intellectual Disability Research, 41*, 126–135.

Fernald, W. E. (1902). The Massachusetts farm colony for the feeble-minded. In I. C. Barrows (Ed.), *Proceedings of the national conference of charities and correction, twenty-ninth annual session* (pp. 487–490). Boston, MA: George H. Ellis Co.

Ferdinand, R., & Marcus, J. (2002). Doing what we had to do in the 1950s: Parents build the foundation. In R. L. Schalock (Ed.), *Out of the darkness and into the light:*

Nebraska's experience with mental retardation (pp. 123–134). Washington, DC: American Association on Mental Retardation.

Fesmire, S. (2003). *John Dewey & moral imagination*. Bloomington, IN: Indiana University Press.

Flaherty, J. A., Gaviria, F. M., Pathak, D., Mitchell, T., Wintrob, R., Richman, J., & Birz, S. (1988). Developing instruments for cross-cultural psychiatric research. *Journal of Nervous and Mental Disease, 176*(5), 257–263.

Forrester-Jones, R., Carpenter, J., Coolen-Schrijner, P., Cambridge, P., Tate, A., Beecham, J. et al. (2006). The social networks of people living in the community 12 years after resettlement from long-stay hospitals. *Journal of Applied Research in Intellectual Disabilities, 19*, 285–295.

Foucault. M. (2006). *History of madness*. New York, NY: Routledge.

Friedman, T. (2015, January 7). Time for a pause. *New York Times* (p. A 1).

Fujiura, G., Park, H. J., & Rutkowski-Kmitta, V. (2005). Disability statistics in the developing world: A reflection on the meanings in our numbers. *Journal of Applied Research in Intellectual Disabilities, 18*, 295–304.

Gardner, H. (1983). *Frames of mind: The theory of multiple intelligences*. New York, NY: Basic Books.

Gardner, J. F., & Carran, D. T. (2005). Attainment of personal outcomes by people with developmental disabilities. *Mental Retardation, 43*(3), 157–174.

Gardner, J. F., Nudler, S., & Chapman, M. S. (1997). Personal outcomes as measures of quality. *Mental Retardation, 35*, 295–305.

Gerdes, K. E., Lietz, C. A., & Segal, E. A. (2011). Measuring empathy in the 21st century: Development of an empathy index rooted in social cognitive neuroscience and social justice. *Social Work Research, 35*, 83–93.

Gleick, J. (2011). *Chaos: making a new science*: open road media.

Glenn, J. C. (2014. September–October). Our global situation and prospects for the future. *The Futurist*, 15–25.

Gómez, L. E. (2010). Evaluación de la calidad de vida en servicios sociales: validación y calibración de la Escala GENCAT [Assessment of quality of life in social services: validation and calibration of the Gencat Scale]. Unpublished doctoral dissertation. Institute on Community Integration (INICO), Universidad de Salamanca. Available at http://gredos.usal.es/jspui/handle/10366/76489

Gómez, L. E. (2014). *Spanish social service recipients*. In A. C. Michalos (Ed.), *Encyclopedia of quality of life and well-being research* (pp. 6251–6258). Dordretch, The Netherlands: Springer.

Gómez, L. E., Arias, B., Verdugo, M. A., Tassé, M. J., & Brown, I. (2015a). *Conceptualization of quality of life for adults with severe disabilities*. Manuscript submitted for publication.

Gómez, L. E., Arias, V. B., Arias, B., Alcedo, M. A., & Verdugo, M. A. (2015b). *The Kidslife Scale: an instrument to assess quality of life for children and adolescents with intellectual disability*. Manuscript in preparation.

Gómez, L. E., Peña, E., Alcedo, M. A., Monsalve, A., Fontanil, Y., Arias, B., & Verdugo, M. A. (2014). El constructo de calidad de vida en niños y adolescentes con discapacidades múltiples y profundas: propuesta para su evaluación [The construct of quality of life concept in children and adolescents with profound and multiple Disabilities: a proposal for its assessment]. *Siglo Cero, 45*(1), 56–69.

Gómez, L. E., Pena, B., Arias, B., & Verdugo, M. A. (in press). Impact of individual and organization variables on quality of life. *Social Indicators Research*.

Gómez, L. E., Verdugo, M. A., & Arias, B. (2010). Calidad de vida individual: avances en su conceptualización y retos emergentes en el ámbito de la discapacidad [Individual quality of life: Advances on its conceptualization and emerging challenges in the disability field]. *Behavioral Psychology, 18*(3), 453–472.

Gómez, L. E., Verdugo, M. A., Arias, B., & Arias, V. (2011). A comparison of alternative models of individual quality of life for social service recipients. *Social Indicators Research, 101*, 109–126.

Gómez, L. E., Verdugo, M. A., & Arias, B. (2015). Validity and reliability of the INICO-FEAPS Scale: An Assessment of Quality of Life for People with Intellectual and Developmental Disabilities. *Research in Intellectual and Developmental Disabilities, 36*, 600–610.

Gómez, L. E., Verdugo, M. A., Arias, B., & Irurtia, M. J. (2011). Evaluación de los derechos de las personas con discapacidad intelectual: estudio preliminar [Assessment of rights of people with intellectual disability: preliminary study]. *Behavioral Psychology, 19*(1), 207–222.

Gómez, L. E., Verdugo, M. A., Arias, B., Novas, P., & Schalock, R. L. (2013). The development and use of Provider Profiles at the organization and systems level. *Evaluation and Program Planning, 40*, 17–26.

Gomez-Vela, M., Verdugo, M. A., Gonzalez-Gil, F., Corbella, M. B., & Wehmeyer, M. L. (2012). Assessment of the self-determination of Spanish students with intellectual disability and other special educational needs. *Education and Training in Autism and Developmental Disabilities, 47*(1), 48–57.

Goode, D. (Ed.). (1994). *Quality of life for persons with disabilities: International perspectives and issues*. Cambridge, MA: Brookline.

Goode, D. (1997). Assessing the quality of life of adults with profound disabilities. In R. I. Brown (Ed.), *Quality of life for people with disabilities: Models, research and practice* (2nd ed.; pp. 72–91). Cheltenham, UK: Stanley Thornes.

Goode, D. A. (1988). *Quality of life for persons with disabilities: A review and synthesis of the literature*. Valhalla, NY: The Mental Retardation Institute/UAP.

Goodey, C. F. (2011). *A history of intelligence and "intellectual disability": The shaping of psychology in early modern Europe*. Farnham, UK: Ashgate.

Goodley, D. (2011) *Disability Studies, An interdisciplinary Introduction*. Los Angeles/London/New Delhi/Singapore/Washington DC: Sage.

Grossman, H. J. (Ed.). (1973). *Manual on terminology and classification in mental retardation*. Washington, DC: American Association on Mental Deficiency.

Groulx, R., Doré, R., & Doré, L (2000). My quality of life as I see it. In K. D. Keith & R. L. Schalock (Eds.), *Cross-cultural perspectives on quality of life* (pp. 23–27). Washington, DC: American Association on Mental Retardation.

Guillemin, F., Bombardier, C., & Beaton, D. (1993). Cross-cultural adaptation of health-related Quality of Life measure: Literature review and proposed guidelines. *Journal of Clinical Epidemiology, 46*(12), 1417–1432.

Guscia, R., Harries, J., Kirby, N., Nettelbeck, T., & Taplin, J. (2006). Construct and criterion validities of the *Service Need Assessment Profile (SNAP)*: a measure of support for people with disabilities. *Journal of Intellectual & Developmental Disability, 31*, 148–155.

Hanamura, H. (1998). *Neils Erik Bank-Middelsen: Father of the normalization principle*. Copenhagen, Denmark: Danish Ministry of Education.

Harley, D., Mpofu, E., Scanlan, J., Umeasiegbu, V., & Mpofu, N. (2015). Disability social inclusion and community health. In E. Mpofu (Ed.), *Community oriented health services: Practices across disciplines* (pp. 207–222). New York, NY: Springer.

Harner, C. J., & Heal, L. W. (1993). The *Multifaceted Lifestyle Satisfaction Scale* (MLSS): Psychometric properties of an interview schedule for assessing personal satisfaction of adults with limited intelligence. *Research in Developmental Disabilities, 14*, 221–236.

Harries, J., Guscia, R., Kirby, N., Nettelbeck, T., & Taplin, J. (2005). Support needs and adaptive behaviors. *American Journal on Mental Retardation, 110*(5), 393–404.

Hart, K. E., & Sasso, T. (2011). Mapping the contours of contemporary positive psychology. *Canadian Psychology, 52*, 82–92.

Hartley S., Finkenflugel H., Kuipers P., & Thomas M. (2009). Community-based rehabilitation: opportunity and challenge. *Lancet, 374*(9704), 1803–1804.

Hartley, S. L., & MacLean, W. E. Jr. (2006). A review of the reliability and Validity of Likert-type scales for people with intellectual disability. *Journal of Intellectual Disability Research, 50*(11), 813–827.

Hassiotis, A., Brown, I., Brown, R., Favila, G., McConkey, R., Jokinen, N., & Lucchino, R. (2011). The IASSID Academy on Education, Teaching and Research and the links with low- and middle-income countries: An international partnership. *Journal of Policy and Practice in Intellectual Disabilities, 8*, 134–138.

Hatton, C. (1998). Whose quality of life is it anyway? Some problems with the emerging quality of life consensus. *Mental Retardation, 36*, 104–115.

Hatton, C., & Emerson, E. (2003). Families with a person with intellectual disabilities: Stress and impact. *Current Opinion in Psychiatry, 16*(5), 497–501.

Haveman, M., Tillmann, V., Stoppler, R., Kvas, S., & Monninger, D. (2013). Mobility and public transport use abilities of children and young adults with intellectual disabilities: Results from the 3-Year Nordhorn public transportation intervention study. *Journal of Policy and Practice in Intellectual Disabilities, 10*(4), 289–299.

Heal, L. W. (1996). Review of *Quality of life for persons with disabilities: International perspectives and issues*. *American Journal on Mental Retardation, 100*, 557–560.

Heal, L. W., Borthwick-Duffy, S. A., & Saunders, R. R. (1996). Assessment of quality of life. In J. W. Jacobson & J. A. Mulick (Eds.), *Manual of diagnosis and professional practices in mental retardation* (pp. 199–209). Washington, DC: American Psychological Association.

Heal, L. W., Rubin, S. S., & Park, W. (1995). *Lifestyle Satisfaction Scale*. Champaign-Urbana, IL: Transition Research Institute, University of Illinois.

Heal, L. W., Schalock, R. L., & Keith, K. D. (1992, July). *Cross-cultural attributions of meaning to quality of life concepts made by mental retardation professionals*. Paper presented at the World Congress of the International Association for the Scientific Study of Mental Deficiency. Brisbane, Australia.

Heine, S. (2012). *Cultural psychology* (2nd ed.). New York, NY: W. W. Norton.

Heinicke-Motsch, K. (2013). Community-based rehabilitation: an effective strategy for rights-based, inclusive community development. In G. Musoke & P. Geiser (Eds.), *Linking CBR, disability and rehabilitation* (pp. 1–119). Bangalore, India: National Printing Press.

Helle, S. (2000). Quality of life: A personal perspective from Finland. In K. D. Keith & R. L. Schalock (Eds.), *Cross-cultural perspectives on quality of life* (pp. 29–31). Washington, DC: American Association on Mental Retardation.

Hensel, E., Rose, J., Stenfert Kroese, B., & Banks-Smith, J. (2002). Subjective judgements of quality of life: A comparison study between people with intellectual disability and those without disability. *Journal of Intellectual Disability Research, 46*, 95–107.

Hickman, L. A. (1990). *John Dewey's pragmatic technology*. Bloomington, IN: Indiana University Press.

Hickson, L., & Khemka, I. (2013). Problem solving and decision making. In M. Wehmeyer (Ed.), *The Oxford handbook of positive psychology and disability* (pp. 198–225). Oxford, UK: Oxford University Press.

Hoffman, K. (1980). *Quality of life as perceived by persons who were classified as mentally retarded* (Unpublished master's thesis). University of Nebraska, Lincoln, NE.

Hoffman, M. L. (1979). Development of moral thought, feeling, and behavior. *American Psychologist, 34*, 958–966.

Hofstede, G. (1984). The cultural relativity of the quality of life concept. *Academy of Management Review, 9*(3), 389–398.

Hofstede, G., & Hofstede, G. J. (2005). *Culture and organizations: Software of the mind*. New York, NY: McGraw Hill.

Hogue, A., & Dauber, S. (2013). Assessing fidelity to evidence-based practices in usual care: The example of family therapy for adolescent behavior problems. *Evaluation and Program Planning, 37*, 21–30.

Hu, X., Summers, J. A., Turnbull, A., & Zuna, N. (2011). The quantitative measurement of family quality of life: A review of available instruments. *Journal of Intellectual Disability Research, 55*, 1098–1114.

Hughes, C., & Hwang, B. (1996). Attempts to conceptualize and measure quality of life. In R. L. Schalock (Ed.), *Quality of life: Volume I: Conceptualization and measurement* (pp. 51–62). Washington, DC: American Association on Mental Retardation.

Hughes, C., Hwang, B., Kim, J., Eisenman, L. T., & Killian, D. J. (1995). Quality of life in applied research: A review and analysis of empirical measures. *American Journal on Mental Retardation, 99*, 623–641.

Hunt, N. (1967). *The world of Nigel Hunt: The diary of a mongoloid youth*. New York, NY: Garrett.

Ingstad, B., & Grut, L. (2007). *See me, and do not forget me: People with disabilities in Kenya*. Retrieved from http://siteresources.worldbank.org/DISABILITY/Resources/Regions/Africa/LCKenya2.pdf

International Research Consortium on Evidence-Based Practices. (2013). *Organization Effectiveness and Efficiency Scale*. Retrieved from: http://www.oeesonline.org

Isaacs, B. J., Brown, I., Brown, R. I., Baum, N., Myerscough, T., Neikrug, S., . . . Wang, M. (2007). The International Family Quality of Life Project *Journal of Policy and Practice in Intellectual Disabilities, 4*(3), pp 177–185.

Ivey, J. K., LeVelle, J. A., Thompson, J. R., Tribble, A., van Loon, J., & Wrigley, S. (2008). *Relating Supports Intensity Scale information to individual service plans*. Washington DC: American Association on Intellectual and Developmental Disabilities.

Jackson, R. (2015). *Who cares? The impact of ideology, regulation and marketization on the quality of life of people with intellectual disability*. Sheffield, UK: The Centre for Welfare Reform.

Jenaro, C., Verdugo, M. A., Caballo, C., Balboni, G., Lachapelle, Y., Otbrebski, W., & Schalock, R. L. (2005). Cross-cultural study of person-centered quality of life domains and indicators: a replication. *Journal of Intellectual Disability Research, 49*, 734–739.

Johnson, H. M. (2003, February 16). Unspeakable conversations. *New York Times*. Retrieved from http://www.nytimes.com/2003/02/16/magazine/unspeakable-conversations.html

Johnson, M. (1993). *Moral imagination: Implications of cognitive science for ethics*. Chicago, IL: The University of Chicago Press.

Kant, I. (1983). *Grounding for the metaphysics of morals* (J. W. Ellington, Trans.). Indianapolis, IN: Hackett Publishing Co. (original work published 1785).

Karr, V. (2011). A life of quality: informing the UN convention on the rights of persons with disabilities. *Journal of Disability Policy Studies, 22*, 66–82.

Keeney, S., Hasson, F., & McKenna, H. (2001). A critical review of the Delphi technique as a research methodology for nursing. International Journal of Nursing Studies, 38, 95–200.

Keith, H. E., & Keith, K. D. (2013). *Intellectual disability: Ethics, dehumanization, and a new moral community*. Chichester, UK: Wiley-Blackwell.

Keith, K. D. (1996). Measuring quality of life across cultures: Issues and challenges. In R. L. Schalock (Ed.), *Quality of life: Volume I. Conceptualization and measurement* (pp. 73–82). Washington, DC: American Association on Mental Retardation.

Keith, K. D. (2001). International quality of life: Current conceptual, measurement, and implementation issues. *International Review of Research in Mental Retardation, 24*, 49–74.

Keith, K. D. (2007). Quality of life. In A. Carr, G. O'Reilly, P. N. Walsh, & J. McEvoy (Eds.), *The handbook of intellectual disability and clinical psychology practice* (pp. 143–168). London, UK: Routledge.

Keith, K. D., & Ferdinand, L. R. (2000). *Project to compare quality of life of Nebraskans with developmental disabilities and citizens without disabilities*. Lincoln, NE: Governor's Planning Council on Developmental Disabilities.

Keith, K. D., Heal, L. W., & Schalock, R. L. (1996). Cross-cultural measurement of critical quality of life concepts. *Journal of Intellectual and Developmental Disabilities, 21*, 273–293.

Keith, K. D., & Schalock, R. L. (1995). *Quality of Student Life Questionnaire*. Worthington, OH: IDS.

Keith, K. D., & Schalock, R. L. (Eds.). (2000). *Cross-cultural perspectives on quality of life*. Washington, DC: American Association on Mental Retardation.

Keith, K. D., Schalock, R. L., & Hoffman, K. (1986). *Quality of life: Measurement and programmatic implications*. Lincoln, NE: Region V Mental Retardation Services.

Kett, M., Lang, R., & Trani, J-F (2009) Disability, development and the drawing of a new convention: A cause for optimism? *Journal of International Development, 21*(5), 649–661.

Kittay, E. (2010). The personal is philosophical is political: A philosopher and mother of a cognitively disabled person sends notes from the battlefield. In E. F. Kittay & L. Carlson (Eds.), *Cognitive disability and its challenge to moral philosophy* (pp. 331–334) Chichester, UK: Wiley-Blackwell.

Kober, R., & Eggleton, I. R. C. (2002). Factor stability of the Schalock and Keith (1993) Quality of Life Questionnaire. *Mental Retardation, 40*, 157–165.

Kromberg, J., Zwane, E., Manga, P., Venter, A., Rosen, E., & Christianson, A. (2008). Intellectual disability in the context of a South African population. *Journal of Policy and Practice in Intellectual Disabilities, 5*(2), 89–95.

Kuhn, T. (1970). *The structure of scientific revolutions* (2nd ed.). Chicago, IL: University of Chicago Press.

Kuhse, H., & Singer, P. (1985). *Should the baby live?* Oxford, UK: Oxford University Press.

Lachapelle, Y., Wehmeyer, M. L., Haelewyck, M. C., Courbois, Y., Keith, K. D., Schalock, R., Verdugo, M. A., & Walsh, P. N. (2005). The relationship between quality of life and self-determination: An international study. *Journal of Intellectual Disability Research, 49*, 740–744.

Langford, C. P. H., Bowsher, J., Maloney, J. P., & Lillis, P. P. (1997). Social support: a conceptual analysis. *Journal of Advanced Nursing, 25*(1), 95–100.

Lante, K., Stancliffe, R. J., Bauman, A., van der Ploeg, H. P., Jan, S., & Davis, G. M. (2014). Embedding sustainable physical activities into the everyday lives of adults with intellectual disabilities: a randomised controlled trial. *BMC Public Health, 14*, 1038.

Larson, S., Hallas-Muchow, L., Hewitt, A., Moseley, C., Sowers, M., Fay, M. L., Aiken, F., Agosta, J., Kardell, Y., & Smith, D. (2014). *In-home and residential long-term supports and services for persons with intellectual or developmental disabilities: Status and trends through 2012*. Minneapolis, MN: Research and Training Center on Community Living, University of Minnesota.

Lee, M., Storey, K., Anderson, J. L., Goetz, L., & Zivolich, S. (1997). The effect of mentoring versus job coach instruction on integration in supported employment settings. *Journal of the Association for Persons with Severe Handicaps, 22*, 151–158.

Lekan, T. (2009). Disabilities and educational opportunity: A Deweyan approach. *Transactions of the Charles S. Peirce Society, 45*, 213–230.

LeVelle, J., & Meche, S. (2008). Individual resource allocation in Louisiana. In R. L. Schalock, J. R. Thompson, & M. J. Tassé (Eds.), *Resource allocation and the Supports Intensity Scale: Four papers on issues and approaches* (pp. 22–23). Washington, DC: American Association of Intellectual and Developmental Disabilities.

Levine, M. (2009). Buddhism. In S. J. Lopez (Ed.), *The encyclopedia of positive psychology*, vol. I (pp. 110–114). Chichester, UK: Wiley-Blackwell.

Li, C., Tsoi, E. W. S., Zhang, A. L., Chen, S., & Wang, C. K. J. (2013). Psychometric properties of self-reported quality of life measures for people with intellectual disabilities: A systematic review. *Journal of Developmental and Physical Disabilities, 25*, 253–270.

Liker, J. (2004). *The Toyota way: 14 management principles from the world's greatest manufacturer*. New York, NY: McGraw-Hill.

Liker, J., & Franz, J. (2011). *The Toyota way to continuous improvement: linking strategy and operational excellence to achieve superior performance*. New York, NY: McGraw-Hill.

Lopez, S. J., & Snyder, C. R. (Eds.) (2009). *The oxford handbook of positive psychology* (2nd ed.). Oxford, UK: Oxford University Press.

Luckasson, R. (1990). A lawyer's perspective on quality of life. In R. L. Schalock (Ed.), *Quality of life: Perspectives and issues* (pp. 211–214). Washington, DC: American Association on Mental Retardation.

Luckasson, R. (1997). Foreword. In R. L. Schalock (Ed.), *Quality of life: Volume II. Application to persons with disabilities* (pp. vii–x). Washington, DC: American Association on Mental Retardation.

Luckasson, R., Borthwick-Duffy, S. A., Buntinx, W. H. E., Coulter, D. L., Craig, E. M., Reeve, A., Schalock, R. L., Snell, M. E., Spitalnik, D. M., Spreat, S., & Tassé, M. J. (2002). *Mental retardation: Definition, classification, and systems of supports* (10th ed.). Washington, DC: American Association on Intellectual and Developmental Disabilities.

Luckasson, R., Coulter, D. L., Polloway, E. A., Reiss, S., Schalock, R. L., Snell, M. E. . . . Stark, J. A. (1992). *Mental retardation: Definition, classification, and systems of supports* (9th ed.). Washington, DC: American Association on Mental Retardation.

Lunsky Y. (2006). Individual differences in interpersonal relationships for persons with mental retardation. In: *International review of research in mental retardation, Vol. 31,* 117–61. San Diego, CA: Elsevier.

Lysaght, R., Siska, J., & Koenig, O. (2015). International employment statistics for people with intellectual disability: The case for common metrics. *Journal of Policy and Practice in Intellectual Disabilities, 12,* 112–119.

Makuwira, J. J. (2013). People with disabilities and civic engagement in Malawi. *Development Bulletin,* No. 75, 66–71.

Manchester, J., Gray-Miceli, D. L., Metcaff, J. A., Prolini, C. A., Napier, A. H., Coogel, C. L., & Owens, M. S. (2014). Facilitating Lewin's change model with collaborative evaluation in promoting evidence-based practices of health professionals. *Evaluation and Program Planning, 47,* 82–90.

Mannan, H, MacLachlan, M., & McAuliffe, E. (2012). The human resources challenge to community based rehabilitation: The need for a scientific, systematic and coordinated global response. *Development, CBR and Inclusive Development, 24,* 6–16.

Mansell, J., Elliott, T., Beadle-Brown, J., Ashman, B., & Macdonald, S. (2002). Engagement in meaningful activity and 'active support' of people with intellectual disabilities in residential care. *Research in Developmental Disabilities, 23*(5), 342–352.

Markus, H., & Kitayama, S. (1991). Culture and the self: Implications for cognition, emotion, and motivation. *Psychological Review, 98,* 224–253.

Matikka, L. (1994). The quality of life of adults with developmental disabilities in Finland. In D. Goode, (Ed.) *The quality of life for persons with disabilities: International perspectives and issues.* Cambridge, MA: Brookline Books.

Matousova-Done, Z., & Gates, B. (2006). *The nature of care planning and delivery in intellectual disability nursing.* Boston, MA: Blackwell Publication.

Matsumoto, D. (2000). Foreword. In K. D. Keith & R. L. Schalock (Eds.), *Cross-cultural perspectives on quality of life* (pp. xxi–xxiv). Washington, DC: American Association on Mental Retardation.

Matsumoto, D., & Hwang, H. S. (2013). Culture. In K. D. Keith (Ed.), *The encyclopedia of cross-cultural psychology*: Volume I (pp. 345–347). Oxford, UK: John Wiley & Sons, Inc.

Matsumoto, D., & Juang, L. (2013). *Cultural and psychology* (5th ed.). Belmont, CA: Wadsworth.

Mayer, J. D., & Salovey, P. (1993). The intelligence of emotional intelligence. *Intelligence, 17,* 433–442.

Mba, P. O. (1995). *Special education and vocational rehabilitation.* Ibadan, Nigeria: Codat.

McConkey, R., & O'Toole, B. (2000). Improving the quality of life of people with disabilities in least affluent countries: Insights from Guyana. In K. D. Keith & R. L.

Schalock (Eds.), *Cross-cultural perspectives on quality of life* (pp. 281–289). Washington, DC: American Association on Mental Retardation.

McFadden, E. S. (2013). The impact of government on quality of life for people with disabilities in the United States and Guatemala. In N. Warren & L. Manderson (Eds.), *Reframing disability and quality of life: A global perspective* (pp. 211–231). New York, NY: Springer.

McKinnon, D. P. (2008). *Introduction to statistical mediation analysis*. New York, NY: Erlbaum.

Mead, G. (1964a). Social consciousness and the consciousness of meaning. In A. Reck (Ed.), *Selected writings of George Herbert Mead*. Chicago, IL: The University of Chicago Press.

Mead, G. (1964b). Social psychology as counterpart to physiological psychology. In A. Reck (Ed.), *Selected writings of George Herbert Mead*. Chicago, IL: The University of Chicago Press.

Meadan, H., Halle, J. W., & Ebata, A. T. (2010). Families with children who have autism spectrum disorders: Stress and support. *Exceptional Children, 77*(1), 7–36.

Memari, A. H., & Hafizi, S. (2015). People with intellectual disability and social-political life participation: A commitment to inclusive policies in less developed countries. *Journal of Policy and Practice in Intellectual Disabilities, 12*, 37–41.

Menolascino, F. J. (1977). *Challenges in mental retardation: Progressive ideology and services*. New York, NY: Human Sciences Press, 1977.

Mill, J. S. (2002). *Utilitarianism* (2nd ed.). Indianapolis, IN: Hackett Publishing Company (original work published 1861).

Millennium Project Report. (2013). Retrieved (December 30, 2014) from: www.millenniumproject.org/millennium/201314SOF

Miller, E., Cooper, S., Cook, A., & Petch, A. (2008). Outcomes important to people with intellectual disabilities. *Journal of Policy and Practice in Intellectual Disabilities, 5*, 150–158.

Mitra, S. (2004). Viewpoint: Disability—the hidden side of African poverty. *Disability World*. Retrieved from http://www.disabilityworld.org/01-03_04/news/africa.shtml

Mitra, S. (2005). Disability and social safety nets in developing countries. *Social Protection Discussion Paper Series No. 0509*. Social Protection Unit, Human Development Network, World Bank. Retrieved November 26, 2009, from http://siteresources.worldbank.org/SOCIALPROTECTION/Resources/0509.pdf

Mittler, P. (2015). The UN convention on the rights of persons with disabilities: Implementing a paradigm shift. *Journal of Policy and Practice in Intellectual Disabilities, 12*, 79–89.

Mpofu, E. (2004). Learning through inclusive education: Practices with students with disabilities in sub-Saharan Africa. In C. de la Rey, L. Schwartz, & N. Duncan (Eds.), *Psychology: An introduction* (pp. 361–371). Cape Town, South Africa: Oxford University Press.

Mpofu, E. (2006). Majority world health care traditions intersect indigenous and complementary and alternative medicine. *International Journal of Disability, Development and Education, 53,* 375–379.

Mpofu, E., Jelsma, J., Maart, S., Levers, L. L., Montsi, M. M. R., Tlabiwe, P., . . . Tchombe, T. M. S. (2007). Rehabilitation in seven sub-Saharan African countries: Personnel education and training. *Rehabilitation Education, 21,* 223–230.

National Core Indicators Website. www.nationalcoreindicators.org

Navas, P., Gómez, L. E., Verdugo, M. A., & Schalock, R. L. (2012). Derechos de las personas con discapacidad intelectual: Implicaciones de la Convención de Naciones Unidas [Rights of persons with intellectual disability: Implications of the United Nation Convention]. *Siglo Cero, 43*(3), 7–28.

Neugarten, B., Havighurst, R., & Tobin, S. (1961). Measurement of life satisfaction. *Journal of Gerontology, 16,* 134–143.

Newton-Smith, W. H. (Ed) (2001). *A companion to the philosophy of science.* London, UK: Blackwell.

Ngaanyatjarra Pitjantjatjara Yankunytjatjara Women's Council. (2014, September). *Provision of services in relation to assisting Indigenous Australians in Anangu Pitjantjatjara Yankunytjatjara (APY) lands to benefit from the National Disability Insurance Scheme (NDIS): Final report.* Retrieved from http://www.ndis.gov.au/document/1331

Nirje, B. (1969). The normalization principle and its human management implications. In Kugel, R. B., & Wolfensberger, W. (Eds.), *Changing patterns in residential services for the mentally retarded* (pp. 181–195). Washington, DC: President's Committee on Mental Retardation.

Nirje, B. (1972). The right to self-determination. In W. Wolfensberger (Ed.), *Normalization: The principle of normalization in human services* (pp. 176–193). Toronto, Canada: National Institute on Mental Retardation.

Nota, L., Ferrari, L., Soresi, S., & Wehmeyer, M. (2007). Self-determination, social abilities and the quality of life of people with intellectual disability. *Journal of Intellectual Disability Research, 51,* 850–865.

Nussbaum, M. C. (2006). *Frontiers of justice: Disability, nationality, species membership.* Cambridge, MA: Harvard University Press, Belknap Press.

Nussbaum, M. C. (2009). The capabilities of people with cognitive disabilities. *Metaphilosophy, 40*(3-4), 331–351.

Nussbaum, M. C. (2011). *Creating capabilities: The human development approach.* Cambridge, MA: Belknap Press of Harvard University Press.

O'Brien, C. L., & O'Brien, J. (2000). The Origins of Person-Centered Planning: A Community of Practice Perspective. In S. Holburn & P. Vietze (Eds.), *Person-centered planning: research, practice, and future directions.* Baltimore, MD: Paul H Brookes.

Ohno, T. (1988). *Toyota production system: beyond large-scale production.* Portland, OR: Productivity, Inc.

Oliver, M. (1996). *Understanding disability: From theory to practice*. New York, NY: St. Martin's Press.

Osgood, C. E., May, W. H., & Miran, M. S. (1975). *Cross-cultural universals of affective meaning*. Urbana, IL: University of Illinois Press.

Otrębski, W. (2000). Quality of life of people with mental retardation living in two environments in Poland. In K. D. Keith & R. L. Schalock (Eds.), *Cross-cultural perspectives on quality of life* (pp. 83–92). Washington, DC: American Association on Mental Retardation.

Otrębski, W. (2005). Variables influencing the ratings of importance and use of quality of life domains and indicators by Polish professionals. *Journal of Intellectual Disability Research, 49*, 750–755.

Oulette-Kuntz, H., & McCreary, B. (1996). Quality of life assessment of persons with severe developmental disabilities. In R. Renwick, I. Brown, & M. Nagler (Eds.), *Quality of life in health promotion and rehabilitation: Conceptual approaches, issues, and applications* (pp. 268–278). Thousand Oaks, CA: Sage.

Parmenter, T. R. (1992). Quality of life of people with developmental disabilities. *International Review of Research in Mental Retardation, 18*, 247–287.

Pelka, F. (2012). *The rights of all people*. Boston, MA: University of Massachusetts Press.

Pell, E. (2014). *NCI performance indicators: Evidence for new HCBS requirements and revised HCBS assurances: Practical tools for states*. Retrieved on 2/17/15 from http://www.nationalcoreindicators.org/upload/core-indicators/HCBS_Reqmts_and_CMS_Assurances_Crosswalk_with_NCI_May_2014_FINAL.pdf

Perry, J., & Felce, D. (1995). Objective assessments of quality of life: How much do they agree with each other? *Journal of Community & Applied Social Psychology, 5*, 1–19.

Perry, J., & Felce, D. (2004). Initial finding on the involvement of people with intellectual disability in interviewing their peers about quality of life. *Journal of Intellectual and Developmental Disabilities, 29*, 164–171.

Perry, J., Felce, D., Allen, D., & Meek, A. (2011). Resettlement outcomes for people with severe challenging behaviour moving from institutional to community living. *Journal of Applied Research in Intellectual Disabilities, 24*, 1–17.

Perske, R. (1972). The dignity of risk. In W. Wolfensberger (Ed.), *Normalization: The principle of normalization in human services* (pp. 194–201). Toronto, Canada: National Institute on Mental Retardation.

Perske, R., & Perske, M. (1980). *New life in the neighborhood: How persons with retardation or other disabilities can help make a good community better*. Nashville, TN: Vanderbilt University Press.

Pink, D. (2011). *Drive: the surprising truth about what motivates us*. New York, NY: Riverhead Books.

Pinker, D. (2005). *A whole new mind: Moving from the information to the conceptual age*. New York, NY: Riverhead Books.

Race, D. (2002). The historical context. In D. G. Race (Ed.), *Learning disability—A social approach* (pp. 23–52). London, UK: Routledge.

Rafael, A. (1991). *Dr. Deming: the American who taught the Japanese about quality.* New York, NY: Carol Publishing Group.

Raphael, D. (1996). Defining quality of life: Eleven debates concerning its measurement. In R. Renwick, I. Brown, & M. Nagler (Eds.), *Quality of life in health promotion and rehabilitation: Conceptual approaches, issues, and applications* (pp. 146–165). Thousand Oaks, CA: Sage.

Rapley, M. (2000). The social construction of "quality of life": The interpersonal production of well-being revisited. In K. D. Keith & R. L. Schalock (Eds.), *Cross-cultural perspectives on quality of life* (pp. 155–172). Washington, DC: American Association on Mental Retardation.

Rapley, M. (2003). *Quality of life research: A critical introduction.* London, UK: Sage.

Rapley, M. (2004). *The social construction of intellectual disability.* Cambridge, UK: Cambridge University Press.

Reinders, H., & Schalock, R. L. (2014). How organizations can enhance the quality of life of their clients and assess their results: The concept of QOL enhancement. *American Journal of Intellectual and Developmental Disabilities, 119,* 291–302.

Renwick, R., Brown, I., & Nagler, M. (Eds.) (1996). *Quality of life in health promotion and rehabilitation: Conceptual approaches, issues, and applications.* Thousand Oaks, CA: Sage.

Renwick, R., Brown, I., & Raphael, D. (2000). Person-centered quality of life: Contributions from Canada to an international understanding. In K. D. Keith & R. L. Schalock (Eds.), *Cross-cultural perspectives on quality of life* (pp. 5–21). Washington, DC: American Association on Mental Retardation.

Riches, V. C., Harman, A. D., Keen, D., Pennell D., Harley, J. H., & Walker, M. (2011). Transforming staff practice through active support. *Journal of Intellectual & Developmental Disability, 36*(3): 156–166.

Riches, V. C., Parmenter, T. R., Llewellyn, G., Hindmarsh, G., & Chan, J. (2009). I-CAN: a new instrument to classify needs for people with disability: Part I. *Journal of Applied Research in Intellectual Disabilities, 22,* 326–339.

Reis, E. (2011). *The lean startup: how today's entrepreneurs use continuous innovation to create radically successful businesses.* New York, NY: Crown Publishing Group.

Rivera, G. (1972). *Willowbrook: The Last Great Disgrace.* WABC-TV.

Rosen, M., Clark, G., & Kivitz, M. (1977). *Habilitation of the handicapped: New dimensions in programs for the developmentally disabled.* Baltimore, MD: University Park Press, 1977.

Ruzgis, P., & Grigorenko, E. L. (1994). Cultural meaning systems, intelligence, and personality. In R. J. Sternberg & P. Ruzgis (Eds.), *Personality and intelligence* (pp. 248–270). New York, NY: Cambridge University Press.

Ryan, R. M., & Deci, E. L. (2000). Self-determination theory and the facilitation of intrinsic motivation, social development, and well-being. *American Psychologist, 55,* 68–78.

Samuel, P. S., Rillotta, F., & Brown, I. (2012). The development of family quality of life concepts and measures. *Journal of Intellectual Disability Research, 56,* 1–16.

Sanders, S. R. (1997). The power of stories. *Georgia Review, 51,* 113–126.

Sands, D. J., & Kozleski, E. B. (1994). Quality of life differences between adults with and without disabilities. *Education and Training in Mental Retardation and Developmental Disabilities, 29,* 90–101.

Santiestevan, H. (1976). *Out of their beds and into the streets.* Washington, DC: American Federation of State, County, and Municipal Employees.

Saxena, S., Thornicroft, G., Knapp, M., & Whiteford, H. (2007). Resources for mental health: Scarcity, inequality, and inefficiency. *Lancet, 370,* 878–889.

Schalock, R. L. (1990a). Preface. In R. L. Schalock (Ed.), *Quality of life: Perspectives and issues* (pp. ix–xii). Washington, DC: American Association on Mental Retardation.

Schalock, R. L. (1990b). *Quality of life: Issues and perspectives.* Washington, DC: American Association on Mental Retardation.

Schalock, R. L. (Ed.). (1996a). *Quality of life: Volume I: Conceptualization and measurement.* Washington, DC: American Association on Mental Retardation.

Schalock, R. L. (1996b). Reconsidering the conceptualization and measurement of quality of life. In R. L. Schalock (Ed.), *Quality of life: Volume I. Conceptualization and measurement* (pp. 123–139). Washington, DC: American Association on Mental Retardation.

Schalock, R. L. (Ed.). (1997). *Quality of life: Volume II: Application to persons with disabilities.* Washington, DC: American Association on Mental Retardation.

Schalock, R. L. (2000). Three decades of quality of life. In M. L. Wehmeyer & J. R. Patton (Eds.), *Mental retardation in the 21st century* (pp. 335–356). Austin, TX: Pro-Ed.

Schalock, R. L. (2001). *Outcomes-based evaluation* (2nd ed.). New York, NY: Kluwer Academic/Plenum Publishers.

Schalock, R. L. (Ed.). (2002). *Out of the darkness and into the light: Nebraska's experience with mental retardation.* Washington, DC: American Association on Mental Retardation.

Schalock, R. L. (2004a). Quality of life from a motivational perspective. *International Review of Research in Mental Retardation, 28,* 303–319.

Schalock, R. L. (2004b). The emerging disability paradigm and its implications for policy and practice. *Journal of Disability Policy Studies, 14,* 204–215.

Schalock, R. L. (2011). International perspectives on intellectual disability. In K. D. Keith (Ed.), *Cross-cultural psychology: Contemporary themes and perspectives* (pp. 312–328). Malden, MA: Wiley-Blackwell.

Schalock, R. L., Bonham, G. S., & Marchand, C. B. (2000). Consumer based quality of life assessment: a path model of perceived satisfaction. *Evaluation and Program Planning, 23,* 77–87.

Schalock, R. L., Borthwick-Duffy, S. A., Bradley, V. J., Buntinx, W. H. E., Coulter, D. L., Craig, E. M., Gomez, S. C., Lachapelle, Y., Luckasson, R., Reeve, A., Shogren, K. A., Snell, M. E., Spreat, S., Tassé, M. J., Thompson, J. R., Verdugo-Alonso, M. A., Wehmeyer, M. L., & Yeager, M. H. (2010). *Intellectual disability: Definition, classification, and systems of supports* (11th ed.). Washington DC: American Association on Intellectual and Developmental Disabilities.

Schalock, R. L., Brown, I., Brown, R., Cummins, R. A., Felce, D., Matikka, L., Keith, K. D., & Parmenter, T. (2002). Conceptualization, measurement, and application of quality of life for persons with intellectual disabilities: Report of an international panel of experts. *Mental Retardation, 40*, 457–470.

Schalock, R. L., Gardner, J. F., & Bradley, V. J. (2007). *Quality of life for person with intellectual and other developmental disabilities: Applications across individuals, organizations, communities, and systems.* Washington, DC: American Association on Intellectual and Developmental Disabilities.

Schalock, R. L., Harper, R. S., & Genung, T. (1981). Community integration of mental retarded adults: Community placement and program success. *American Journal of Mental Deficiency, 85*, 478–488.

Schalock, R. L., & Keith, K. (1993). *Quality of Life Questionnaire.* Worthington, OH: IDS.

Schalock, R. L., Keith, K. D., & Hoffman, K. (1990). *1990 Quality of Life Questionnaire: Standardization Manual.* Hastings, NE: Mid-Nebraska Mental Retardation Services.

Schalock, R. L., Keith, K. D., Verdugo, M. A., & Gómez, L. E. (2010). Quality of life model development and use in the field of intellectual disability. In R. Kober (Ed.), *Enhancing the quality of life of people with intellectual disabilities: From theory to practice* (pp. 17–32). Dordrecht, Netherlands: Springer.

Schalock, R. L., Lee, T., Verdugo, M. A., Swart, K., Claes, C., van Loon, J., & Lee, C. (2014a) An evidence-based approach to organization evaluation and change in human service organizations evaluation and program planning. *Evaluation and Program Planning, 45*, 110–118.

Schalock, R. L., Lee, T., Verdugo, M. A., & van Loon, J. (2014b). *Continuous Quality Improvement Strategies Referenced to the Perspective of the Customer, and the Organization's Growth, Financial Analyses, and Internal Processes. OEES Manual Supplement #2.* Retrieved from: http://oees-inico.usal.es.

Schalock, R. L., Lemanowicz, J. A., Conroy, J. W., & Feinstein, C. S. (1994). A multivariate investigative study of the correlates of quality of life. *Journal on Developmental Disabilities, 3*, 59–73.

Schalock, R. L., & Luckasson, R. (2013). What's at stake in the lives of people with intellectual disability? Part I: The power of naming, defining, diagnosing, classifying, and planning supports. *Intellectual and Developmental Disabilities 51*(2), 86–93.

Schalock, R. L., & Luckasson, R. (2014). *Clinical judgment* (2nd ed.). Washington, DC: American Association on Intellectual and Developmental Disabilities.

Schalock, R. L., Luckasson, R., Bradley, V., Buntinx, W. H. E., Lachapelle, Y., Shogren, K. A., Snell, M. E., Thompson, J. R., Tassé, M. J., Verdugo-Alonso, M. A., and Wehmeyer, M. L (2012). *User's guide to intellectual disability: Definition, classification, and systems of supports.* Washington DC: American Association on Intellectual and Developmental Disabilities.

Schalock, R. L., & Verdugo, M. A. (2002). *Handbook on quality of life for human service practitioners.* Washington, DC: American Association on Mental Retardation.

Schalock, R. L., & Verdugo, M. A. (2008). Quality of life from concept to application in the field of intellectual disability. *Evaluation and Program Planning, 31*, 181–190.

Schalock, R. L., & Verdugo, M. A. (2012a). A conceptual and measurement framework to guide policy development and systems change. *Journal of Policy and Practice in Intellectual Disabilities, 9*, 70–79.

Schalock, R. L., & Verdugo, M. A. (2012b). *A leadership guide for today's disabilities organizations: Overcoming challenges and making change happen*. Baltimore, MD: Paul H. Brookes.

Schalock, R. L., & Verdugo, M. A. (2013a). The impact of the quality of life concept on the field of intellectual disability. In M. Wehmeyer (Ed.), *The Oxford handbook of positive psychology and disability* (pp. 37–47). Oxford, UK: Oxford University Press.

Schalock, R. L., & Verdugo, M. A. (2013b). The transformation of disabilities organizations. *Intellectual and Developmental Disabilities, 51*(4), 273–286.

Schalock, R. L., & Verdugo, M. A. (2014). Quality of life as a change agent. In R. I. Brown & R. Faragher (Eds.), *Challenges for quality of life: Application in education and other social contexts* (pp. 60–72). New York: Nova Science.

Schalock, R. L., Verdugo, M. A., & Gómez, L. E. (2011). Evidence-based practices in the field of intellectual and developmental disabilities: An international consensus approach. *Evaluation and Program Planning, 34*, 273–282.

Schalock, R. L., Verdugo, M. A., Gómez, L. E., & Reinders, H. (2016). Moving us toward a theory of individual quality of life. *American Journal on Intellectual and Developmental Disabilities, 112*, 1–12.

Schalock, R. L., Verdugo, M. A., Jenaro, C., Wang, M., Wehmeyer, M., Xu, J., & Lachapelle, Y. (2005). A cross-cultural study of quality of life indicators. *American Journal on Mental Retardation, 110*, 298–311.

Schmidt, S., Power, M., Green, B., Lucas-Carrasco, R., Eser, E., Dragomirecka, E., & Fleck, M. (2013). Self and proxy rating of quality of life in adults with intellectual disabilities: Results from the DISQOL study. *Research in Developmental Disabilities, 31*, 1015–1026.

Schunk, D. H., & Bursuck, W. D. (2013). Self-regulation and disability. In M. Wehmeyer (Ed.), *The Oxford handbook of positive psychology and disability* (pp. 265–279). Oxford, UK: Oxford University Press.

Seligman, M. E. P. (1999). The President's address. *American Psychologist, 54*(8), 559–562.

Seligman, M. E. P., & Csikszentmihalyi, M. (2000). Positive psychology: An introduction. *American Psychologist, 55*, 5–14.

Serpell, R., Mariga, L., & Harvey, K. (1993). Mental retardation in African countries: Conceptualization, services and research. *International Review of Research in Mental Retardation, 19*, 1–34.

Shearn, J., & Todd, S. (2000). Maternal employment and family responsibilities: the Perspectives of mothers of children with intellectual disabilities. *Journal of Applied Research in Intellectual Disabilities, 13*(3), 109–131.

Shogren, K. A. (2013). Positive psychology and disability: A historical analysis. In M. Wehmeyer (Ed.), *The Oxford Handbook of positive psychology and disability* (pp. 19–33). Oxford, UK: Oxford University Press.

Shogren, K. A., Lopez, S. J., Wehmeyer, M. L., Little, T. D., & Pressgrove, C. L. (2006). The role of positive psychology constructs in predicting life satisfaction in adolescents with and without cognitive disabilities: An exploratory study. *Journal of Positive Psychology, 1,* 37–52.

Shogren, K. A., Luckasson, R., & Schalock, R. L. (2014). The definition of "context" and its application in the field of intellectual disability. *Journal of Policy and Practice in Intellectual Disabilities, 11,* 109–116.

Shogren, K. A., Luckasson, R., & Schalock, R. L., (2015). Using context as an integrative framework to align policy goals, supports, and outcomes in intellectual disability. *Intellectual and Developmental Disabilities, 53,* 367–376.

Shogren, K., Palmer, S., Wehmeyer, M. L., Williams-Diehm, K., & Little, T. (2012). Effect of intervention with the *Self-Determined Learning Model of Instruction* on access and goal attainment. *Remedial and Special Education, 33*(5), 320–330.

Shogren, K. A., & Turnbull, H. R. (2010). Public policy and outcomes for persons with intellectual disabilities: Extending and expanding the public policy framework of the 11th edition of intellectual disability: Diagnosis, classification, and systems of supports. *Intellectual and Developmental Disabilities, 48,* 387–392.

Shogren, K. A., & Turnbull, H. R. (2014). Core concepts of disability policy, the Convention on the Rights of Persons With Disabilities, and public policy research with respect to developmental disabilities. *Journal of Policy and Practice in Intellectual Disabilities, 11*(1), 19–26.

Shogren, K. A., Wehmeyer, M. L., Lang, K., & Niemiec, R. M. (2015). *The application of the VIA Classification of Strengths to youth with and without disabilities.* Manuscript submitted for review.

Shogren, K. A., Wehmeyer, M. L., Palmer, S. B., Rifenbark, G., & Little, T. (2015). Relationships between self-determination and postschool outcomes for youth with disabilities. *Journal of Special Education, 48*(4), 256–267.

Shogren, K. A., Wehmeyer, M. L., Pressgrove, C. L., & Lopez, S. J. (2007). The application of positive psychology and self-determination to research in intellectual disability: A content analysis of 30 years of literature. *Research and Practice for Persons with Severe Disabilities, 31,* 338–345.

Singer, P. (1993). *Practical ethics* (2nd ed.). Cambridge, UK: Cambridge University Press.

Singer, P. (2010). Speciesism and moral status. In E. F. Kittay & L. Carlson (Eds.), *Cognitive disability and its challenge to moral philosophy* (pp. 331–344). Chichester, UK: Wiley-Blackwell.

Skevington, S., Bradshaw, J., & Saxena, S. (1999). Selecting national items for the WHO-QOL: Conceptual and psychometric considerations. *Social Sciences and Medicine, 48,* 473–487.

Smith, C., Felce, D., Jones, E., & Lowe, K. (2002). Responsiveness to staff support: Evaluating the impact of individual characteristics on the effectiveness of active support training using a conditional probability approach. *Journal of Intellectual Disability Research, 46*(8), 594–604.

Smith P. M., & Dean, S. (2002). The Pilot Parent Program. In R. L. Schalock (Ed.), *Out of the darkness and into the light* (pp. 63–72). Washington, DC: American Association on Mental Retardation.

Sofair, A., & Kaldjian, L. (2000). Eugenic sterilization and qualified Nazi analogy: The United States and Germany, 1930–1945. *Annals of Internal Medicine, 132,* 312–319.

Stainton, T. (2001). Reason and value: The thought of Plato and Aristotle and the construction of intellectual disability. *Mental Retardation, 39,* 452–460.

Stainton, T., & Clare, I. C. H. (2012). Human rights and intellectual disabilities: an emergent theoretical paradigm? *Journal of Intellectual Disability Research, 56*(11), 1011–1013.

Stancliffe, R. J. (2000). Proxy respondents and quality of life. *Evaluation and Program Planning, 23,* 89–93.

Stancliffe, R. J. (2005). Semi-independent living and group homes in Australia. In R. J. Stancliffe & K. C. Lakin (Eds.), *Costs and outcomes of community services for people with intellectual disabilities* (pp. 129–150). Baltimore, MD: Paul H. Brookes.

Stancliffe, R. J., Abery B. H., & Smith, J. (2000). Personal control and the ecology of community living settings: Beyond living-unit size and type. *American Journal on Mental Retardation, 105,* 431–454.

Stancliffe, R. J., Bigby, C., Balandin, S., Wilson, N. J., & Craig, D. (Epublication 11/12/14). Transition to retirement and participation in mainstream community groups using active mentoring: A feasibility and outcomes evaluation with a matched comparison group. *Journal of Intellectual Disability Research.* doi: 10.1111/jir.12174.

Stancliffe, R. J., Jones, E., Mansell, J., & Lowe, K. (2008). Active support: A critical review and commentary. *Journal of Intellectual & Developmental Disability, 33*(3), 196–214.

Stancliffe, R. J., & Lakin, K. C. (2007). Independent living. In S. L. Odom, R. H. Horner, M. Snell, and J. Blacher (Eds.), *Handbook on developmental disabilities* (pp. 429–448). New York, NY: Guilford Publications, Inc.

Stancliffe, R. J., McVilly, K. R., Radler, G., Mountford, L., & Tomaszewski, P. (2010). Active Support, participation and depression. *Journal of Applied Research in Intellectual Disabilities, 23,* 312–321.

Stancliffe, R., & Wehmeyer, M. L. (1995). Variability in the availability of choice to adults with mental retardation. *The Journal of Vocational Rehabilitation, 5,* 319–328.

Stancliffe, R. J., Wilson, N. J., Bigby, C., Balandin, S., & Craig, D. (2014). Responsiveness to self-report questions about loneliness: A comparison of mainstream and intellectual disability-specific instruments. *Journal of Intellectual Disability Research, 58,* 399–405.

Sternberg, R. J. (1986). *Intelligence applied: Understanding and increasing your intellectual skills.* San Diego, CA: Hartcourt Brace Jovanovich.

Sternberg, R. J. (1996). *Successful intelligence: How practical and creative intelligence determine success in life.* New York, NY: Simon & Schuster.

Super, C. M., & Harkness, S. (1982). The infants' niche in rural Kenya and metropolitan America. In L. L. Adler (Ed.), *Cross-cultural research at issue* (pp. 47–55). New York, NY: Academic Press.

Sutherland, J. (2014). *SCRUM: the art of doing twice the work in half the time.* New York, NY: Crown Publishing Group.

Svraka, E., Loga, S., & Brown, I. (2011). Family quality of life: Adult school children with intellectual disabilities in Bosnia and Herzegovina. *Journal of Intellectual Disability Research, 55,* 1115–1122.

Tagaya, M. (1985). Administration of institutions for mentally retarded persons. In Japan League for the Mentally Retarded (Ed.), *Services for people with mental retardation* (pp. 98–102). Tokyo, Japan: Japan League for the Mentally Retarded.

Taylor, S. J. (1994). In support of research on quality of life, but against QOL. In D. Goode (Ed.), *Quality of life for persons with disabilities: International perspectives and issues* (pp. 260–265). Cambridge, MA: Brookline.

Taylor, S. J., & Blatt, S. D. (Eds.) (1999). *In search of the promised land: The collected papers of Burton Blatt.* Washington, DC: American Association on Mental Retardation.

Temple University Developmental Disabilities Center Research & Quality Assurance Group (1990). *Final report: Report on state and territorial developmental disabilities councils: 1990 national consumer survey.* Washington DC: National Association of Developmental Disabilities Councils.

Terry, L. (Producer/Director) (1968). *Out of darkness and into the light* [documentary]. Omaha, NE: KETV.

The Arc of Nebraska. (2003). *Nebraska developmental disabilities service provider profiles.* Lincoln, NE: Author.

Thompson, J. R., Bradley, V. J., Buntinx, W. H., Schalock, R. L., Shogren, K. A., Snell, M. E., . . . Yeager, M. H. (2009). Conceptualizing supports and the support needs of people with intellectual disability. *Intellectual and Developmental Disabilities, 47*(2), 135–146.

Thompson, J. R., Bryant, Brian R., Campbell, Edward M., Craig, Ellis M. (Pat), Hughes, Carolyn M., Rotholz, David A., Schalock, Robert L., Silverman, Wayne P., Tassé, Marc J., & Wehmeyer, Michael L. (2004). *Supports Intensity Scale User's Manual.* Washington, DC: American Association on Intellectual and Developmental Disabilities.

Thompson, J. R., Bryant, B. R., Schalock, R. L., Shogren, K. A., Tassé, M., Wehmeyer, M. L., Campbell, E. M., Craig, E. M., Hughes, C., & Rotholz, D. A. (2015). *Supports Intensity Scale—Adult Version User's Manual.* Washington, DC: American Association on Intellectual and Developmental Disabilities

Thompson, J. R., Schalock, R. L., Agosta, J., Teninty, L., & Fortune, J. (2014). How the supports paradigm is transforming service systems for persons with intellectual disability and related developmental disabilities. *Inclusion, 2*(2), 86–99.

Thorndike, E. L. (1917). The curve of work and the curve of satisfyingness. *Journal of Applied Psychology, 1,* 265–267.

Thorndike, E. L. (1939). *Your city*. New York, NY: Harcourt, Brace & Co.

Throne, J. M. (1972). The assessment of intelligence: Towards what end? *Mental Retardation, 10*(5), 9–11.

Tiberius, V., & Mason, M. (2009). Eudaimonia. In S. J. Lopez (Ed.), *The encyclopedia of positive psychology*, vol. I (pp. 351–355). Chichester, UK: Wiley-Blackwell.

Ticha, R., Qian, X., Larson, S., & Stancliffe, R. (In Press) Alignment between the convention on the rights of persons with disabilities and the national core Indicators. *Journal of Policy and Practice in Intellectual Disabilities*.

Tizard, J. (1964). *Community services for the mentally handicapped*. London, UK: Oxford University Press.

Tomlinson, M., Tasamy, M. T., Emerson, E., Officer, A., Richler, D., & Saxena, S. (2014). Setting global research priorities for developmental disabilities, including intellectual disabilities and autism, *Journal of Intellectual Disability Research, 58*(12), 1121–1130.

Townsend-White, C., Pham, A. N. T., & Vassos, M. V. (2012). A systematic review of quality of life measures for people with intellectual disabilities and challenging behaviors. *Journal of Intellectual Disability Research, 56*, 270–284.

Trent, J. W. (1994). *Inventing the feeble mind: A history of mental retardation in the United States*. Berkeley, CA: University of California Press.

Tsai, W. H., Chou, W. C., & Hsu, W. (2009). The sustainability balanced scorecard as a framework for selecting socially responsible investment. *Journal of Operational Research Society, 60*, 1396–1410.

Turnbull, H. R., & Stowe, M. (2014). Outcomes-driven policy development. *Intellectual and Developmental Disabilities, 54*, 120–134.

Udoh, S., Gona, J., & Maholo, C. (2013). Evidence base for CBR. In G. Musoke & P. Geiser (Eds.), *Linking CBR, disability and rehabilitation*, (pp. 89–105). Kyambogo, Uganda: CBR Africa Network.

Umeasiegbu, V. I., Bishop, M., & Mpofu, E. (2013). The conventional about disability conventions: A reflective analysis of United Nations Convention on the Rights of Persons with Disabilities. *Rehabilitation Education, Policy and Research, 27*(1), 58–72.

United Nations (1948). *Universal declaration of human rights*. Retrieved from http://www.un.org/en/documents/udhr/ (retrieved 9 February 2015).

United Nations (1975). Declaration on the rights of persons with disabilities. Retrieved from http://www2. Ohchr.org/english/law/res3447.htm (retrieved 9 February 2015).

United Nations (1993). Standard rules on the equalization of opportunities for disabled persons. United Nations General Assembly, New York, NY.

United Nations (2006). Convention on the rights of persons with disabilities. Retrieved from http://www.in.org/disabilities/convention/conventionfull.shtml (retrieved 9 February 2015).

United Nations enable (2015). Rights and dignity of persons with disabilities: Latest developments. Retrieved from http://www.un.org/disabilities/latest.asp?id=169

Vail, D. J. (1967). *Dehumanization and the institutional career.* Springfield, IL: Charles C. Thomas.

van Gennep, A. (2007). *Waardig leven met beperkingen. Over veranderingen in de hulpverlening aan mensen met beperkingen in hun verstandelijke mogelijkheden.* Antwerpen, Belgium-Apeldoorn, Netherlands: Garant.

van Loon, J. (2005). *Emancipation and self-determination of people with intellectual disabilities: Dismantling institutional care.* Gent, Belgium: Leuven-Apeldoorn Garant.

van Loon, J., Bonham, G. S., Peterson, D., Schalock, R. L., Claes, C., & Decramer, A. (2013). The use of evidence based outcomes in systems and organizations providing services and supports to persons with intellectual disabilities. *Evaluation and Program Planning, 36,* 80–88.

van Loon, J., Claes, C., Vandevelde, S., Van Hove, G., & Schalock, R. L. (2010). Assessing individual support needs to enhance personal outcomes. *Exceptionality,* 18:1–10, 2010.

van Loon, J., & Van Hove, G. (2001). Emancipation and self-determination of people with learning disabilities and down-sizing institutional care. *Disability & Society,* 16, 233–254.

van Loon, J. H. M., Van Hove, G., & Schalock, R. L. (2009). The use of SIS data/items for the development of an individual supports plan. In R. L. Schalock & J. Thompson, *The SIS Implementation Guide* (pp. 80–92). Washington, DC: American Association on Intellectual and Developmental Disabilities.

van Loon, J., van Hove, G., Schalock, R. L., & Claes, C. (2008). Measuring quality of life: The complex process of development of the *Personal Outcomes Scale. Journal of Intellectual Disability Research,* 52, 789–789.

van Loon, J., Van Hove, G., Schalock, R. L., & Claes, C. (2008). *Personal Outcomes Scale.* Gent, Belgium: University of Gent.

Verdugo, M. A., Arias, B., Gómez, L. E., & Schalock, R. L. (2010). Development of an objective instrument to assess quality of life in social services: Reliability and validity in Spain. *International Journal of Clinical and Health Psychology, 10*(1), 105–123.

Verdugo, M. A., Canal, R., & Bermejo, B. G. (1997, May). *Enhancing residential services for persons with mental retardation and extensive support needs.* Paper presented at the annual meeting of the American Association on Mental Retardation, New York, NY.

Verdugo, M. A., Gómez, L. E., Arias, B., Navas, P., & Schalock, R. L. (2014). Measuring quality of life in people with intellectual and multiple disabilities: validation of the *San Martin Scale. Research in Developmental Disabilities, 35*(1), 75–86.

Verdugo, M. A., Navas, P., Gómez, L. E., & Schalock, R. L. (2012). The concept of quality of life and its role in enhancing human rights in the field of intellectual disability. *Journal of Intellectual Disability Research,* 56, 1036–1045.

Verdugo, M. A., Prieto, G., Caballo, C., & Peláez, A. (2005). Factorial structure of the Quality of Life Questionnaire in a Spanish sample of visually disabled adults. *European Journal of Psychological Assessment, 21*, 44–55.

Verdugo, M. A., Schalock, R. L., Keith, K. D., & Stancliffe, R. J. (2005). Quality of life and its measurement: important principles and guidelines. *Journal of Intellectual Disability Research, 49*(10), 707–717.

Waddington, L. (2001). Evolving disability policies: From social-welfare to human rights: An international trend from a European perspective. *Netherlands Quarterly of Human Rights*, 141–165.

Wanderi, M. P., Mwisukha, A., & Bukhala, P. W. (2009). Enhancing the full potential of persons with disabilities through sports in the 21st century with reference to Kenya. *Disability Studies Quarterly, 29*. Retrieved from http://dsq-sds.org/article/view/1010/1167

Wang, M., & Kober, R (2011). Embracing an era of rising family quality of life research. *Journal of Intellectual Disability Research, 55*, 1093–1097.

Wang, M., McCart, A., & Turnbull, A. (2007). Implementing positive behaviour support with Chinese American families: Enhancing cultural competence. *Journal of Positive Behaviour Interventions, 9*, 38–51.

Wang, M., Schalock, R. L., Verdugo, M. A., & Jenaro, C. (2010). Examining the factor structure and hierarchical nature of the quality of life construct. *American Journal on Intellectual and Developmental Disabilities, 115*, 218–233.

Ward, N. (2000). The universal power of speaking for oneself. In K. D. Keith & R. L. Schalock (Eds.), *Cross-cultural perspectives on quality of life* (pp. 33–36). Washington, DC: American Association on Mental Retardation.

Watson, S. M. R., & Keith, K. D. (2002). Comparing the quality of life of school-age children with and without disabilities. *Mental Retardation, 40*, 304–312.

Webb, O. M. (2002). Call me by my name. In R. L. Schalock (Ed.), *Out of the darkness and into the light: Nebraska's experience with mental retardation* (pp. 55–61). Washington, DC: American Association on Mental Retardation.

Wehmeyer, M. L. (Ed.). (2013). *The story of intellectual disability: An evolution of meaning, understanding, and public perception*. Baltimore, MD: Paul H. Brookes.

Wehmeyer, M. L., Bersani, H., & Gagne, R. (2000). Riding the third wave: Self-determination and self-advocacy in the 21st Century. *Focus on Autism and Other Developmental Disabilities, 15*, 106–115.

Wehman, P., Brooke, V., Lau, S., & Targett, P. (2013). Supported employment. In M. Wehmeyer (Ed.), *The Oxford handbook of positive psychology and disability* (pp. 338–364). Oxford, UK: Oxford University Press.

Wehmeyer, M. L., Buntinx, W. H. E., Lachapelle, Y., Luckasson, R. A., Schalock, R. L., Verdugo, M. A., . . . Yeager, M. H. (2008). The intellectual disability construct and its relation to human functioning. *Intellectual and Developmental Disabilities, 46*(4), 311–318.

Wehmeyer, M. L., & Metzler, C. (1995). How self-determined are people with mental retardation? The National Consumer Survey. *Mental Retardation, 33,* 111–119.

Wehmeyer, M. L., & Schalock, R. (2001). Self-determination and quality of life: Implications for special education services and supports. *Focus on Exceptional Children, 33*(8), 1–16.

Wehmeyer, M. L., & Schwartz, M. (1998). The relationship between self-determination, quality of life, and life satisfaction for adults with mental retardation. *Education and Training in Mental Retardation and Developmental Disabilities, 33,* 3–12.

Whitney, E. A. (1949). The historical approach to the subject of mental retardation. *American Journal of Mental Deficiency, 53,* 419–424.

WHOQOL Group. (1995). The definition of quality of life and development of international quality of life assessment instruments. *Social Science and Medicine, 41,* 1403–1409.

WHOQOL Group. (1998). The World Health Organization Quality of Life Assessment (WHOQOL): Development and general psychometric properties. *Social Science and Medicine, 46,* 1569–1585.

Williams, P., & Schoultz, B. (1982). *We can speak for ourselves.* London, UK: Souvenir Press.

Wober, M. (1974). Toward an understanding of the Kiganda concept of intelligence. In J. W. Berry & P. R. Dasen (Eds.), *Culture and cognition* (pp. 261–280). London, UK: Methuen.

Wolfensberger, W. (1969). The origin and nature of our institutional models. In R. B. Kugel & W. Wolfensberger (Eds.), *Changing Patterns in Residential Services for the Mentally Retarded* (pp. 59–171). Washington, DC: President's Committee on Mental Retardation.

Wolfensberger, W. (1972). *The principle of normalization in human services.* Toronto, Canada: National Institute on Mental Retardation.

Wolfensberger, W. (1975). *The origin and nature of our institutional models.* Syracuse, NY: Human Policy Press.

Wolfensberger, W. (1980). A brief overview of the principle of normalization. In R. J. Flynn & K. E. Nitsch (Eds.), *Normalization, social integration, and community services* (pp. 7–30). Baltimore, MD: University Park Press.

Wolfensberger, W. (1994). Let's hang up "quality of life" as a hopeless term. In D. Goode (Ed.), *Quality of life for persons with disabilities: International perspectives and issues* (pp. 285–321). Cambridge, MA: Brookline.

Wolfensberger, W. (2002). Why Nebraska? In R. L. Schalock (Ed.), *Out of the darkness and into the light: Nebraska's experience with mental retardation* (pp. 23–52). Washington, DC: American Association on Mental Retardation.

Wolfensberger, W., & Kugel, R. (1969). *Changing patterns in residential services for the mentally retarded.* Washington, DC: President's Committee on Mental Retardation.

World Health Organization. (2001). *International classification of functioning, disability, and health*. Geneva, Switzerland: Author.

World Health Organization. (2010). *Community-based rehabilitation: CBR guidelines*. Geneva, Switzerland: Author.

World Health Organization (2011). World report on disability. Retrieved on 2/15/15 from http://www.who.int/disabilities/world_report/2011/en/

World Health Organization, UNESCO, ILO, and International Disability and Development Consortium (2010). *CBR guidelines introductory booklet: Towards community-based inclusive development*. Geneva: World Health Organization.

Wu, H.-Y., Lin, Y.-K., & Chang, C.-H. (2011). Performance evaluation of extension education centers in universities based on the balanced scorecard. *Evaluation and Program Planning, 34*, 37–50.

Xiang, Y., Xu, J., & Wang, M. (2007). Reexamining the key indicators of quality of life for Chinese individuals with mental retardation. *Chinese Journal of Special Education, 89*, 41–48.

Xu, S. (2010). *A study on self-determination of your people with intellectual disabilities*. Unpublished dissertation: East China Normal University.

Yount, L. (2000). *Physician-assisted suicide and euthanasia*. New York, NY: Facts on File.

Zimmermann, M., & Endermann, M. (2008). Self-proxy agreement and correlates of health-related quality of life in young adults with epilepsy and mild intellectual disabilities. *Epilepsy and Behavior, 13*, 202–211.

Zuna, N. J., Summers, J. A., Turnbull, A. P., Hu, X., & Xu, S. (2011). Theorizing about family quality of life. In R. Kober (Ed.), *Enhancing the quality of life of people with intellectual disability: From theory to practice* (pp. 241–278). Dordrecht, Netherlands: Springer.

GLOSSARY

Adaptive behavior The collection of conceptual, social, and practical skills that have been learned and are performed by people in their everyday lives.

Active support Direct support from caregivers for active participation and increased engagement in meaningful everyday activities.

Agenda A plan of action that has a clearly stated goal, a rationale that reflects the current zeitgeist, an empirical basis, and specific action steps.

Alignment Placing or bringing critical organization functions into line. Alignment involves applying a logic model that includes input, throughput, and output components. Alignment positions the service delivery component of an organization into a logical sequence for the purposes of reporting, monitoring, evaluation, and continuous quality improvement.

Capabilities approach The notion that individual and social wellbeing depends on the capability of individuals to function well in society, rather than only on economic affluence. It includes the idea that there is no moral threshold of capability required for participation in the activities of normal life, and that quality of life is based on recognition of potential and opportunities of the individual, independent of the total or average well-being of the group.

Catalyst A factor or condition that brings about change but is not consumed in the process.

Change catalysts Entities that facilitate change; with regard to disability, change catalysts often include such constructs as values, leadership, empowerment, and technology.

Community-Based Rehabilitation (CBR)   A strategy based on a community development framework stressing poverty reduction, equalization of opportunities, rehabilitation, promoting and protecting human dignity, and social inclusion for people with a disability.

Context   The totality of circumstances comprising the milieu of human life and human functioning. Context can be viewed as an independent variable, an intervening variable, or an integrative construct. The context of QOL application is composed of the approach to disability, organization transformation and systems change, professional education and support provider development, and research.

Contextual factors   Influences that define the context of quality of life. These factors include approaches to disability, organization transformation and systems change, professional education and support provider development, and research.

Continuous Quality Improvement   An integrative, sequential, and participatory process that is based on best practices, and whose primary purpose is to enhance an organization or system's effectiveness or efficiency from a multiple, performance-based perspective. The sequential quality improvement components vary among quality improvement models, but generally involve either a plan-do-check-act cycle or an assess-plan-do-evaluate cycle.

Cross-cultural   An approach to research or study that compares how behavior or other social/psychological phenomena occur in different cultural groups. Cross-cultural approaches often seek to identify processes or phenomena that are universal (etics) and those that are culture-specific (emics).

Cross functional teams   See High performance teams.

Culture   Behaviors, attitudes, values, and traditions shared by a group and enduring from one generation to the next.

Delphi Method   A structured research process by which several rounds of data collection are used to achieve consensus about a complex problem.

Domains   See Quality of life domains

Developmental disability   Disability often associated with intellectual disability, but may also result from cerebral palsy, epilepsy, autism, or other neurological conditions producing impairment of normal functioning. This disability originates before age 18.

Ecological   A focus on the person-environmental interaction and its effect on human functioning. Human functioning is facilitated by the congruence between personal competence and environmental demands and the provision of individualized supports.

Ecological model of disability   A perspective recognizing that disability can be defined not simply as a characteristic of the individual, but that it is the interaction between person and environment. In this way, disability may be seen as dynamic and context-related. The environment can serve to mitigate disability and enhance ability.

Effectiveness The degree to which an organization's intended mission and results are achieved.

Efficiency Extent to which an organization produces planned results in relation to the expenditure of resources.

Emic A culture-bound or culture-specific psychological phenomenon or process; applicable or valid in a single culture.

Etic A universal psychological phenomenon or process; applicable or valid across multiple (or all) cultures.

Evaluation The process of carefully and systematically appraising the status of objective, evidence-based performance indicators. The three primary purposes of evaluation are to: (a) provide information for data-based decision making and managing for results, (b) provide data for continuous quality improvement, and (c) determine the significant predictors of personal and organization outcomes.

Evidence-based outcomes Personal and organization outcomes indicators that are assessed via a broad class of objective evidence related to personal and organization outcomes.

High performance teams Horizontally structured work groups that focus on teamwork, synergy, raising the performance bar, focus on "us" accountability, and promoting a learning culture. High performance teams are organized around performing six primary functions: assessment; individual support plan development, implementation, and monitoring; data gathering, processing, analysis, and reporting; outcomes evaluation; continuous quality improvement; and crisis management. They are characterized by involvement, information, organization, accountability, and empowerment.

Human functioning dimensions A multidimensional model of human functioning that includes five dimensions: intellectual abilities, adaptive behavior, health, participation, and context. These five dimensions are used both descriptively and as outcome categories. Each is positively affected by the provision of appropriate individualized supports.

Inclusion The notion that all people, without regard to disability, should be freely and openly accommodated, without discrimination or pity, by their cultures.

Indicators See **Quality of life indicators**

Individual supports plan (ISP) The integration of personal goals and assessed support needs with individualized support strategies based on a system of supports, support objectives, and desired personal outcomes. A quality of life framework is often used to organize ISP components.

Intellectual disability A disability characterized by significant limitations in both intellectual functioning and in adaptive behavior as expressed in conceptual, social, and practical adaptive skills. This disability originates before age 18.

Intellectual functioning A broader term than either intellectual abilities or intelligence. The term reflects an understanding that what is considered intellectual behavior is dependent on other dimensions of human functioning: the adaptive behavior one exhibits, the person's mental and physical health, the opportunities to participate in major life activities, and the context within which people live their everyday lives. Some cultures have construed intelligence as harmonious social relations, participation in the activities of family, or cooperative, obedient, and socially responsible behavior.

Intelligence A general mental capability. It traditionally includes reasoning, planning, solving problems, thinking abstractly, comprehending complex ideas, learning quickly, and learning from experience. However, intelligence is increasingly viewed in broader terms, often encompassing social and adaptive capacities. Cross-culturally, intelligence may include cooperation, obedience, effort, determination, and participation in family life, among other characteristics.

Macrosystem The larger culture or society within which the individual resides.

Mediator variable A phenomenon that influences the relation between independent and outcome variables and exhibits indirect causation, connection, or relation.

Mental models Deeply ingrained assumptions, generalizations, and images used to understand the world. Mental models form the lens through which one sees the world and forms the vision and culture of individuals, organizations, systems, and societies.

Mesosystem The neighborhood, community, or organizations providing supports or services.

Microsystem The immediate social setting, including the person, family, peers, and/or advocate(s).

Moderator variable A phenomenon that alters the form or strength of the relation between two variables.

Monitoring At the organization level, monitoring is an oversight and interactive process that has four primary purposes: (a) to demonstrate compliance with the organization's policies and practices, (b) to ensure that the input, throughput, and output service delivery components are in place and functioning as anticipated, (c) to provide benchmarks for self-comparison, standards for evaluating current organization performance, and goals that direct quality improvement efforts, and (d) to ensure the precision, accuracy, and integrity of the information that is used for reporting, evaluation, and continuous quality improvement. The monitoring of performance indicators is the basis for performance management. At the individual level, monitoring ensures that the individual support plan is developed on the basis of personal goals and assessed support needs and employs a system of supports to enhance personal outcomes.

Moral community A group of people who take part in moral decision making (either as active agents or recipients). In this book we have suggested the importance of a new moral community based on relationships and individual growth, in lieu of traditional notions of inert intelligence and rationality.

Moral philosophy Area of philosophy concerned with principles of ethics and morality.

Multicultural An approach to understanding distinct cultural groups within an organization or society. The United Kingdom and the United States, for example, are multicultural countries, to the extent that multiple cultural groups make up the larger society.

Multiple Performance-Based Perspective A balanced scorecard approach to organization assessment, planning, evaluation, and change based on the perspectives of the consumer, and the organization's growth, financial analysis, and internal processes.

Multivariate research Research methodologies that allow analysis of the effects of, or relations among, multiple variables or influences. In quality of life research, investigators have studied not only numerous factors that contribute to quality of life (e.g., health, satisfaction, social belonging), but also the relation of quality of life measures to other factors (e.g., cognitive ability, employment, nature of housing).

Organization outcomes Organization-related outcomes that result from the resources a program or organization uses to achieve its goals and the actions implemented by the organization to produce these outcomes. Organization outcomes are frequently presented as a "balanced scorecard," reflecting the perspectives of the customer, and the organization's growth, financial analyses, and internal processes.

Organization self-assessment The use of collaborative evaluation to assess an organization's key performance indicators or quality improvement needs. Organization self-assessment can be used to determine what is important *to* the organization in terms of values and mission, and what is important *for* the organization in terms of quality improvement needs related to the perspective of the customer, and the organization's growth, financial analyses, and internal processes.

Organization transformation Changes that come about in organizations as a result of continuous quality improvement activities. Characteristics of a transformed organization are its customer-centeredness, use of horizontally-structured high performance teams, use of collaborative self-assessment, engagement in outcomes evaluation, and implementation of continuous quality improvement activities.

Outcome predictors Variables that are statistically associated with (predict) personal outcomes. Predictors are considered independent or intervening variables, and personal outcomes are considered dependent variables.

Outcomes evaluation Assessing personal, family, or societal changes or benefits that follow as a result or consequence of some activity, intervention, or service.

Paradigm A constellation of beliefs and techniques that reflect an approach to an issue and provide a pattern or example.

Participatory action research An approach to research that attempts to effect social change by addressing issues significant to those who participate in the research.

Person-centered planning An individual person-focused approach to planning based on the unique needs, capacities, and goals of the person.

Personal outcomes The benefits derived by program recipients that are the result, direct or indirect, of program activities, services, and supports. Within the text, personal outcomes are related to quality of life domains and measurable indicators associated with each domain.

Personhood The quality or condition of being an individual human being. Moral personhood often denotes an individual who is worthy of equal moral or legal treatment.

Plan-Do-Check-Act (PDCA) cycle A commonly used quality improvement cycle that involves plan (i.e. identify gaps to goal, analyze root issues, and formulate strategies) do (i.e. develop implementation process), check (i.e. monitor progress and measure impact), and act (i.e. identify improvement needs, standardize best practices, and spread best practices).

Positive Psychology Study of human flourishing—the pursuit of understanding optimal human functioning and well-being. Important positive psychology constructs include self-determination, self-regulation, problem-solving skills, decision making, hope, character strengths, optimism, resilience, and creativity.

Pragmatism Philosophical perspective that emphasizes the importance of practical consequences as a standard for determining truth or value, with a focus on an empirical approach. Pragmatism is characterized by integration of theory and practice, a view of human nature as evolving, and a view of truth that is experimental and fallible.

Provider profile A description of the services and supports offered by a service provider, including an overview of the organization's quality improvement and quality assurance activities, and a summary of aggregated quality of life outcome measures for service recipients.

Quality management Management strategies that focus on organization performance indicators and valued personal outcomes.

Quality of life A multidimensional phenomenon composed of core domains influenced by personal characteristics and environmental factors. These core domains are the same for all people, although they may vary individually or culturally in relative value and importance. Assessment of quality of life domains is based on culturally sensitive indicators, and generally takes into account general health, well-being, and happiness.

Quality of Life Conceptual Model A model of individual QOL depicting QOL domains, moderator and mediator variables, and quality enhancement techniques.

Quality of life domains The set of factors that constitute personal well-being. The set represents the range over which the quality of life concept extends and, thus, defines a life of quality.

Quality of life indicators Quality of life-related perceptions, behaviors, and conditions that give an indication of the person's well-being.

Quality of Life Language of Thought and Action A language that includes a cast of basic concepts, a set of relationships, a family of causal relationships, and the concept of a goal.

Relational supports Instrumental support strategies based on emotion, affiliation, and information. These types of supports are interlinked with the overall collectivistic worldview of mutually advantaging the self and others

Relational well-being A worldview rooted in collectivistic-relational culture in which quality of life is explained and realized with and for the well-being of self and others.

Relational world view The beliefs that: (a) one "is" because others "are"; and (b) a satisfying life is one in which one is a means of life satisfaction for others.

Reliability The measurement consistency of a test or assessment instrument.

Report by others Assessment of an individual based on the view of one or more informants/respondents (other than the individual) of an individual's quality of life-related perceptions, behaviors, and conditions.

Resource allocation A current approach to distributing financial resources based on a system that incorporates assessed support needs and other cost drivers.

Right-to-left thinking Beginning with desired outcomes and then asking, "What needs to be in place for these outcomes to occur?"

Self-advocacy Civil rights movement for people with intellectual disability. This includes the right to speak or act on behalf of oneself or others in matters of personal concern or of public policy.

Self-determination Ability of an individual to make decisions and choices based on personal interests and preferences. This includes personal control of supports, services, and other assistance.

Self-report Self-assessment by an individual of his/her quality of life-related perceptions, behaviors, and conditions.

Social entrepreneurship A systematic process to service/support delivery that builds on values, opportunities, innovation, and maximized resources. Successful entrepreneurial strategies result in creating social value by improving peoples' lives, building community, and improving society.

Social construction of disability The notion that disability reflects not just characteristics of an individual, but also cultural views and attitudes toward the individual—that disability is what a particular culture says it is.

Strengths-based Approach to disability from the perspective of human potential, human capabilities, and a social-ecological (i.e., person-environment) model of disability.

Support needs A psychological construct referring to the pattern and intensity of supports necessary for a person to participate in activities linked with normative human functioning. Support needs can be assessed with a standardized support needs assessment instrument.

Support objective Statement that details the procurement or provision, means, and outcome of a needed support. A support objective has three elements: an action verb, a support strategy, and the intended results of the strategy.

Support strategies The actual techniques used to bridge the gap between "what is" and "what can be." Support strategies can be grouped into a system of supports.

Supports Resources and strategies that aim to promote the development, education, interests, and personal well-being of a person and that enhance individual functioning.

Supports paradigm An approach to service delivery that emphasizes an individual's assessed support needs, individualized supports planning and provision, and the incorporation of a system of supports.

Sustainability Ability to keep up, prolong, and nourish. Sustainability reflects an organization's ability to adapt and change, and thus provide an ongoing range of sound service delivery opportunities and practices.

System of supports The planned and integrated use of individualized support strategies and resources, such as natural supports, technology, prosthetics, education (new skills), environmental accommodation, incentives, personal strengths/assets, and professional services. A system of supports model provides a structure to enhance human performance that is interdependent and cumulative.

Theory An integrative construct in which investigators arrive at the level of explanation and prediction based on their specific observations and/or systematic inquiries. A theory is used to explain relationships, generate hypotheses, and guide application.

Utilitarian philosophy Utilitarianism is a philosophical perspective that includes the ideas that actions are judged to be good or bad depending on their consequences, and that morally good actions are those that are good for the greatest number of people. Thus, utilitarian approaches have sometimes suggested that such actions as withholding treatment from infants with significant disability would serve the greater good of families and the wider society.

Validity The extent to which a test or assessment instrument measures what it claims to measure.

Zeitgeist Defining mood of the time; reflected in ideas and history of an era.

SUBJECT INDEX

A

active support, 22, 134, 138–142, 251
adaptive behavior, 10, 77, 135–139, 145, 251
alignment, 24, 70, 82–85, 90–93, 114, 115, 150, 163, 168, 170, 196, 197, 251
application. See QOL application
assessment, 3, 5, 7, 8, 9, 12, 16, 22–25, 30, 61, 70–80, 84, 86, 88, 90, 91, 93, 100, 109, 112–117, 134–138, 141–142, 149, 152, 162, 187, 193, 200
    administrative procedures, 74
    organizational, 255
    parallel process, 70, 94, 107
    personal outcomes, 72–76
    psychometric properties, 59, 73, 77–78, 91, 188
    scoring metric, 73, 76
    See also QOL guidelines, reliability and validity, self-report, report of others, QOL measurement instruments

C

capabilities approach, 251
Championship Formula Inventory, 100, 103
change catalysts, 149–159, 165, 251
communication tools, 56, 161
community-based rehabilitation, 176, 178–179, 180, 205, 208, 211, 252

contextual factors, 9–12, 63, 123, 191, 193, 196, 200, 201, 252
continuous quality improvement, 23, 69–70, 79, 80, 93, 97, 116, 119, 149, 151–155, 157, 162–164, 181, 200, 210, 252
    application in business and industry, 94–95
    application in human service organizations, 96, 99
Convention on the Rights of Persons with Disabilities. See UN Convention
cross-cultural approach, 252
culture and support, 134–135, 141

D

deinstitutionalization, 29, 70, 109–111, 117
developing world, 25, 119, 176–180
    challenges regarding services and supports, 179
    evolution of quality of life perspectives, 176–178, 188

E

ecological matrix, 70, 85–88, 90
empowerment, 1, 5, 7, 20, 34, 40, 45, 49, 50, 52, 57, 69, 85, 93, 117, 147, 149, 151, 161, 165, 168–169, 179, 181, 209, 213

evaluation, 21–24, 25, 50, 61–62, 69, 71, 76, 79, 80, 84, 91, 93, 94, 95, 109, 112, 115–119, 125, 127, 131, 142, 147, 149–150, 159, 169, 182, 184–185, 195, 200–201, 205, 211, 253

F

family quality of life, 59, 187, 188
    concept, 188
    scales, 59, 61, 62

G

global community, 183, 188, 189
guidelines, 1, 7, 69, 71, 110–111, 118, 129, 205, 214
    QOL outcomes assessment, 72, 76

H

human functioning, 33, 81, 85, 134–135, 144–148, 169, 193, 210, 253
humanity, 14–15, 17, 144, 175, 204
    characteristics of, 144, 175
human rights. See Convention on the Rights of Persons with Disabilities
hypotheses, 191, 196, 199

I

indicators. See quality of life
individual supports plan, 23, 83, 97, 113–115, 211, 253
    important to vs. important for, 8–9, 23, 86, 163
    planning process, 83–86
    quality of life framework, 115, 118, 254
intellectual disability, 5, 17, 19, 35, 41, 44–45, 65, 109, 119, 133, 143, 145, 184, 203
intelligence, 12, 14–17, 145–146
    definition, 254
    multiple, 15–16, 254
    types, 15–16, 254
International Association for the Scientific Study of Intellectual Disability (IASSID)
    Academy, 26
    SIRG-QOL, 3, 4

International Classification of Functioning (ICF), 135, 137, 187
    relation to outcome measurement, 129
interviewing
    skills, 34, 49, 52
    strategies, 52–53, 56, 57

L

leadership, 4, 23, 26–27, 93, 100, 122, 149, 151–153, 155–157, 159, 161–165
logic model, 24, 81, 151–153, 165, 210

M

measurement, 1, 3–8, 11–12, 21–24, 27, 34, 61, 71–72, 76, 92, 113, 119, 121–123, 125, 128–129, 141–142, 171, 174, 182, 184–186, 188, 193, 214
    peer interviewers, 8, 186
    report of others, 74–78
    self-report, 74–78
mediator variables, 192–200, 208, 214–215, 254
mental models, 21, 25, 159, 211–213, 254
moderator variables, 195, 200, 215, 254
monitoring, 50–52, 91, 94, 129, 200, 211, 213, 254
moral community, 2, 13–17, 255

N

National Core Indicators, 125–132
natural supports, 82, 91, 139, 196
new millennium, 61, 183, 185, 188
normalization, 20, 29, 30, 122, 143

O

openness, 95, 97, 99
organization, 2, 8–10, 18–19, 23–28, 33, 40, 43, 50–51, 53, 60–72, 77, 79, 80–86, 90–100, 107–120, 134, 142, 144, 149–164, 178–182, 193–196, 200–216, 255
    effectiveness, 96, 100, 105, 116
    efficiency, 96, 100, 105, 116
    self-assessment, 112, 116–117, 255–256

organization and systems transformation, 19, 21, 109–110, 203, 206–207, 210, 216, 255
outcomes evaluation, 21, 69, 71, 80, 84, 116, 142, 149, 169, 182, 195, 200–201
    definition, 256
    uses of outcome infomation, 80
    uses of outcome information, 79

P

PDCA cycles, 94–97, 99, 100, 107, 256
personal involvement, 34, 49–52, 56–57, 181, 193, 195, 210, 214
personal outcomes, 9, 20–21, 27, 70–73, 76, 78–80, 82–85, 93, 107, 111–117, 140, 151–153, 162–163, 169, 187, 193–194, 196, 209–210, 214, 256
personhood, 16, 17, 256
policy development, 19, 23–24, 182, 194, 196–197, 203, 206, 209, 216
Positive Behavior Interventions and Supports, 146
positive psychology, 119, 143–148, 201, 206, 213, 256
    and intellectual disability, 145–146
    and quality of life, 147, 198
prediction, 182, 191, 195, 201
professional education, 9–10, 19, 182, 193, 198, 203, 205–206, 208, 211, 213, 216
professional responsibility, 211, 216

Q

quality improvement, 9, 12, 23, 69–70, 76, 79–80, 93–94, 97, 107, 116–117, 119, 122, 126–129, 149, 151–153, 155, 157, 162–164, 181–182, 200–201, 210, 252
quality management, 70, 112, 116, 127, 256
quality of life
    agenda, 143, 181
    application, 10, 194
    assessment instruments, 7, 23–24, 70–72, 74, 78, 80, 86, 91, 100
    conceptualization principles, 4
    conceptual model, 192, 257
    contextual factors, 9–12, 63, 191, 193, 200–201, 252
    definition, 257

quality of life (*continued*)
    domains, 160, 192, 257
    enhancement strategies, 120, 192–201, 205, 214
    factor structure, 6, 74
    global perspective, 182–183
    indicators, 212, 257
    journeys, 2, 18–30
    language of thought and action, 20–21, 213, 257
    measurement approach, 7
    measurement principles, 7
    outcome predictors, 9, 12, 256
    test develoment guidelines, 7
    test development guidelines, 8
    theory, 194
    use of information, 7–9, 12, 116–117, 159

R

reasoning, 14, 254
relational QOL perspective, 120, 176
relational supports, 175–176, 205, 257
reliability, 73
report of others, 74–78, 100, 114, 193
research, 9–13, 19, 21–28, 45, 49, 59, 69, 79, 111, 122–123, 128, 132, 139, 142, 145–146, 153, 170, 182–186, 193, 196, 198–200, 203, 205–206, 208, 210–216
resource allocation, 23, 134–138, 142, 152, 177, 179, 257
right-to-left thinking, 69, 80, 111, 119, 209, 257

S

self-advocacy, 1, 20, 35–36, 40, 42–46, 144, 181, 205–206, 210, 257
self-advocates, 21–22, 26–28, 35, 40, 49, 121–123, 158, 169–170, 185, 205
self-determination, 1, 4–5, 20, 27, 35–36, 38, 41, 42, 44, 46, 49, 63–64, 66, 69, 80, 85, 93, 111–112, 117, 141, 143–147, 150, 159, 160, 163, 178–179, 181, 184, 186, 195, 208–210, 213, 257
self-report, 8, 12, 72–80, 100, 114, 186, 193, 258

social-ecological model of disability, 21, 23, 131, 136, 147, 206, 213
support needs assessment, 136, 258
support objectives, 24, 85–86, 90–91, 258
support planning, 83, 92, 112
support provider development, 182, 203, 206, 208, 211, 213, 216
supports, 6, 9, 17, 19–27, 46, 50–51, 57, 59–60, 69–71, 78, 80, 81–93, 97, 100, 109–123, 127, 131–137, 141–142, 145–150, 160, 168–171, 176–182, 187–188, 193–197, 200–201, 204–216, 258
supports matrix, 70, 85, 88–90
supports paradigm, 21, 59, 70, 81, 110, 112–113, 116–117, 133–135, 142, 145, 187–188, 200, 206, 208, 215, 258
supports plan. *See* individual supports plan
systems-level outcome indicators, 119, 149, 181, 205
systems of supports, 19–20, 82–83, 85–86, 90, 93, 117, 120, 147, 194, 196, 216

T

teams, 24, 41–42, 51, 53, 70, 82, 85, 94–95, 97–99, 111, 117, 126, 152–153, 156, 159, 161, 164, 179, 208, 210
    cross-functional, 97–99, 252
    high performance, 93, 99–100, 157, 253

theory, 14, 21, 71–73, 77, 94, 182, 191, 193–197, 200–201, 203, 215, 258
transformation, 25, 84, 93–94, 96, 110, 117, 161, 165, 193
    organizations, 10, 19, 21, 70, 80, 93, 107, 109–112, 118, 182, 203, 206–207, 210, 216
    systems, 10, 19, 149, 182, 193, 203, 206–207, 210, 216

U

United Nations Convention on the Rights of Persons with Disabilities, 40, 50, 64, 83, 112–113, 128–132, 167–173, 186
    Articles, 171–173
    relation among UN convention articles, QOL domains and measureable indicators, 169, 174
    relation to core indicators, 172
    relation to national core indicators, 173
    relation to QOL domains, 169, 172–173

V

validity, 73, 74, 77–80, 151, 186, 259
values, 20, 30, 69, 74, 75, 82, 85, 90–96, 109, 117, 147, 149, 151–153, 159–160, 164–165, 169, 197–198, 201, 205, 207, 209, 211, 213